"Learn How To Learn"
STUDY SKILLS

By
Herman Ohme, Ed.D.

Published By

CALIFORNIA EDUCATION PLAN
942 Acacia Avenue
Los Altos, CA 94022

ACKNOWLEDGEMENT & DEDICATION

To my wife, Jean, whose careful, meticulous editing and wise counsel contributed immeasurably to the quality and content of this book.

"Learn How To Learn" STUDY SKILLS
Copyright © 1986 by Herman Ohme

ISBN 0-936047-00-3

Library of Congress Catalog Card Number: 86-091520

Printed in the United States of America

10 9 8 7 6 5 4 3 2 1

Cover Design by Rogandino & Associates

Table of Contents

KNOW SOMETHING!

DO SOMETHING!

BE SOMETHING!

INTRODUCTION

Why would anyone need to "learn" how to learn?

Isn't learning natural, something we're born with? Do birds have to go to school to learn how to fly? Who has to teach a baby how to cry, or crawl?

Why is learning English or Math so different?

Why would anyone have to *learn* how to do something as natural and obvious as *learning*? Why was *school* ever invented in the first place?

To begin with, we aren't birds, nor are we babies any longer. What we learned through the process of physical growth, and as imitators of adult and other models--does not represent the kind of blueprint that we need for the intellectual growth and development required for success in the real world.

Learning Skills Equal Success

Your success in the real world will depend to a large extent on how well you can:

- **Learn**

- **Remember** what you learn

- Use what you have learned

These are called *learning skills*. Some of your teachers may help you acquire these skills, while others may assume that you already have them. However, none of this should be left to chance. This **MANUAL** will remove that possibility. It will help you understand, **perfect**, and **use** *learning skills*. As a result, the quality of your work should improve, and you will truly experience the *joy of learning*.

Contents Of The Manual

The **MANUAL** consists of ten Chapters plus two Supplements. The ten Chapters deal with the basic learning skills that will help you improve your performance in all subjects. The Skills are:

- **Organization**
- **Time Management**
- **Concentration**
- **Notetaking**
- **Report Preparation**
- **Test Taking**
- **Reading**
- **Memory**
- **Critical Thinking**
- **Motivation**

SUPPLEMENT A will show you how to analyze and improve your own performance in any subject.

SUPPLEMENT B is a cross referenced **Grammatical Glossary** of terms you need to understand in order to be successful in learning a Foreign Language.

How To Use The Manual

The most effective way to begin is to become very familiar with Chapter One--ORGANIZATION. This is actually an *Umbrella* Chapter, which contains enough information on the learning skills you will need for practically any assignment or project you may have.

You don't have to read through the entire Manual before beginning to help yourself.

For example, there are nine basic functions needed for efficient *Organization*. Each of these is described in detail in separate Chapters of the **MANUAL**. However, the information, examples, and exercises in **Chapter One** will give you the working knowledge you need to become a more effective, efficient, and skilled learner. These are:

1. The *description* of the assignment.

2. The *specific tasks*.

3. The *teacher's expectations*.

4. *Key words* and *concepts*.

5. The importance of *managing your time*.

6. The use of *required* and **support** materials.

7. The best ways to *remember* what you need to know.

8. The *quizzes*, *tests*, or *examinations* you will take.

9. The best *place(s)* to study.

Brief Description Of Chapters
Two Through Ten

CHAPTER TWO - TIME MANAGEMENT

How to get more done in less time. You will learn to use:

The *Master Time Chart*. See at a glance how to make the best use of free time during a one week period.

The *Assignment Log*. Keep track of all your assignments: when due, and when completed.

The *To-Do-List*. Be certain that you take care of all daily obligations, both big and small.

CHAPTER THREE - CONCENTRATION

How to keep working on an assignment until done.
You will learn to:

Control your work space so that you have the best possible place(s) to study and concentrate.

Take care of your *physical* and *mental needs* so that you are distracted as little as possible.

Generate *interest* in the subject so that you will *want* to stay with it.

CHAPTER FOUR - NOTETAKING

How to get the most out of textbooks, lectures, and other sources of information. You will learn how to:

Select the proper information from any written material you are required to read.

Listen, analyze, and select *important facts* from a demonstration (science and math classes), lecture or other visual or spoken source of information.

Take *good notes* on all information, then summarize your notes in the form of a *Visual Map*, or whatever notetaking device works best for you.

CHAPTER FIVE - REPORT PREPARATION & PRESENTATION

How to prepare and present written and oral reports.
You will learn how to:

Make the best *choice* of a subject.

Research the subject you have chosen.

Organize, select, and *condense* information.

Draft and *revise* your report.

Make the best possible *presentation.*

CHAPTER SIX - TEST TAKING

How to prepare for and take all types of tests and examinations. You will learn:

The main *purposes* for taking tests

How best to *prepare* for the different types of tests.

Tips and *techniques* for getting the best results.

What *to do* in unusual circumstances.

3) Who is buried in
   Grant's tomb?

☐ a) James Grant

☐ b) Ulysses Grant

☐ c) Sally Grant

☐ d) all of the above

☐ e) none of the above

CHAPTER SEVEN - READING

How to measure and increase speed and comprehension.
You will learn how to:

Use *hand pacing* to control reading speed.

Quickly *locate the main facts* in different
types of writing.

Use *different reading speeds* for different
study purposes.

Overcome distractions such as music or television.

Break subvocalizing and single word reading habits.

CHAPTER EIGHT - MEMORY

How to improve your memory. You will learn the following:

Visual memory methods such as *Mapping,* a way to list
topics and subtopics according to their importance
and relationships to each other.

Mnemonics, a rhyming device that helps you to
remember concepts and spelling combinations.

Association, which helps you remember a series of different concepts.

CHAPTER NINE - CRITICAL THINKING

Critical Thinking involves *problem solving, creative thinking,* and how to make the best *judgments* about what you *read, hear,* or *observe.* The thinking skills that will help you most are:

The development of systems: how to reorganize problems for clearer understanding; how to use hypotheses for trial solutions; how to rule out the irrelevant; how to set up criteria; how to estimate the amount of time necessary to solve a problem.

$E = MC^2$

The creative thinking process: what it is, and how to use it to solve problems. How to remove conventional limits, invent, explore, rearrange, and seek out the most challenging options. You will also gain greater insight into your own originality, and how you can make the best use of your instincts.

CHAPTER TEN - MOTIVATION

How *setting goals* can affect your performance in a positive way. You will learn the significant differences between *short, intermediate,* and *long range goals.* You will learn the *A,B,C Priority System:*

A - Most Important

B - Important

C - Least Important

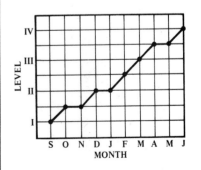

You will also learn how *Purpose* and *Self Initiation* relate to *Goals* and *Goal Setting.*

SUPPLEMENT A - THE PERFORMANCE PROFILE

How to *collect,* and *analyze* information that will help you identify the areas of your academic performance that need improvement. How to develop strategies for improvement in:

MOTIVATION - Well directed energy and the incentive to use it constructively. This consists of:

> *Goal Setting*
>
> *Purpose*
>
> *Self Initiation*

SELF MANAGEMENT - The best possible use of:

    Time

    Place

    Resources

ESSENTIAL SKILLS - Those most needed for success:

    Listening

    Reading Comprehension

    Computation

    Communication (Speaking and Writing)

    Concentration (Staying on Task)

    Research

    Note Taking

    Test Taking

ESSENTIAL SKILLS (For Students of Foreign Language)

    Speaking

    Listening/Hearing

    Understanding

    Writing

    Knowledge of Grammar

CRITICAL THINKING

    Problem Solving

    Analytical Reasoning

ACCOUNTABILITY

    Behavior

    Participation

    Homework and *Classwork*

SUPPLEMENT B - FOREIGN LANGUAGE LEARNING SKILLS AND GRAMMATICAL GLOSSARY

This **SUPPLEMENT** contains important information on the skills of *Speaking, Listening, Understanding, Reading,* and *Writing*.

There is also a complete **Glossary** of all the grammatical terms you need to know in order to succeed in learning a Foreign Language. The **Index** is cross-referenced so that you can find a definition very quickly. The definitions will also help you understand the differences and similarities between English grammar and the grammar of the language you are studying.

How To Use the Margin Space

You will notice that each page has a line drawn down the right or left margin. I have set this space aside for illustrations and brief summaries of the major concepts. As you examine each page, use the information in the margins as a guide to the content on the page.

Use any of the blank space for notes of your own about the content on the page. It works well as a good recall device, and it can also be a model for notetaking from certain types of textbooks you may be using.

Read what is written in this space and add your own notes and comments.

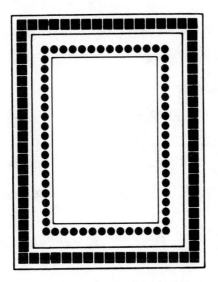

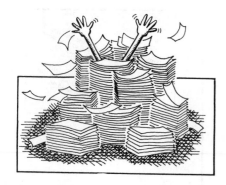

1

ORGANIZATION

"The well organized student gets work done faster and better."

This chapter has the information you need to get off to a good start.

In this chapter, we will introduce you to everything you need to know about completing an assignment from start to finish. Much of what is presented will be taken up in greater detail in other parts of the **MANUAL**. The purpose here is to get you started without your having to complete the entire book before you can begin an assignment. This first chapter will make it possible for you to use the **MANUAL** immediately, and with positive results so that your organizational efforts will be worthwhile.

Once you become familiar with these basic skills, you will find that you automatically work more efficiently and effectively every time you have an assignment. There are nine key questions to ask yourself:

Be able to answer each of these questions for all your assignments.

1. What is the precise *description* of the assignment?

2. What am I supposed *to do*?

3. What does the *teacher expect*?

4. Do I understand all the *key words* and *concepts*?

5. How should I *manage my time* so that I can do the work properly, without "last minute" pressure?

6. How and why should I go beyond the *minimum requirements*?

7. How will I be able to *remember* everything I need to know?

8. How will I be *tested* or *evaluated*?

9. *Where* am I most able to do my best work?

These are nine basic questions that you need to answer before beginning an assignment. At first, you will use these nine questions as a check list. After you form the habit of "organizing yourself," you won't need the list any longer. The questions will automatically occur every time you have a project or assignment.

Let's look at the basic questions and examples of what you need to do.

Description of the Assignment

The most important starting point is knowing exactly what the assignment consists of in precise, specific terms. For example, a math assignment is 20 problems on page 134 of the math textbook. It is to be turned in the following day, on lined notebook paper. Know the answers to these questions before beginning.

How much? 20 problems

What? Addition of fractions

Where? Page 134 in the math textbook

When? It is due the following day

Form? On lined notebook paper

There is nothing really difficult about understanding an assignment. You simply have to know **how extensive** it should be (1 page, 10 pages, 20 problems) **what** it is, **where** to find the content, the **proper format**, and when the work is due. As simple as it may seem, students often overlook some of these points and as a result have their grades lowered. Don't let it happen to you.

Use any of the following assignment examples as a starting point for completing the Worksheet on page 12.

ENGLISH

1. *Grammar/Usage Exercises.* Which personal pronouns to use after prepositions.

2. *Spelling.* When to double a consonant as in "sto*p*," and "sto*pp*ing."

3. *Vocabulary.* Words from a story you are reading.

4. *Reading.* A chapter from a novel.

5. *Composition.* Your opinion of a movie you have seen in class.

6. *Term Paper.* On John Steinbeck's **Cannery Row.**

Be sure you understand exactly <u>what</u> the assignment is.

Examples.

9

SOCIAL STUDIES

1. *Definitions.* Identify and describe the different "freedoms" mentioned in the First Amendment to the United States Constitution.

2. *Reading.* Chapter Three in the World History text: "The Golden Age of Greece."

3. *Interpretation and Analysis.* What caused the Southern States to secede from the union?

4. *Geogreaphy.* Locate all the boundaries of the countries of modern Europe.

5. *Map Reading.* Give the names, latitude, and longitude of six islands in the Pacific Ocean.

6. *Discussion.* Give supporting arguments for your position on the "Right To Life" Amendment to the Constitution.

7. *Research.* Obtain as much information as possible on the discovery of gold in California.

MATHEMATICS

1. *Word Problems.* Read and solve problems on the use of percentages.

2. *Interpretation.* How to get and use information from analyzing different types of graphs.

3. *Construction.* Put numerical facts in the form of a descriptive Information Table.

4. *Estimation.* How much would it cost to produce a specific item?

5. *Computer Program.* Create a program to be used to repeat certain mathematical functions.

6. *Project.* Describe the mathematics of stellar navigation.

7. *Games.* Invent a Game of Chance that makes practical use of the "laws of probability."

8. *Puzzle.* Explain mathematically how much you would weigh if you lived on the moon.

SCIENCE

1. *Nomenclature*. Identify and define all the terms associated with cell division.

2. *Reading*. Chapter Seven on the topic of "Cell Division."

3. *Laboratory Experiment*. The use of fruit flies to understand certain genetic concepts.

4. *Investigation*. What factors are important for seed germination?

5. *Analysis*. Identify the different molecules present in a prepared solution.

6. *Special Project*. What is the scientific explanation for "Color Blindness?"

7. *Research Project*. How does nicotine affect plants?

8. *Group Activity*. How do plants and animals interact in a balanced aquarium?

FOREIGN LANGUAGE

1. *Vocabulary*. Memorize list of new words.

2. *Verb Drill*. Learn how to form the Imperfect tense.

3. *Dialogue*. Memorize expressions.

4. *Grammar Review*. Do exercises on the use of relative and interrogative pronouns.

5. *Translation*. Translate sentences into the language you are studying.

6. *Translation*. Translate passage into English.

7. *Reading*. Read a story in the textbook.

8. *Composition*. Write an account of the story you are reading in the textbook.

9. *Culture*. What kind of food would you expect to eat in a French restaurant?

10. *Recitation*. Memorize and recite a poem.

Examples.

Examples.

DESCRIPTION OF THE ASSIGNMENT - WORKSHEET

Use an assignment of your own or any of the preceding examples of assignments in English, Social Studies, Math, Science, or Foreign Language. Use as much detail in your description as necessary. Make as many copies of this Worksheet as you like.

SUBJECT_____**TEACHER**_____**PERIOD**____

How much do you have to do?

_____

_____

What do you have to do?

_____

_____

_____

Where is the assignment (book, pages, etc.)?

_____

_____

When is it due?

_____

What form does the teacher expect (pen, graph, etc.)?

_____

Notes

_____

_____

_____

_____

_____

What Are You Required To Do?

After you fully understand your assignment, you need to know exactly what *to do* to complete the assignment. Take some time to write down the specific things you should do. Use the following examples as a guide:

ENGLISH: Grammar/Usage Exercises. Which personal pronouns to use after prepositions.

1. *Review* the use of prepositions in Warriner's *English Grammar and Composition*, p. 185, 10d.

2. Prepare Exercise 6, p. 185, for *oral recitation.*

3. *Write* the correct prepositional phrases in Exercise 7.

4. *Follow the instructions* and complete Review Exercise A.

SOCIAL STUDIES: Describe the sequence of events that took place before, during, and immediately after the attack on Pearl Harbor, December 7, 1941.

1. *Read* Chapters 93 and 94, pages 576 to 593 in the textbook, *Building the United States*

2. *Define* the terms on pages 581 and 593, and add the definitions to your U. S. History notebook.

3. *Locate* all the countries on your map.

4. *List* the main events that took place prior to the attack on Pearl Harbor.

5. *Describe* the reaction of the President and Congress of the United States.

6. *Be prepared* to discuss the main ideas.

7. *Connect* the past events with the present.

MATHEMATICS: Read and solve problems on the use of percent.

1. *Review* the classroom information that was given on how to do problems that deal with percent.

2. *Review* the information on pages 278-279 in your text on the use of percent.

The specific tasks for each assignment.

Examples of what to do.

Examples of what to do.

Examples of <u>what</u> to do.

3. *Solve* problems 1 through 9.

4. *Write an explanation* for each step in the process.

5. For *extra credit*, do problems 10 through 20.

SCIENCE: Unit On Heredity

1. *Construct* a Trait Chart similar to the one on page 417 of your textbook.

2. *Place a check* after all the traits you have.

3. *List* any of your classmates who have the traits listed in the chart.

4. *Predict* whether the traits listed are dominant or recessive.

5. *Answer* questions 1 through 8 on page 417.

FOREIGN LANGUAGE: Grammar

Examples of <u>what</u> to do.

1. *Read* the paragraph in Section H on page 110 in your French *Workbook*.

2. *Rewrite* the paragraph changing all verbs in the present tense to the passe compose.

3. *Do Exercises* A and B on page 359 of the textbook.

4. *Repeat* everything several times orally.

WHAT ARE YOU REQUIRED TO DO - WORKSHEET

List all of the tasks you need to do for each of your assignments. At first, this will seem a bit tedious, but after a while it will become second nature. You will do it automatically, and soon you will be that much better organized.

SUBJECT_____**TEACHER**_____**PERIOD**_____

_____

_____

_____

_____

_____

_____

_____

_____

_____

_____

_____

_____

_____

_____

_____

_____

_____

What Does the Teacher Expect?

What are the
PERFORMANCE Objectives?

In addition to the parts or tasks in each assignment, the teacher has another reason for giving the assignment. The teacher wants *something to happen* as a result of giving the assignment. This is called the *outcome*, or the *objective(s) of the assignment*.

The *objectives* are usually based on *performance*. You have to show that you can *do* something, *remember* something, *recite* something, *explain* something, *discuss* something, *use* something, *understand* something, and finally *take a test* to show that you know the material.

The *performance objectives* of an assignment should in some way be connected to overall learning. For example, by doing 20 problems on percents in a math class, you will be able to use that knowledge in the next unit on decimal equivalents. This in turn will prepare you for more advanced calculation needed in higher levels of learning.

When you know what your teacher expects, it is easier to organize your work and you won't be in for a big surprise at exam time.

Some *teachers* assume that you know what *they expect*. But you may not be sure. You should make absolutely certain that when you have any doubts about teacher expectations, that you ask questions. Don't be bashful. See the teacher after class, if necessary. Don't leave anything to chance. Following are examples of *Performance Objectives* from an English vocabulary assignment.

What does the teacher want you to <u>demonstrate</u> from doing the assignment?

1. Know the *definition* of each word in the list.

2. *Use* each word in a sentence.

3. Be able to *spell* each word correctly.

4. *Locate* each word in the reading selection from which the words were taken.

5. Give the *derivation* of each word.

6. *Recite* the meaning or usage of each word when called upon in class the next day.

Notice that each of the above expectations is actually a *performance objective*. It means that learning and doing are very closely associated with each other.

16

WHAT DOES THE TEACHER EXPECT - WORKSHEET

Use this space to list everything your teacher expects you to "learn" when doing an assignment. Think of "learn" as being the same as "perform." In other words, you haven't really learned anything *until you can demonstrate* what you have learned by some sort of *performance*. Remember that "knowing" is not enough; you have to be able "to do" what you know. Think of "performance" as you list what your teachers expect in each of your assignments:

SUBJECT_____**TEACHER**_____**PERIOD**___

_____

_____

_____

_____

_____

_____

_____

_____

_____

_____

_____

_____

_____

_____

_____

Understanding Key Words and Concepts

Be sure you <u>know</u> the meaning of <u>all</u> important words and concepts.

The next organizational step is to be certain that you understand all of the key words and concepts. For example, you have a *Map Analysis* to do for Social Studies. You have to locate boundaries of countries, rivers, and other bodies of water, agricultural and industrial regions, trade routes (rail, water, air), and population centers. The textbook uses terms like:

- scale, representative fraction

- political map, reference map

- legend

- parallel, latitude, longitude

- terrain

- projection: azimuth, gnomic, mercator, conic

You may not need to know all of these terms, but a Map assignment could well include many of them. The important thing is that you find out what you need to know *before* you begin any serious work on the assignment.

What do you do when you don't know the meaning of a term or concept? Try one or more of the following:

1. Look for the meaning or explanation in your *textbook*, or in the Glossary of terms contained at the end of the chapter in many textbooks.

2. Ask the *teacher*.

3. Use a *reference*: encyclopedia, dictionary, Index.

4. Use what is usually known as a *Wordbook*. These include the following: Acronyms, Abbreviations and Symbols, Thesaurus, Foreign Words and Phrases, Guide to Synonyms, Cliches, Linguistics, Literary Terms, and American Dialect Terms.

   You should be able to obtain any of these at your school or community library.

5. Subject matter *glossaries*. These are available in all academic subjects. The best glossary of grammatical terms for students taking a foreign language is in **SUPPLEMENT B** of this **MANUAL**.

UNDERSTANDING KEY WORDS AND CONCEPTS - WORKSHEET

Take each assignment separately and list all the terms and concepts that you should know and remember. Keep all of these definitions and examples in your notebook. Refer to them as often as necessary, particularly before any test or examination. You will be pleased with how much easier your assignments become as you constantly increase your special knowledge of terms and concepts in each of the subjects you are taking.

SUBJECT_____**TEACHER**_____**PERIOD**___

_____

_____

_____

_____

_____

_____

_____

_____

_____

_____

_____

_____

_____

_____

_____

_____

Managing Your Time

Plan <u>how</u> <u>much</u> time you need for an assignment and <u>when</u> you will find the time.

Use the WEEKLY TIME CHART on page 32.

Now that you know exactly what you are required to do: the goals, objectives, expectations, key terms and concepts--the next step is to set aside enough time to complete the assignment.

Remember, one expectation that practically every teacher insists on is that the assignment be completed **on or before** the due date. Here is where many of you fool yourselves. You think you have more time than you actually have. The result is, even with the best of intentions, that you wait to the "last minute." You may get the work done, but the quality may be less than it should be, and the work itself turns out to be pure drudgery. It also becomes a habit and like all habits, this one becomes more difficult to break.

You can begin to break the habit now by forming new habits described briefly here, and in greater detail in Chapter Two, Time Management.

1. Examine the **WEEKLY TIME CHART** on page 32, and the example on page 36. The purpose of this **CHART** is to give you a *visual picture* of how much time you actually have in a typical week during the school year.

2. Fill in all of your *known* commitments: classes, sports, job, family obligations, etc. At a glance you can quickly *see* how much free time you have.

3. List all of your current "homework" assignments in the space below, and estimate how much time each assignment *should* take:

SUBJECT   TIME REQUIRED

_____

_____

_____

_____

_____

_____

_____

20

4. Enter the hours you need to complete your current assignments on the **WEEKLY TIME CHART**. After you do this, notice how crowded the hours become when you **see** all your commitments and obligations. You realize how busy you can be. You must *plan carefully* to make the best use of your time. There just aren't that many "last minutes" to rely on.

   Remember, *careful planning* can become a habit, the kind that helps you organize yourself for work.

5. List all of your *on-going assignments* meaning those subjects in which you have regular work three or four nights each week. You need to plan for a certain amount of time on these subjects on a daily basis. Foreign language and math are good examples.

6. Be sure you make enough copies of the **WEEKLY TIME CHART** to last you for a semester or year. Don't hesitate to improve on the form if you can think of anything that might work better for you. That applies to any other form in the **MANUAL** as well. Don't ever be shy about using your imagination.

7. Examine the **ASSIGNMENT LOG** and the **TO-DO-LIST** in Chapter Two. How might you use them along with the **WEEKLY TIME CHART**?

Finding Time You Never Knew You Had

How would you feel if you found a $100 bill on the street, with no one in sight to whom it might belong? What a sudden feeling of freedom! You can go out and buy something you never thought you could afford. What fun!

The same feeling applies to *time*. When you manage your time well, you have more of it, and it's even better than "found money," because the time you get is really yours. You can do things with it that you never thought possible. Even better, once good time management becomes automatic, you will always be "finding" time for extra activities, leisure, or whatever you like.

Ask Yourself Lakein's Question

Alan Lakein wrote one of the best books on *Time Management* that I have ever found, entitled *How To Get Control Of Your Time And Your Life.* He told his readers to ask themselves, "*What is the best use of my time right now*?" I encourage you to do the same. Make it a habit, and practice it regularly. It will not only help you get things done, but it will add to your pleasure as well.

When you make plans, get in the habit of using the WEEKLY TIME CHART.

Well managed time gives you <u>more</u> free time.

Beyond the Minimum Requirements

By doing <u>more</u> than the teacher expects, you learn more and the result is a better grade.

Over the years I have found that the best students often do more than the minimum. They go beyond reading the chapter in the text, answering the assigned questions or whatever else is expected.

Right or wrong, students constantly compete with each other. It is a fact of life, and if you are to succeed in school, you have to know how to compete effectively. I recommend the following:

1. Be sure you know the basic or minimum requirements for the assignment. Consider that as the *starting point.* Most students think of the basic or minimum requirements as all they have to do. When you go beyond the minimum, you give yourself a competitive edge.

2. Ask about *supplenentary materials.* This could be articles from periodicals, reference books, or anything else the teacher might suggest.

3. Ask about "*extra credit.*" Some teachers offer this regularly, others do not. There is no harm in asking.

4. Always know *the importance* of each assignment, project, or activity. *Importance* means how it will affect your grade. How much "weight" will it have? Obviously, the more *importance*, the more attention you will want to give.

5. *Review past assignments* to see how you can improve. Learn why the teacher gave you a certain grade that was lower than you thought it should be.

6. *Compare* what you do with what the most successful students in the class are doing. They may be doing something you aren't.

7. *Identify yourself* with the top students. Let them be the pace setters. Always work to the highest possible standard.

Important Note: Please Read This

You may have the impression from what I have written on this topic that the most important thing about school is the *grade you get,* and that I want you to become bloodthirsty competitors! That is not at all what I want to see happen.

There are two important outcomes that I want you to achieve: the first is *to learn,* and the second is *to get a good grade.* In my opinion, they are *both equally important.* I would be doing you a disservice if I emphasized one and not the other. This **MANUAL** is designed to help you become an efficient learner so that you will experience the real pleasures of *learning.* I also want you to get the best possible grades, and I will give you as much as I can to help.

In summary, *learning* is important. *Good grades* are also important. There is no reason why you can't have both.

In the space below, list everything you can think of that would take you beyond the minimum requirements of your current assignments:

Knowledge <u>and</u> good grades are what you want.

English

_____

_____

_____

Social Studies

_____

_____

_____

Mathematics

_____

_____

_____

Science

_____

_____

_____

Foreign Language

_____

_____

_____

Remembering What You Need To Know

If I were to rank the importance of the various study skills, I would put *Notetaking* at or near the top of the list. A student without a good recall system is like a car without gas or a tape recorder without tape. The development of a good recall system does not happen by itself. It must be learned, and equally important, practiced regularly. A good recall system can make your life much more pleasant.

Recall Skills You Can Learn

Good note taking which helps you remember important information is more than simply writing down the main points from what you read, see, or hear. There are four related skills involved:

1. *Speed.* Write quickly. This means using some sort of abbreviated but legible and understandable script. If your school has a course in *Speedwriting*, it might be worth taking. Otherwise develop your own system; be sure you can read what you write.

2. *Screening Information.* Separate out what is important. You don't have time to write anything unnecessary, unimportant, or irrelevant. This can be most difficult. In the beginning you might tend to write too much or too little, and then perhaps not use any of it. Refer to Chapter Four on *Notetaking* for more explanation and examples on this skill.

3. *Format/Graphics.* The purpose is to remember. Use any technique that does the job. Use pictures, color, bold letters, stars, underline, or whatever causes you to recall the fact, idea, or concept that you want to remember. The *Format* and *Graphics* you use should help you remember important information from minimal clues.

   Be sure that you include a *reference* component. In other words, put the page number, the date, place, time of an observation, or something significant about the setting of a lecture. If necessary, you want to be able to get to an original source to fill in important details easily and quickly.

4. *Mapping.* If you have taken good notes, you can make a visual *Map* of the information to help you with immediate recall. Pick out important topics and sub-topics and draw lines that indicate how they relate to each other. See page 68.

Test Taking

The mention of the word *test* causes some degree of anxiety in nearly everybody. The *test* day can be a day of reckoning, a moment of truth, doomsday, or a confrontation with the inevitable. The worst part is waiting for the *test* to happen. In my opinion, tests are among the main causes of school stress, especially during mid-terms and finals.

Know well in advance what kinds of tests your teacher gives, <u>and</u> how much they count toward your grade.

Although tests will always strike some amount of fear in your heart, I hope I can help you approach the event with more self confidence and reassurance. There are *two* important *types* of *knowledge* you need in order to do your best on any kind of test. They are:

1. Knowledge of the *subject*.

2. Knowledge of *how to take a test*.

Most of you probably assume that all you really need to know is the subject. Believe me, that is only half the battle--in some ways the easier half. The other (equally important) half has to do with *test taking* skills. Good test taking skills will relieve a lot of the stress you feel when taking a test. There are two important points:

1. Always know the *teacher's purpose* for giving the test. What are you expected to know? Why? What are you expected to demonstrate? See Chapter Six for more details on the purpose of tests.

2. How should you *prepare* for the test? What kind of test will it be: essay, short answer, true-false, multiple choice? The following guidelines should help you prepare:

   • Identify and pinpoint the *subject matter*.

   • *Review* notes, handouts, past exams, and anything else that might be helpful.

   • *Plan* your review *time*. Log the hours on your **WEEKLY TIME CHART**.

   • Know in advance *details* such as penalties for guessing, length of the test, use of pen or pencil, and how the test will be graded.

Refer to Chapter Six on **TEST TAKING** for further information.

Where Do You Do Your Best Work?

Find <u>and</u> use the best places to do schoolwork.

This could be a real key to your success. No matter how good your intentions, if you do not have a place to go for quiet concentrated study, your efforts will be wasted. If you have good study conditions at home, so much the better. Most of you, however, may not. Don't give up. Some of the best of us had to deal with this problem and were able to handle it. Remember, your goal is **to succeed**. Don't let anything get in your way.

Form A Habit

Studying, like many other activities, has a lot to do with *habit forming*. That is why you are reading this **MANUAL**. To form new habits. However, some habits are good, and some are not so good. Your job is to form good ones.

Knowing how and where to find the right kind of study places can become a habit. You should study where you can work without distractions. Remember, nothing is ever perfect. What you want to do is find the best places even though you may have to learn how to tolerate some noise.

The interesting thing about noise is that you notice it a lot less when you are not directly concerned with it. For example, when you can hear the TV set or loud talking among persons in another room, possibly your friends, or members of your own family, it may be very difficult to concentrate. On the other hand, you could be in a room overlooking the busiest Los Angeles freeway and hardly notice the sound of the cars streaming by.

The first step then is to find a place where noise or distraction does not affect you directly. Once you use these places regularly, you begin to form a habit.

Have you ever noticed how you tend to take the same seat in many of your classrooms? Or in the library? Or in the movie theater? These are the habits I speak of. As patterns emerge, you always feel more comfortable doing the same thing.

Suppose we look at some possible study places that are frequently available to you.

The *Community Library* comes immediately to mind. All the resources are there, and libraries are usually open when you need to study. The drawback is that the Community Library may also be a place to socialize, which is fine if you want to socialize, but not so good if you want to study. Find out which hours are best for you, and plan your schedule accordingly.

The *School Library* is also good, but most school libraries are only open when you are usually in class. The School Library may tend to be a social gathering place during lunchtime, and at other times when classes are not in session.

Your *teacher's classroom* may be available at certain times before, during, or after school. Talk to your teachers about coming in at times. They ordinarily don't mind at all. Remember, the more work you get done during school hours, the more time you will have for other activities.

Other places to investigate would include the *local YMCA*, a *church* or *synagogue*, friends' or relatives' homes, and even some businesses. The point is, *don't* ever throw up your hands and think you do not have a good place to go where it is quiet enough to study.

Organization - Chapter Summary

There is enough information in this Chapter for you to begin improving and practicing the study skills you need for top performance in your school subjects. Use the examples as models, and the *Worksheets* for practice.

The goal is to form new habits. In other words, every time you get an assignment you will automatically ask yourself the following questions:

Get in the habit of answering these questions for all your assignments.

1. What is the *description* of the assignment

2. What exactly am I supposed *to do*?

3. What does the *teacher expect*?

4. Do I understand all the *key words* and *concepts*?

5. How should I *manage my time* so that I can do the work properly without any last minute pressure?

6. How do I go *beyond* the *minimum requirements*?

7. What are the best ways *to remember* what I need to know?

8. How do I *prepare* for and *take tests*?

9. Where are the *best places to study*?

This can become an automatic part of your study routine. The more practice you get in forming these habits, the more organized and successful you will become in all of your school work.

When you need more information on any of the skill categories, refer to other parts of the MANUAL where the subjects are treated in greater detail.

Chapter Two will provide you with the forms and techniques for a very complete TIME MANAGEMENT system.

2

TIME MANAGEMENT

"Time Management is the enemy of Procrastination"
(Author Unknown)

Time Management, for our purposes, means getting the most amount of work done in the least amount of time, and with the best possible results (grades). It's that simple, but it requires conscious and continuous effort on your part. However, once you understand the tools to use and how to use them, the job becomes easier. In fact, you could very well become fondly addicted to these skills because of their importance to your success in school. The first Time Management step is a full understanding of the *planning process*.

Managing time takes <u>planning</u>.

Planning

Planning is as natural as breathing. You make plans every day; you couldn't get much done otherwise. You *plan* to go to a ball game, a dance, the movies. You *plan* to take a vacation, become a life guard, buy a new stereo, or sometimes just relax for an hour or two. You also make plans to work in an office, become an auto mechanic, go to college, study law, medicine, or whatever interests you. Whatever you do, it is usually the result of some sort of plan that you have made in advance or on the spur of the moment. There are two types of planning that I refer to: *informal* and *formalized planning*. Both are important, and you need to understand their purposes and how they differ from each other.

The difference between formal and informal planning.

   Informal planning is what most of you usually do. This kind of planning is simple and uncomplicated. There is no elaborate or involved structure. It tends to be somewhat limited in terms of consequence. For example, you plan to go to a dance and something happens that prevents your going. It won't likely make much difference in the long run; there will be other dances that you can go to. Your life will not change one way or the other

Informal planning is mostly <u>short range</u>, associated with "here and now."

Informal planning is least complicated.

Informal planning is also associated with what I call **linear outcomes**: between the plan and the outcome is a straight (linear) line. For example, you plan to go to a movie. The **movie** is what you want, or what the **outcome** should be. The **plan** is aimed **straight** at the **outcome.** Although you may also have to plan about getting enough money and transportation, the most important part of the plan is whether or not you see the movie.

Formal Planning. Although Informal planning may be acceptable for many of your day to day needs, if you want to succed in school, you need a **formalized** planning system which includes:

Formal planning is longer in range, and well thought out.

1. *Important Purpose*

2. *Interrelationships*

3. *Structure*

Formal planning has a definite purpose.

Important Purpose. This implies that there is a serious reason for the planning. There are also important consequences. For example, you have a term paper to do for your English class. The grade on the term paper will count toward one third of the final grade in the course. That is important. The purpose is that you want to do well and get the best possible grade. You can't leave any of this to chance. You need to make a formal plan.

Formal planning is directly related to priorities and time commitments.

Interrelationships. In formalized planning, nearly everything is interrelated. Your time commitment for a job after school, piano lessons, or swimming practice are all related and limit the amount of time you have to do the work at hand. You therefore have to make decisions which in turn affect other outcomes. You will need to **set priorities** to make the best use of your time. This involves:

● The *importance* of the *commitment*

● The amount of *time required.*

An activity that takes very little time might have a low priority. Under certain circumstances, however, it could be worth doing just to get it out of the way and clear the deck. You will have to make these decisions constantly. It will become easier with practice, as you learn how to pick and choose what to do first.

Formal planning is most effective when you use A WEEKLY TIME CHART, a TO-DO-LIST, and an ASSIGNMENT LOG.

Structure. The **Time Charts, Assignment Logs,** and **To-Do-Lists** in this MANUAL will help you effectively structure your time. You can keep track of your assignments, your progress and your achievement. Nothing of any importance is ever left to chance. At first using these tools may seem complicated, but after regular use, the most intricate planning will seem natural and easy to do.

Following are three parts of a good Time Management System.

The Weekly Time Chart (page 32)

In order to plan your weekly activities and study sessions, it is helpful to see at a glance your time commitments and what hours you can use for study. The **WEEKLY TIME CHART** helps you plan more efficiently and effectively. Refer to it often, and keep it as handy as possible. Experience has shown that the *one week* Time Chart is the most useful.

Make enough copies to last you for 2 or 3 months. Keep the used copies in your files for reference. You will be surprised when you look back after a month or so at how much more skilled you are in using the **WEEKLY TIME CHART**. Don't hesitate to make changes in the Time Chart if you feel there are ways to improve it. Always do what works *best for you.*

Make copies of the WEEKLY TIME CHART on page 32. See the example on page 36.

The Assignment Log (page 33)

Record all of your major classroom assignments, projects, and activities on the **ASSIGNMENT LOG**. Be sure that all of these are also accounted for on the **WEEKLY TIME CHART**. This should be done for all work requiring one or more hours of outside class time.

Make copies of the ASSIGNMENT LOG on page 33. See the example on page 37.

The To-Do-List (page 34)

The third leg of the Time Management System is the **TO-DO-LIST**. These are the daily things that you must do, and which you might forget without a reminder. Appointments with teachers, phone calls, meetings, errands, and anything else that could be a problem if not attended to at the right time.

Make copies of the TO-DO-LIST on page 34. See the example on page 38.

Personally, I dislike making phone calls. I tend to put them off, and if I don't have a reminder, I will often forget them. Every morning I have a list of important phone calls that I have to make. That becomes my first obligation (*to do*) of the day. Be sure you list your obligations, especially the ones you will be most likely to forget.

Pages 32-34 are blank forms that you should copy for your own use. I have also included typical examples on pages 36-38 that you can use as a reference.

Keep your forms up to date; refer to them often, and make entries every time new obligations and time commitments come up. These aids will help you get rid of that nasty old persistent enemy: *PROCRASTINATION*.

WEEKLY TIME CHART

DATES: From_____Through_____

Time	M	T	W	Th	F	S	Sun
7-8							
8-9							
9-10							
10-11							
11-12							
12-1							
1-2							
2-3							
3-4							
4-5							
5-6							
6-7							
7-8							
8-9							
9-10							
10-11							

ASSIGNMENT LOG

Fill in your major assignments for the next 2 to 4 weeks.
Keep 2 or 3 of these sheets with you and update them as needed.

DATES: From_____**To**_____

Subject	Assignment	Due	Comp ✓	Time Needed/Comments

_____

_____

_____

_____

_____

TO-DO-LIST

Write down the important things you have to do today. Be sure to note at what time these things should be done. Keep this with you and use it every day.

Day_____**Date**_____

What Must Be Done	When	Done ✓	Notes

_____

_____

_____

_____

_____

Time Manangement Models

On the following pages are examples of completed Time Management Forms. They are meant mainly for you to see how three students planned the most efficient use of their time. It will take some practice on your part to become skilled in managing your time and you will then discover what good management can do for you.

- You will save time.

- Your work will be better.

- You will have more time to relax.

- You will feel more relaxed.

- You won't forget things.

- You will be able to do more.

- Your grades will improve.

- Your parents will appreciate you more.

- You will impress your teachers.

- You will make better preparations for the future.

- You will become better organized.

- Your study habits will improve.

- You will get greater satisfaction from your work.

- You will be more motivated.

- You will have a better attitude about yourself.

- You will have more self confidence.

- You will not procrastinate.

- You will have a greater sense of personal freedom.

- Your concentration will improve.

- You will find other rewards and gratification associated with success in school.

This can happen when you make good use of your time.

WEEKLY TIME CHART

10th Grade Student
DATES: From _____ Oct. 7 _____ Through _____ Oct. 13 _____

Time	M	T	W	Th	F	S	Sun
7-8							
8-9	X	X	X	X	X		
9-10	X	X	X	X	X		
10-11	X	X	X	X	X	ENGLISH REPORT	
11-12	X	X	X	X	X	"	
12-1	FREE	FREE	FREE	FREE	FREE		
1-2	X	X	X	X	X		
2-3	X	X	X	X	X		
3-4	FOOTBALL PRACTICE	F—— P——	F—— P——	F—— P——	GAME		
4-5	"	"	"	"	"		BEGIN SCIENCE PROJECT
5-6	FREE	FREE	FREE	FREE	FREE		"
6-7	DINNER	D——	D——	D——	D——	D——	D——
7-8	STUDY FRENCH	STUDY FRENCH	STUDY FRENCH	STUDY FRENCH	FREE		ENGLISH REPORT
8-9	US HIST MATH	ENGLISH TEST MATH	US HIST QUIZ	TEST ENGLISH MATH	FREE		"
9-10	BIOLOGY	BIOLOGY QUIZ	MATH	QUIZ BIOLOGY	FREE		MATH

"X" - Indicates class time
"FREE" - Used for relaxation or other choices
BLANK SPACES - For study and/or other pursuits

ASSIGNMENT LOG

Fill in your major assignments for the next 2 to 4 weeks.
Keep 2 or 3 of these sheets with you and update them as needed.

DATES: From _Sept. 23_ To _Oct. 18_

8th Grade Student

Subject	Assignment	Due	Comp ✓	Time Needed/Comments
English	Book Report on Call of the Wild	Oct. 10		15-20 Hours 1000 Word Minimum
Social Studies	Map of European Countries	Oct. 1	Sept. 27	2 Hours Include Symbols
Math	Daily			45 Minutes
Spanish	Daily			30 Minutes
Science	Plant Project	Oct. 15		3 Hours - Visit a Plant Store List Plants Sold There

Science - Extra Credit - Make a Small Portable Garden

TO-DO-LIST

Write down the important things you have to do today. Be sure to note at what time these things should be done. Keep this with you and use it every day.

Day **MON.**   Date **NOV. 3**

11th Grade Student

What Must Be Done	When	Done ✓	Notes
PICK UP GROCERIES	AFTER SCHOOL		
AUTO REPAIR	"		MAY NEED NEW MUFFLER
ASK TEACHERS FOR FUTURE ASSIGNMENTS	BEFORE/ AFTER CLASS		PREP FOR FAMILY TRIP 11/7 - 11/13
SET DATE TO MEET WITH CLASS OFFICERS	DURING LUNCH		MAKE PLANS FOR X-MAS DANCE
MAKE APPT. TO SEE COUNSELOR	BEFORE SCHOOL	✓	GET PSAT SCORES
PHONE JOHN AT HOSPITAL	AFTER SCHOOL		
GET BOOK ON CIVIL WAR FROM LIBRARY	3RD PERIOD	✓	
WATCH TV SPECIAL FOR SCIENCE CLASS	8:00 - 9:00 PM		COUSTEAU

WISH GINNY "HAPPY BIRTHDAY"

Time Management - Chapter Summary

Time Management means getting the most done in the least amount of time, with the best possible results. This involves both *formal* and *informal planning*, and the use of a **WEEKLY TIME CHART**, an **ASSIGNMENT LOG**, and a daily **TO-DO-LIST**.

Informal planning relates to most of what you do from day to day. Although the plans may seem important at the time, they don't usually have much long range importance.

Formal Planning requires:

- *Purpose*, which means that you should have a good reason for the plan.

- *Interrelationships*, which means taking everything possible into account: time, other obligations, and setting *priorities*.

- *Structure*, which requires the use of the *Time Chart*, the *Assignment Log*, and the daily *To-Do-List*.

The **WEEKLY TIME CHART** shows you at a glance all your time commitments for a one week period.

The **ASSIGNMENT LOG** is a record of all your current assignments, projects and activities that you have to complete within approximately a 4 week time period.

The **TO-DO-LIST** is a daily reminder of all your important obligations such as appointments, phone calls, meetings, errands, etc.

Good Time Management habits will give you more free time, help you become a better student, and make your work more enjoyable.

Remember how <u>precious</u> your time is. Do all you can to save it, guard it, and use it wisely.

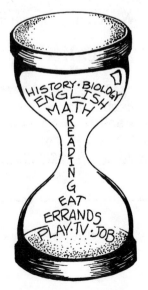

3

CONCENTRATION

"Concentration is mental magic"

You concentrate better when you have a good reason or purpose to do the work.

I f there is one single skill that students find difficult to master, it is the skill of *concentration*: how to get started and focus on an assignment until it is done. How do you avoid daydreaming and mind wandering? How do you stay on the job without getting tired, fidgety, hungry, thirsty, distracted, or so frustrated that you put aside the work you need to do?

Why is it so difficult? What does it really take to be able to concentrate? Why is it so easy for some people and difficult for others? The answer to all of these questions can be found in each of the 5 categories listed below:

- *Purpose and Practicality*: The reason(s) for doing the assignment.

- *Interest*: The power of curiosity and personal benefit.

- *Control:* Eliminating distracting conditions.

- *Consequence I:* What happens when you fail.

- *Consequence II*: What happens when you succeed.

Purpose and Practicality

You _can_ learn how to concentrate better.

Do you usually know why you are doing a particular assignment? For example, your Spanish teacher has assigned ten sentences that you have to translate from English to Spanish. Why? Is there some grammatical concept to practice in order to understand how to apply it? Is it to practice some new vocabulary words?

The enemy of concentration for this type of exercise is to think that there is no reason for the assignment, other than that the assignment is busy work. Following are typical assignments which include purposes and practical reasons for doing the work.

English Assignment: Read the Introduction to *JULIUS CAESAR* by Shakespeare. (Why? For what reasons?)

1. To become familiar with the author and what life was like when he lived and wrote.

2. To become familiar with the background of the play and the main characters.

3. To become familiar with Shakespearean English.

4. To learn how this play relates to the present day.

5. To understand characterization and motivation.

Examples of Purpose: English.

Mathematics Assignment: Do 10 word problems dealing with percents and decimals. The purposes are:

1. To become more adept in solving word problems.

2. To improve critical problem solving ability.

3. To become familiar with the practical side of using percents and decimals.

4. To become skilled in applying concepts.

5. To demonstrate problem solving capability.

Examples of Purpose: Math.

Social Studies Assignment: Read the chapter on "The Hopi Indians." The purposes are:

1. To understand the Hopi social conditions.

2. To appreciate Hopi artistic creations.

3. To appreciate the historical facts of Hopi contributions to the United States.

4. To relate Hopi culture to other native American cultures.

5. To find a topic for further research and a term paper.

Examples of Purpose: Social Studies.

Science Assignment: Start Unit on "Cells and Tissues." The purposes are:

1. To learn the basic parts of a cell and how it lives.

2. To understand the mechanics and principal parts of the microscope.

3. To learn how to use the laboratory to investigate and verify scientific principles.

4. To understand the process of cell division.

5. To understand how DNA, RNA, and enzymes regulate the life activities of a cell.

6. To understand the functions of tissues.

Foreign Language Assignment: Use of the Relative Pronoun. Translate ten English sentences into French. The purposes are:

1. To demonstrate knowledge of what a Relative Pronoun is.

2. To demonstrate knowledge of the forms of Relative Pronouns.

3. To demonstrate ability to select the correct Relative Pronoun under all circumstances.

4. To understand the pitfalls of English use of the Relative Pronoun compared to French use.

Notice that every one of the purposes listed above begins with the expression "*To*" do something. "*To* understand," "*To* learn," "*To* appreciate," "*To* demonstrate," "*To* become familiar with," and so on. All of these expressions imply being able to "perform" in some way or other as a result of the knowledge you gain from doing the assignment.

When you think of "purpose," always think of how it relates to "performance." Being able "*To* do something." Think of it this way:

First • You learn something (knowledge).

Next • You do something (purpose).

Last • You become something. (use).

PURPOSES OF THE ASSIGNMENT - WORKSHEET

List the major purposes for each of your assignments:

English

_____

_____

_____

Social Studies

_____

_____

_____

Math

_____

_____

_____

Science

_____

_____

_____

Foreign Language

_____

_____

_____

Notes

_____

_____

_____

Interest In the Assignment

If you get off to a good start, you will have a better chance to become interested in what you are doing.

Interest in what you have to do is without a doubt the single most positive motivating force in getting you started and helping you keep your attention on your work. When interest is high, the time goes by quickly and you usually get a lot done. "But," you will probably ask, "how can I become interested in something I absolutely hate to do, like translating ten silly sentences from English into Spanish? What buttons do I press so that I can sit down and do the work?"

Unfortunately, there are no buttons to press. If your background and current knowledge of the subject are limited, this can be a drawback, especially in subjects like foreign language or mathematics. In these subjects, what you learn today is the building block for tomorrow's lesson. This is called cumulative knowledge. You may be able to open a social studies book, an English book, and in many instances, a science book to any page and begin reading without any real difficulty. Not so in mathematics or foreign language. If you haven't thoroughly mastered Chapter One in these subjects, you cannot go on to Chapter Two. By the time you get to Chapter Five, the situation could become absolutely hopeless.

There is little or no way to become interested when you fall hopelessly behind in a subject. You will need other solutions such as special help from your teacher or a private tutor, or even a change in your program. The point I would like to stress is the importance of a *good beginning* in all classes, especially subjects that build like mathematics and foreign language.

Do whatever you can to become interested. Be creative and inventive.

But suppose you have a reasonably good background in a subject. What do you do then to become interested in a particular assignment? The following are some suggestions:

Fun.

1. *Make it fun* by using your imagination. In the case of the ten sentences to be translated from English to Spanish, try to make a story out of the sentences. The sillier the better.

   Reword the math problems using far out expressions for all of the quantities, percents, or other parts of the problem.

   If you are artistic, draw pictures or cartoons of the social studies assignment on the characteristics of the American voter. An added bonus is that this could be a big help to you when recalling the information.

   Think of what might happen if you changed a laboratory experiment in some bizarre way.

2. *Make it a game*. Compete with yourself. Time yourself with a math problem and then try to do better with the next and the next. In a map exercise, plan it like a trip and give yourself points for different stops, and for knowing the names of places. How many points would you give Brutus for his big speech in ***JULIUS CAESAR***? Marc Antony for his big speech? How would you measure the points?

   Try conjugating an irregular verb in five seconds, four seconds, three seconds.

   Think of "trivia" questions as part of a science assignment.

   Invent your own "games." Share them with your friends and teachers.

3. *Make it relevant*. Try to develop as many relation-ships between your work and your goals for the future. If you plan to study engineering, the more math and science you take, the better.

   Associate your work with outside interests, a job, career, travel, hobbies, or current events.

4. Use your knowledge for ***potential profit***. Your knowledge of various subjects, particularly math, science and foreign languages, may qualify you to tutor other students for a fee. You not only make money, but you learn a lot. There is always a need for good tutors, and if you are good at it and like it, you might want to become an educator.

5. *Form a study group*. Get together with other students in the class to discuss the work, compare notes, and quiz each other.

6. *Expand your knowledge*. Find other information on the subject using resources such as magazine articles, movies, TV programs, tapes, trips, lectures, etc. This will give you greater exper-tise and depth as well as heightened interest.

Games.

Useful.

Profitable.

Work with other students.

Learn as much as you can.

45

Try short cuts and study
aids.

Make your work count in
as many ways as possible.

7. ***Make use of study aids***, such as ***Cliff Notes***,
summaries, outlines, translations, reviews, and
other condensed forms of analysis and information.
A warning, however, that you should be aware of is
that the ***study aid*** is just that, an aid. It is
not, I repeat, ***not***, a substitute for what the
teacher requires and expects you to do.

8. "***Kill two birds with one stone***." If you are
studying <u>***JULIUS CAESAR***</u> in English, and you are also
doing a unit on Roman Civilization in your World
History class, the two can benefit each other.
Find ways for it to happen. The same goes for
science, math, and many other combinations.

Knowledge does not exist in a vacuum. Always look
for connections that can provide interest, save
time, and provide you with greater understanding in
your classes.

INTEREST IN THE ASSIGNMENT - WORKSHEET

Use the suggestions I have given you about generating interest as a starting point for your own ideas. Think of how you might become more enthused about the work you have to do in each of your classes. Use imagination and creativity.

English

_____

_____

_____

Social Studies

_____

_____

_____

Math

_____

_____

_____

Science

_____

_____

_____

Foreign Language

_____

_____

_____

Control

Take charge!

Your ability to concentrate also depends on your internal and external control, plus organizational factors. Suppose we examine these separately.

Internal Control. This is really "self control." Who's in charge? You? Or something else? When you sit down to begin an assignment, is the stage set for work? Have you pre-arranged for distractions that will prevent you from doing your work? For example, consider the following questions before you get started on an important assignment:

What to avoid <u>before</u> you get started.

- Are you *tired*?

- Are you *hungry*?

- Are you *thirsty*?

- Are you *hot*?

- Are you *cold*?

- Are you *cramped*?

- Are you *uncomfortable*?

- Are you *miserable*?

- Are you *excited*?

- Are you *anxious*?

- Are you *distraught*?

If you answered "Yes" to any of the above questions, you are not ready to begin concentrating on your assignments. Everything mentioned in the questions is something *you can control*. Don't sabotage yourself.

What can you do if you have any of the above *symptoms*? Step #1-Be *aware* of the condition. Be aware of what it could do to your ability to concentrate. Then before you get started, do whatever you can to eliminate the condition. Be as positive and effective as possible. Don't try to delude yourself. You can't concentrate when you lack sufficient *self control*.

External Control. These are factors outside of yourself. You can control them, but they are not part of you personally. Remember, you can sabotage concentration as easily with external distractions as with internal ones. Don't let it happen. For example, consider what control you have over the following:

Make some thoughtful choices about your study environment.

- The **study place**. Is it the best you can find?

- The **stereo**. How distracting is this to you when you study? Is it more distracting for some subjects, and less for others?

- Outside **noise**. How much can you tolerate? How much can you eliminate?

- The **lights**. Can you see well enough, or do you frequently have to strain your eyes?

- The **heat**. Can you control it? How much does it bother you?

- The **learning materials**. Is everything you need easily available?

When you consider all the possible internal and external types of distractions, you can quickly realize why it can be difficult to concentrate. The important thing is *for you to be in control*. You do this by confronting distractions head on, and not letting yourself be fooled or defeated.

Organizational control. This takes you back to Chapter One on **ORGANIZATION**. You may overcome all possible distractions, but if you aren't properly organized for an assignment, you could be wasting your time.

Remember what you learned in the chapter on ORGANIZATION.

Review the nine items in Chapter One to be sure that you will not have organizational problems. Now you are ready to concentrate on your work with a minimum of difficulty. The quality of your work should improve remarkably.

CONTROL - WORKSHEET

In the space below, list all the areas you need to control for the best possible concentration.   Use the examples on the preceeding two pages as a starting point. If you think of any others, list them also.

Internal or Self Control

_____

_____

_____

_____

_____

External Control

_____

_____

_____

_____

_____

Organizational Control

_____

_____

_____

_____

_____

Consequence I - If Nothing Else Works

If all else fails, the last resort for improving your concentration is knowing what will happen if you don't do the work, or do it poorly. This is the "bottom line," the "fear factor," which also has its place in the domain of concentration.

The bad news.

The most obvious consequence of inability to concentrate on an assignment is failure. You fail a test, a class, or you might even fail to get a diploma. That's pretty powerful stuff, enough to motivate many students to get down to business. If, however, none of the consequences matter, and there are some students for whom there are no consequences, then the problems are outside the realm of this **MANUAL**. Surprisingly, there are many students who seldom take the trouble to think of consequences. If they did, the results could be quite different.

I never cease to be amazed when I ask a student why he or she has failed to turn in assignments and the answer is, "I forgot," or "I just didn't make time to do it," or other answers that indicate a real absence of any thought about the consequence of not doing the assignment.

In some ways, this relates to the first part of this section on *Purpose*. Many assignments are never done because students don't believe there is any real reason for doing them. The students may feel that some assignments are just "busy work," so why should they do them?

If you get in the habit of skipping assignments because they don't seem important, you might tend to see nearly all of your assignments that way. The consequences are obvious; don't let it happen to you. Use as much information in this Chapter as possible to help you succeed in everything you do.

Consequence II - Success Becomes A Habit

The good news.
THIS IS FOR YOU!

Now I want you to forget everything I said under **Consequence I**, and think about *success*. What does it mean to you? What would happen if your teacher told you your work was among the best in the class? How would that affect your confidence? How would your parents react? Your friends? Do you think you could handle it? Of course you could.

Does it sound like a fantasy? It isn't. It can happen, and it will happen if you want it to, and if you are willing to believe it, work for it, and not let anything or anyone discourage you.

Remember, *success*, like anything else, can become a habit, and when it does, it will be as difficult as any other habit to break. Think about what it will mean to you, and then *Go for it!*

51

Concentration - Chapter Summary

There are five basic factors that determine how well you can concentrate on your work:

Reason.

1. PURPOSE AND PRACTICALITY

Why are you doing the assignment? What are the purposes, reasons, expectations and specific outcomes?

How will your work help you with whatever else you have to learn? How does it <u>fit in</u> to the overall requirements of the course?

"Turn On."

2. INTEREST

Make it *fun*.
Make it a *game*.
Make it *relevant*.
Form a *study group*.
Expand your knowledge.
Use study *aids*.
"Kill two birds with one stone."
   Use the *same assignment* for
   two subjects.

Take charge.

3. CONTROL

Internal control means all the conditions within yourself that you can control such as being hungry, thirsty, tired, hot, cold, cramped, anxious, depressed, etc.

External control means the place, noise, lights, materials, etc.

Results.

4. CONSEQUENCE I - *Failure*

What to expect if nothing mentioned above can be made to work.

5. CONSEQUENCE II - *Success*

What can happen if *success* becomes a *habit* you cannot break.

4

NOTETAKING

"The palest ink is better than the most retentive memory"
(Chinese Proverb)

Learning requires remembering. It doesn't do much good to spend hours reading, studying, listening, watching, solving problems, doing research, or anything else if you don't have a tried and true system to retain and recall what you have learned. Your social studies teacher gives you a test on a textbook unit which you read carefully and seriously, but you get a mediocre grade on the test. Ditto for most of your other subjects. Why? The reason is all too obvious: you try hard enough, but when the time comes to prove what you know, you don't remember enough. It happens all the time. The solution: you need a better system, one that really works.

You need a good <u>system</u> to remember everything you need to know.

The core of the recall system is **Notes**. Those comments, reminders, lists, ideas, statements, references, facts, and whatever else you write down in order to help you remember information without constantly having to refer to an original source.

In the broader sense, a textbook should be considered as **written course content**. Some teachers use one textbook as their main source, while others may use a number of written materials. It makes no real difference to you since you have to learn whatever is required.

Two Types Of Textbooks

I have divided textbooks into two groups. The first consists of those that do not require prior knowledge of each chapter before going on to subsequent chapters: English and Social Studies texts. The second group requires a knowledge of each chapter before going on to subsequent chapters: examples are Mathematics, Foreign Language, and most Science textbooks. Let's begin with the first group.

Textbook differences.

ENGLISH AND SOCIAL STUDIES TEXTBOOKS

You have a social studies assignment to read a chapter in your U. S. Government textbook. If you are like many students, you will probably read the chapter once and assume that you have completed the assignment, or if the teacher gave the class a study guide in the form of a list of questions, many of you may have **read only what was necessary for the answers to those questions.**

Afterwards, you may have felt that you **adequately** prepared for the assignment. That is when you experience the shock. If the teacher were to give an exam on the material, there is so much you don't remember that you wonder whether you read the right chapter.

What really happened is that as soon as you finished reading the chapter, you began to forget what you read. Within a few days, you could well forget from 70 to 90% of the material, particularly if you thought that all you had to do was read the chapter once.

In order to retain information, **reading** is only the first of four steps. Without the other three, reading is of little value. The following are the four steps that will help you understand and remember most of what you read.

Notetaking Steps:

1. Read the material first for a general overview.

Step 1. The first time, read the designated material to get an overview of the content. Make some notes regarding major themes and concepts. The purpose is to get some first impressions and a feeling for what the author is trying to say. In the sample that I selected from a U. S. Government text (pages 57-63 in this **MANUAL**), the authors, in my opinion, want to impress the reader with the dilemma of how Americans regard their constitutional right to vote. The author's approach is a challenge to the reader to get not only the facts, but also some insight into the problems.

How should these problems be solved? What can happen if the problems remain unsolved, or even worse, neglected? This is what goes through my mind as I read the chapter for the first time. I am not simply turning pages, I am involved in the issues. It helps me understand them better, and when I read the chapter again for the purpose of taking notes, (*Step 2)* I will have a point of view, and some paths to follow.

Turn to page 57, and read 2 or 3 pages of the sample chapter as described in this *Step*. It should not take more than five or ten minutes.

Step 2. Re-read the material, this time taking notes on the important concepts, ideas, and issues. Use the left margin of your notebook to write down page numbers which you can refer to later, if necessary. Keep in mind what you feel the author is trying to say, what the problems are, and what kind of a critical approach you might want to take later on. Be sure to get the essential facts and arguments on each of the issues. Remember, these notes are for you. Use any technique that will help you remember what you write. Be graphic, artistic, spontaneous, creative, whatever works best for you. Take as much time as you like, then turn to page 63 in the **MANUAL** and compare your notes with those made by a social studies teacher.

2. Re-read more carefully and take notes.

What are the most obvious differences, similarities? Do you wonder why the teacher didn't take more notes? How many notes did you take? The following is a brief analysis of the teacher's notes with some questions about your notetaking. The page numbers listed below are from the sample material in the U. S. Government textbook. The pages in the **MANUAL** are in parentheses.

●Page 278 (57)

See the examples:

Start with the sample Chapter, pages 57-63.

Except for the Introduction Statement, the teacher listed 3 questions. Why? Because the authors asked these questions. Also, teachers like to use questions from the author or the text on exams and quizzes.

●Page 279 (58)

The teacher is still taking notes in the form of questions. Is this a good technique for you with this type of material?

Do you think the teacher got the essential information in the notes? Do you think the teacher left out anything that you might have included?

Would it be helpful for you to see how your teacher would take notes on this chapter? Why?

●Pages 280, 281, 282, 283, 284 (59, 60, 61, 62, 63)
This is a large section of the chapter. Notice how few notes the teacher took. Notice the format. The series of points the teacher numbered on several of the issues. I will come back to this when I discuss the use of *Mapping* as part of the notetaking process.

If you had your teacher's notes, could you make up the exam? How close might it be to the actual exam?

Look at the notes on the sample Chapter, pages 64-66.

This exercise should give you some idea of how a teacher might take notes on a chapter. Keep in mind that teachers are as different as students, and they don't all act in the same way. As you become more skilled in notetaking, you will learn how to determine what your teacher believes is important. This will then be reflected in your notes, and very likely in the grades you get on quizzes and exams.

Keep in mind also that ***notetaking is a skill***, and it will take time and practice for you to become an expert. As I pointed out at the beginning of this chapter, notetaking is probably one of the most useful skills you will ever acquire. Get in the habit of taking notes whenever there is something that you read or see that you want to remember.

# Chapter 10
Political
behavior:
the american
voter

"Elections are a mystery," writes Gerald M. Pomper. "Although we consider elections crucial to the functioning of democracy, we have little knowledge of their true significance. Americans choose half a million public officials through the ballot, but the extent of popular control of government policy decisions is undetermined. Throughout the world as well, governments proclaim themselves democracies and hold mass elections, but the meaning of the ballot remains cloudy to the Soviet worker and the Mississippi Negro."[1]

The mystery deepens when we try to look inside the mind of the voter. What causes some people to go to the polls and vote when others do not? Why are so many Americans merely spectators? How do we decide to vote the way we do? Does voting have any kind of rational pattern, or is it a crazy-quilt of vagrant and emotional actions?

278

[1]*Elections in America* (Dodd, Mead, 1968), p. 1.

Burns/Peltason/Cronin, **GOVERNMENT BY THE PEOPLE,** 9th Edition, Basic Edition, ©1975, pages 278-284. Reprinted by permission of **Prentice-Hall, Inc.,** Englewood Cliffs, New Jersey

The right to vote as one wishes, without interference from the government or from other persons, is supposed to be the great glory of democracy and the ultimate safeguard of it. The fact that Americans choose half a million public officials, according to some critics of American political arrangements, does not necessarily mean popular control of government. They contend that voters do not generally see the relation between elections and their own interests; that they do not usually get a meaningful choice between candidates; that what candidates promise and what they do in office is often quite different; in short, that voting is not the great foundation of democracy that many Americans assume it to be.

One reason for the controversy over the importance of voting is that scholars are making only slow progress in unraveling the nature of it. But we are steadily gaining new insights into the way relations among members of groups, between leaders and followers, and among members of families affect political activity.

Who votes?

The history of suffrage in the United States has been a long struggle to extend the right to vote from a small group of property-owning males — perhaps one person out of every twenty or thirty — to the great mass of the people. In this chapter we will consider who actually votes and how and why, rather than who has the right to vote. But note that we could not even be discussing voting behavior if many men and women had not fought to extend the right to vote over the last century and a half.

Three great struggles have been fought over this issue. The first was against *property tests* for voting. Conservatives like Chancellor Kent of

The great struggle for equal voting rights for women (left) was finally rewarded with passage of the Nineteenth Amendment. The women at right are voting for the first time.

New York argued that universal male suffrage would jeopardize the rights of property, that if poor people gained the right to vote they would sell their votes to the rich. The democratic, egalitarian mood of America, eastern immigration and the western frontier, and the eagerness of politicians to lower voting barriers so they could pick up votes — all these led to the end of property (and taxpaying) restrictions by the middle of the nineteenth century.

The second great struggle was for *women's suffrage*. Husbands and fathers once argued that women had no place at the polling booth, that husbands could vote for the interests of the whole family — but these arguments had a hollow ring. The aroused women conducted noisy parades, drew up petitions, organized a Washington lobby, picketed the White House, got arrested, went on hunger strikes in jail. They won the vote in some states and finally achieved a breakthrough with the passage of the Nineteenth Amendment in 1920.

The third great struggle — for the right of black Americans to vote — has been mainly won (see Chapter 7). The most recent major extension of the suffrage has been to youths eighteen to twenty years old. Unlike the earlier expansions of the suffrage, this was hardly the result of a struggle by young people. It was in part a recognition by those twenty-one and older that younger persons were being educated to a point where they could vote intelligently. It was also a response to the widespread protest during the 1960s among the young, especially college students, against governmental and other "establishments"; adults realized that they could hardly urge young persons to forsake violence and confrontation and use peaceful political processes if the young lacked even the right to vote. It also seemed unfair that those "old enough to die for their country" could not "vote for their country." This most recent extension of suffrage was embodied in the twenty-sixth Amendment, ratified in 1971.

By the mid-seventies the overwhelming number of Americans, including women, blacks, and the young, possessed the right to vote. What do they do with it?

MILLIONS OF NONVOTERS

On the average, the proportion of Americans who vote is smaller than that of the British, French, Italians, West Germans, Scandinavians, or Canadians. Talk as we will about democratic suffrage, the fact remains that millions of Americans do not choose to vote or somehow fail to get to the polls on election day. Our record has not always been so poor. Voting was generally high (among those legally *able* to vote) during the latter nineteenth century; in 1876, 86 percent of the adult enfranchised males voted. In this century our voting ratio has been erratic. Turnout dropped between the early 1900s and the mid-twenties, rose in the late 1920s and 1930s, declined in the mid- and late 1940s, climbed in 1952 and 1956, and has decreased in the last three presidential elections—

three elections, incidentally, that were thought to be unusually significant and compelling.

Americans have an absolute right *not* to vote. But in a democracy where voting is considered a civic virtue and a prudent means of self-defense, the extent of nonvoting is startling. In the last two presidential elections about 40 percent of the eligible voters did not go to the polls. *Over 60 percent* of them stayed home in the congressional elections of 1974. Participation in state and local elections is usually even *lower*.

Why do people fail to vote? Aside from outright denials of the right to vote—happily no longer a significant factor—important reasons are registration requirements and being absent from the voting district on election day. As we noted in Part Three, registering to vote (not required in many other democracies) is bothersome and time-consuming and often compels a potential voter to initiate action long before he or she faces election issues.[2] Although the Supreme Court has ruled that states may not impose residency requirements of longer than fifty days, almost a third of the potential voters are not even registered to

[2]See Stanley Kelley, Jr., Richard E. Ayres, and William G. Bowen, "Registration and Voting: Putting First Things First," *American Political Science Review* (June 1967), pp. 359–77.

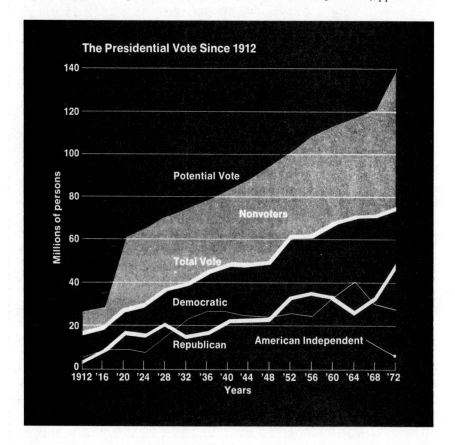

60

vote. Disturbed by the low turn-out, Congress in 1970 established for *presidential elections* a uniform thirty-day residency requirement and set simpler procedures for absentee voting.

The *prime* reasons for not voting, however, are not institutional. They are *personal*. Millions of Americans are just not interested enough to go to the polls to vote for president, and even fewer vote for state and local candidates. They feel—if they think about the matter at all—that politics is not important, or that there is no real choice between candidates, or that they do not know enough to vote, or that they are "disgusted with politics." Some fear losing business or wages if they go to the polls. Much nonvoting probably results from a combination of low interest and inconvenience: An elderly person might vote if the polls were around the corner—but actually they are two miles away and he or she lacks transportation. Of course, sometimes the inconvenience is simply a rationalization for basic lack of interest.

Should such apathy surprise us? When students mobilized for action after President Nixon's Cambodia "incursion" of 1970, it was estimated that half a million of them would take part in the ensuing national elections. In fact only a tiny minority was active. That minority was effective in a number of congressional elections, but the vast majority of interested students did more talking than electioneering. Some were alienated from the whole election process; most were simply not interested in the issues of the day.[3] Indeed, of all major categories of voters, the lowest percentage of voter turnout in the 1964 and 1968 presidential elections was among the eighteen to twenty-year-olds in the states that permitted them to vote.

WHO FAILS TO VOTE?

The extent of voting varies among different types of persons, areas, and elections. Voting studies generally agree on the following patterns, which are listed here roughly in order of declining importance:

1. People with high incomes are more likely to vote than people with low ones. Why do low-income people vote in fewer numbers than the wealthy? They have less economic security; they feel less of a sense of control over their political environment; they feel at a disadvantage in social contacts; and their social norms tend to deemphasize politics. Their nonvoting thus is part of a larger political and psychological environment that discourages political activity, including voting.[4]

2. The college-educated are more likely to vote than the noncollege-

[3]Walter T. Murphy, Jr., "Student Power in the 1970 Elections: A Preliminary Assessment," *Political Science* (Winter 1971), pp. 27–32. See also Sidney Hyman, *Youth in Politics* (Basic Books, 1972).

[4]See Angus Campbell, Philip E. Converse, Warren E. Miller, and Donald E. Stokes, *The American Voter* (John Wiley, 1960).

educated. High school alumni are more likely to vote than those with only a grade school education. "Practically speaking," writes Warren Miller, "almost everybody who has been to college votes."[5] Even college-educated persons who profess little interest in or knowledge about political issues turn out to vote. People with college backgrounds exist in a climate of opinion in which voting is considered a civic duty; they tend to be more exposed to ideas, active people, newspapers, political leaders. The college education itself may have an independent effect in exposing the graduates to political ideas and personalities.

3. Middle-aged people are more likely to vote than the younger and older. Many young people are busy getting established, moving about, having babies, raising young children. The new husband is occupied with getting ahead; the young wife is immersed in home affairs, or has a job of her own. They find little time for politics. The more established, between thirty-five and fifty-five, are more active; then voting falls off sharply in the sixties and seventies, owing partly to the infirmities of old age.

4. Men are more likely to vote than women. This variation—not very great in most elections—exists in many foreign countries as well. In recent presidential elections about 61 in every 100 women have voted, about 75 in every 100 men. Women feel less social pressure to vote than men. Morality issues such as birth control, however, generally bring out a high women's vote, and college-educated women tend to be more active in political party work than college-educated men. There are indications that the traditional difference in the rate of voting between men and women is decreasing.

5. Partisans are more likely to vote than independents. "By far the most important psychological factor affecting an individual's decision to vote is his identification with a political party."[6] When the election outcome is doubtful, strong partisanship is even more likely to induce a person to vote. A partisan is likely to have a personal interest and to be concerned about the outcome. If partisanship has this influence, however, the recent decline in party feeling and loyalty could bring a decline in voting turnout.

6. Persons who are active in organized groups are more likely to vote. This is especially true when the organized groups are themselves involved in community activity.[7] People in groups are more likely to be exposed to stimuli that engage them with civic and political problems.

Summing up, if you are a young woman with a low income and little

[5]Warren Miller, "The Political Behavior of the Electorate," *American Government Annual, 1960–1961* (Holt, Rinehart & Winston, 1960), p. 50.

[6]*Report of the President's Commission on Registration and Voting Participation* (U. S. Government Printing Office, 1963), pp. 9–10.

[7]Sidney Verba and Norman H. Nie, *Participation in America* (Harper & Row, 1972), pp. 197–200.

Choosing a presidential candidate at the Democratic convention in 1972. Robert Abrams reads the New York delegation's vote for the presidential nomination.

sense of partisanship, the chances that you will turn out even for an exciting presidential election are far less than if you are a wealthy man in your fifties, a strong partisan, and a member of a civic group. Thus nonvoting influences are cumulative. But there also appear to be psychological or attitudinal differences between nonvoters and voters. Even when sex, age, education, and income are controlled, the chronic nonvoter, more characteristically than the voter, is a person with a sense of inadequacy, more inclined to accept authority, more concerned with personal and short-range issues, less sympathetic toward democratic norms, and less tolerant of those who differ from himself.

EFFECT OF DIFFERENT TYPES OF ELECTIONS

Political institutions have their impact on nonvoting. So does the total political context. Note these tendencies:

1. National elections bring out more voters than state or local campaigns. Presidential elections attract the greatest number of voters. Off-year congressional elections almost invariably draw fewer persons to the polls. City and other local elections tend to attract an even smaller number.[8] And participation is lowest in party primaries. Even when voters are marking a ballot that offers a variety of national and local contests, some voters will check their presidential choice but not bother with others.

[8]On the variation of turnout in cities, and some reasons for it, see Robert R. Alford and Eugene C. Lee, "Voting Turnout in American Cities," *American Political Science Review* (September 1968), pp. 796–813.

284

Chapter 10 - Political Behavior
The American Voter

278-301

P. 278

Introduction

Elections are a mystery!
(500,000) Public officials elected
annually

Questions:

1. Why do people go to the polls?
2. Why do they not go?
3. How does the voter decide?

P. 279

(Controversy)

☆ Is voting really the great
foundation of American Democracy?

WHO votes?

HOW do they vote?

WHY do they vote? (This has
nothing to do with the right to vote

64

Three struggles over the issue:

P.280
1. **Property Tests** If poor could vote they would sell their rights to the rich.

2. **Women's Suffrage**
19th Amendment passed in 1920

3. Right of Black Americans also. Voting age reduced to 18

Non Voters

Small percentage of Americans vote. About 40% in the 1968 and 1972 elections (presidential)

P.281

Reasons for Non-Voting

P.282
1. Have to register
Residency requirement

2. Personal reasons

1. Not interested
2. Not important
3. No real choice
4. Don't know enough
5. Disgusted with politics
6. Must take time off from work

WHO FAILS TO VOTE ?

P.283
1. Lower income persons
2. Less educated
3. Younger voters
4. Women 61%
   Men   75%
5. Independents — have no cause
6. People with no affiliation

Effect of Different Types of Elections

P.284
1. National Elections — brings out most of the voters

Party Primaries bring out least

66

Step 3. Re-read your notes very soon (immediately if possible) after writing them. This helps your memory. Forgetting takes place continually, and most of it right after the learning has occurred. By re-reading your notes within a short time you will retain the information longer and in greater detail.

Have your notes available as an easy and quick reference at all times. Remember, the more you refer to them, the more you will remember.

As you re-read your notes, if anything new or important occurs to you, include it. If you think you took too many notes then take out what is not important. In other words, streamline your notes so that they represent what is essential for recall.

If you have doubts about whether you are taking the right kinds of notes, show them to your teacher and ask him or her to criticize them for content. This will also help you learn what your teacher thinks is important. Don't be bashful. In fact, learn how to be assertive, but at the same time be very tactful. You will find that your teachers admire anyone who shows that much interest in learning.

Step 4. Make a *Map* of the chapter *from your notes*. The *Map* should contain key points, numbered for easier reference, of all the major topics and sub-topics. *If you cannot make a Map from your notes, then you have not taken good notes.* When you look at the *Map* you should be able to get a complete view of the entire chapter. Maps can be excellent references to use just before exams.

Look at the example of the *Map* on page 68. Notice the form. Major topics are written on lines that are perpendicular to the chapter heading. Sub-topics are perpendicular to the topic lines. This arrangement of lines represents relationships and inter-relationships of the ideas and concepts. It is not the only way to represent these relationships. You may think of better ways to do it. By all means, be as creative and imaginative as you can. Do whatever works best *for you.*

Summary of the Four Steps in Textbook Notetaking
Social Studies and English

Step 1. Read the material for general understanding.
Step 2. Re-read and take notes.
Step 3. Review notes as soon and as often as possible.
Step 4. Make a *Map* of the material from the notes.

Although this may take more time than you planned at first, as you become more skilled, it will take less time, you will become more confident, more motivated, and more successful.

3. Re-read your notes as soon as possible and as often as necessary.

4. Make a Map from your Notes. See page 68.

MAP- CHAPTER 10

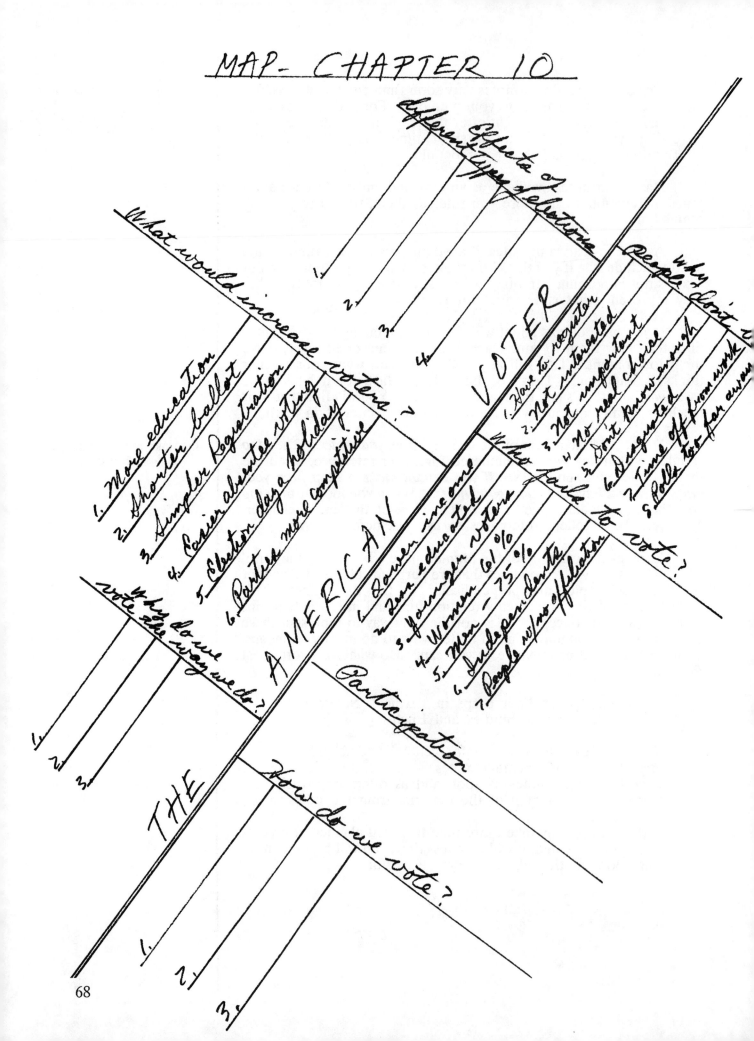

Effects of different types of elections
1.
2.
3.
4.

What would increase voters?
1. More education
2. Shorter ballot
3. Simpler Registration
4. Easier absentee voting
5. Election day a holiday
6. Parties more competitive

VOTER

Why people don't vote
1. Have to register
2. Not interested
3. Not important
4. No real choice
5. Don't know enough
6. Disgusted
7. Time off from work
8. Polls too far away

Who fails to vote?
1. Lower income
2. Less educated
3. Younger voters
4. Women 61%
5. Men — 75%
6. Independents
7. People w/ no affiliation

AMERICAN

Why do we vote the way we do?
1.
2.
3.

Participation

THE

How do we vote?
1.
2.
3.

MATHEMATICS, SCIENCE, FOREIGN LANGUAGE TEXTBOOKS

These subjects have one important thing in common: they are "cumulative," which means that you build your knowledge from the ground up, brick by brick, in the same way that you build a house. You must have a good foundation before you can make progress.

You cannot skip chapters in math, science, and foreign language textbooks.

You can open a history or English book at any page and have no problem understanding the material. Information in the previous chapters might be helpful for you to know, but it is not crucial. This is not true for mathematics, foreign language, and most sciences. In these subjects, *you must start at the beginning*. Your progress will be determined by how well you master each learning step.

Overlearning. Mathematics, foreign language, and science require overlearning. It is not enough to figure out how to conjugate an irregular verb, it must be repeated over and over again until you can do it *instinctively*, the same way a typist types without looking at the keyboard, or thinking where the letters are. Science and math formulas must be recalled *instinctively* or you haven't *learned* them. Your recall system must be geared to this, otherwise you will suffer and fall behind. The teacher will continue to move at the established pace; you will succeed only if you keep up by continually *overlearning* the material.

Math, science, and foreign language <u>must</u> be <u>overlearned</u>.

I mentioned the skill of typewriting as an example of *overlearning*. You do it also in sports, performing arts, shops, and practical arts. If the tennis coach demonstrates the backhand, you might understand it perfectly--the moves, the position of the racket, and everything else. But you would not have *learned the backhand* until you practiced doing it for thousands of times, under all conditions. The same is true of *learning* math, foreign language, and science.

The textbook becomes your practice guide. Every page is important. Every fact, problem, explanation, concept, must be thoroughly understood and reinforced so that you could almost write the text yourself. In addition to taking notes from the textbook, you should write and re-write conjugations, formulas, solutions, and anything else that will help you *overlearn*.

Remember, your response has to become *instinctive*, without any thought or interference, like playing a musical instrument, or doing the backhand in tennis. You don't think about it, you do it, and eventually (sooner than you think) you will reach the point when you do things right, automatically. It comes with lots of practice, and once you *overlearn* something, it becomes difficult to forget. For example, would you ever *forget* how to ride a bicycle?

Taking Notes During A Lecture

Taking notes during a lecture is different from taking notes from a textbook.

There are four specific skills you need to develop in order to take good notes during a lecture, demonstration, interview, or observation. They are:

1. **LISTENING** to what is being said or discussed.

2. **ANALYZING** what is being said or discussed.

3. **SELECTING** what to write.

4. **WRITING** what you need to remember in the proper form and at a proper speed. This means putting down specific statements, concepts, ideas, and clues that can serve as reminders later on.

LISTENING

Listening Skills.

We tend to assume that *listening* is as natural as breathing. We have ears, we have a nose and a mouth, and what difference is there between breathing or hearing? Do we have to learn how to breathe? Why is *hearing* so special? Or *listening*? What's the difference? What is there to learn? Why would *listening* or *hearing* be considered a skill?

Listening is definitely a skill. It requires that you not only *hear* what is being said, but that you *observe* everything possible about the speaker that might give you additional clues to what the speaker is trying to say. A good listener gets information from sounds, gestures, the speaker's style, the tone of voice, movement, and anything else that might help you understand what the speaker wants you to know.

Hearing: "Tune in."

Hearing. Tune in to the speaker. Concentrate on the speaker's style. There are always lots of clues as to what is important. You can relax when the speaker starts telling you about growing up on a farm in Idaho, but be on your toes when he comes back to the subject.

As quickly as possible, try to get into the speaker's "rhythm." This means getting a feel for the pace, for the way ideas are emphasized, the way the words flow--smooth or choppy, the sequence of ideas and so forth.

Try to identify main ideas and themes. When a list of items is read, try to get as many as you can on your note page.

Don't let anyone or anything distract you from what you are doing. *If you begin to get bored or tired, ask a question or make a comment about something*. Stay with it and "keep your ears open."

Observing. Watch the speaker closely. There will always be clues, if you are alert enough to observe them. These can be in the form of gestures, facial expressions, items written on the chalkboard, certain types of pauses, the way the speaker emphasizes and illustrates a point or concept--vocally, dramatically, quietly, or with some particular device like a picture, slide, object, etc.

Observing: Notice all possible details.

Lectures, like textbooks, are a mixture of important and unimportant filler material. Observation will help you know the difference. Your attention, however, must be completely focused on what is happening in front and also around you at all times.

ANALYZING/INTERPRETING WHAT YOU SEE AND HEAR

This involves knowing what the speaker is trying to say, and the relative importance of what is being said. Try to imagine the outline the speaker is following. Structure the topics, subtopics, details, extraneous comments and other statements into a form that not only helps you but makes sense out of what you hear. Fit the pieces into a sensible pattern of information for good notetaking. This will help you later on when you re-read your notes. It will also make it possible for you to separate important from unimportant remarks, as well as any straying from the subject.

Interpreting: Get the important facts and meanings.

As you become more skilled in knowing what ideas and concepts are most important, you will find that you have a much greater sense of knowing what to write, and how to phrase your notes in the least number of words, while still retaining the full meaning.

Remember: Visualize the outline of the speaker's talk. What is he trying to say. Get an overview as quickly as possible of the main ideas and concepts.

SELECTING WHAT TO WRITE

If you have been listening and analyzing properly, knowing what is important will follow naturally. You write down what is important, and what you believe you should know. Nothing else. You don't have time to clutter up your notes with anything unnecessary or umimportant. If in doubt, however, put it down. You can cross it out later. You will know how good you are at *selecting* after every test you take. If you took down the right information, you will enjoy that pleasant feeling of knowing and remembering all that is expected. Make that your goal.

What: Become very aware of the differences between important and unimportant remarks.

WRITING DOWN WHAT YOU NEED TO REMEMBER

Writing or recording the information is easy for some students and difficult for others. If you try to write too carefully, you may not get everything down. If you try to write too much, you lose the trend of the speech. If you write too little, your notes won't be worth much.

Get the information on paper--legibly.

Practice some form of speed writing. Your notes have to be legible *to you* only. Use whatever speed techniques work best for you. If possible, take a course in some form of Speedwriting, or get a book on the subject and teach yourself. You will know how good you are when you see that what you want on paper is there.

★   ★   ★   ★   ★

Reminder.

REVIEW YOUR NOTES AS SOON AS POSSIBLE AFTER THE LECTURE. DO THIS SEVERAL TIMES, AND ADD ANYTHING THAT COMES TO MIND THAT YOU MIGHT HAVE MISSED DURING THE LECTURE. USE THE LEFT SIDE OF THE PAPER FOR COMMENTS OR OTHER HELPFUL HINTS.

★   ★   ★   ★   ★

On the following page is an example of the recommended note taking procedure to use when the math instructor explains how to do a problem. The important part is to write down the explanation for each of the steps in the solution. Refer to your notes when you have math problems to do at home, particularly when you get confused.

PROCEDURE FOR NOTETAKING WHEN MATH TEACHER
DOES A SAMPLE PROBLEM ON THE CHALKBOARD

Problem: Find the area of a circle that has a diameter of 12".

Teacher's work at the board	Your notebook explanation
(circle with 12" diameter) (circle with 6" radius) πR^2 $A = \frac{22}{7} \times 6^2$ or $\frac{22}{7} \times \frac{36}{1}$ $\frac{22}{7} \times \frac{36}{1} = \frac{792}{7}$ $A = 113.14$ sq. in.	DIAMETER IS 12" RADIUS IS 6" FORMULA FOR AREA OF CIRCLE CONVERT π TO $\frac{22}{7}$ 6^2 TO 36 MULTIPLY DIVIDE

Know the importance of <u>every</u> step in the process.

Write down the explanation.

Although this is a fairly easy problem, the procedure would be the same regardless of difficulty. Don't just copy down what the teacher does no matter how well you think you understand the steps. Your added explanations will help you form the habit of following a logical procedure, and it should help overcome stumbling blocks. You can now systematically review all the steps to find where you might have made an error.

This type of notetaking might also be useful during certain types of scientific experiments and demonstrations.

Notetaking - Chapter Summary

The core of a good recall system is **Notetaking**. Properly prepared written notes will save time, and give you a permanent source of information that will help you remember nearly everything you need to know for exams. You should take notes from textbooks, from lectures, demonstrations, interviews, or observations.

TEXTBOOKS. There are two basic types:

1. Little or **no prior knowledge necessary**. Examples: **English** and **Social Studies**. You can open them to any chapter or lesson and understand the material without having read the previous chapters.

2. The information is **cumulative**. You must start at the beginning and move ahead only when you understand the preceding material. Examples are **Mathematics**, **Foreign Language** and to a large extent, **Science**.

There are 4 steps in taking notes from textbooks:

1. **Read** the entire selection once to get the general ideas.

2. **Re-read** the selection, taking notes of the important ideas, concepts, events, and facts.

3. **Review** the notes often and as soon after taking them as possible.

4. Make a **Map** of the material from your notes. (See page 68 of the **MANUAL**)

LECTURE, DEMONSTRATION, INTERVIEW, OBSERVATION

There are four skills:

1. **Listening**.

2. **Analyzing** and **Interpreting**.

3. **Selecting** what to write.

4. **Writing down** what you need to remember.

4 steps for notetaking from textbooks.

Taking notes on what you hear and see.

5

REPORT PREPARATION AND PRESENTATION

"The reports of my death are greatly exaggerated"
(Mark Twain)

When you have to prepare either an oral or written report, it can be both good and bad news. The good news is that the report will probably not be due for two weeks or longer, so you don't have to worry about it for a while.

The bad news is that time goes by faster than you think, and before you know it, the report is due and you haven't begun any serious work. By the time you do it may be too late to spend as much time on it as you should. As a result, you suffer through an unpleasant experience. Some of the main reasons may be:

• You aren't interested in the subject.

• You don't like to write.

• You don't like to read.

• You can't seem to get organized.

• You don't like to speak in front of a class.

Well, don't worry. With reasonable effort, you can learn all you need to know about properly preparing and presenting both written and oral reports. It is not difficult, but it does require following some rules and procedures. We will begin with *five basic steps*:

Report writing becomes easier when you understand the process.

1. **CHOOSING** a subject.

2. **RESEARCHING** your work.

3. **ORGANIZING** your work.

4. **WRITING** the report.

5. **PRESENTING** the report.

Choosing A Subject

Consider carefully whether there is *enough information* on the subject, and whether the information is easily *available*.

What to avoid.

AVOID subjects that are:

- *too recent* to have much information. For example, the effects of a law just passed would not allow you enough time to gather the information.

- *too specialized* to provide you with enough information. For example, "The Nocturnal Habits of Siamese Cats in Wyoming."

- *too generalized or broad* to allow you to focus on anything specific enough to write about. For example, "Political Problems in South America."

- *too difficult, sensitive, or controversial* to deal with objectively. For example, "The Firing of A Popular Teacher by the School Board."

- *too complex* for you to understand completely. For example, "The Long Term Effects of Acid Rain on Corn Production in the Midwestern United States."

Be guided in your selection.

CHOOSE a subject you know something about. The following guidelines should be helpful:

- *Something you enjoyed studying.* It could be a biography, an important event in history, or something connected with a trip you might have taken to some historical place. For example, a trip to the fields at Gettysburg.

- *Any hobbies or special interests* you may have. Sports, computers, music, drama, cars, etc. For example, "The Political Influence in the 1980 Olympic Games."

76

• *A subject based on a group you happen to belong to.* It could be ethnic, religious, economic, or a place where you lived. For example,"Growing Up in Appalachian Country." Always be as objective as possible.

• *Something you might have experienced personally.* This could be an event in your life that had special meaning for you. For example, "My First Extrasensory Experience."

• *Something related to another course you are taking.* This would give you a chance to help yourself in two subjects, and reduce your work load. For example, you are studying World War II in your U. S. History class, and you are also reading 20th Century novelists in your English class. Since both teachers require a term paper, you might use Herman Wouk's The Winds of War as the major source material for both papers.

THE THESIS STATEMENT

The *thesis statement* is your personal point of view regarding the subject of your report. It helps you understand **why** you are writing the report, **why** you selected this subject rather than some other subject. *It is the underlying theme of your report.* Everything you write in some way should relate to your *thesis*.

Thesis is your own personal view. It makes it easier to write your report.

For example, if you were writing on the *Discovery of Gold In California*, you might choose the following thesis statement to guide you: "The discovery of gold in California was without a doubt the most important single event in the history of the state." All headings would relate to this statement.

Another *thesis statement* could be: "The desire to get rich quick is universal." How much difference is there between these two statements? which would be more interesting to you personally? Why?

The *thesis statement* is important for both you and the reader. Put yourself in the position of the reader. You would want to know what the author has in mind and what he or she wants to impress on you. You should do the same when you are the writer.

As you prepare your report, the *thesis statement* should be firmly in your mind at all times. It will keep you from wandering from the subject and will help you prepare a well structured, interesting report.

LIMITATIONS

One of the most common difficulties that students have in selecting a topic to write on has been pointed out under the types of subjects to avoid. I refer to subjects that are too general or too broad. You should not overburden yourself with an endless amount of material to review. The opposite is also true: avoid subjects on which you will have difficulty getting information. The following can guide you in your selection:

Know all of this before you start your report.

• How much *time* can you devote to the work? If your answer is 5 to 10 hours, then you should plan on about a five page paper, double spaced. You would probably have time to review 4 to 6 outside sources.

Your teacher will be the best person to tell you how much time you should expect to spend on the work. if you aren't sure what the expectation is, then ask.

• What *percentage of your grade* will the paper represent? This will also be a good gauge to determine how much time to spend on the paper.

• What are the *minimum* and *maximum* length requirements as set by the teacher? Be sure to get this information in *number of words* rather than pages. If you type your work (which you should definitely do) then the number of words can vary according to the size of the typewritten letters: pica or elite. Handwriting is even more variable.

• *When* is the paper due? The warning here is to avoid the last minute rush. Plan your time carefully, and then *follow the plan*.

• Are you working *alone or with other(s)*? If it is a group effort, select the member(s) carefully. You want persons who will contribute equally, and who will be a real help in the overall work.

• Is there a specific *format*? If so, what is it?

These are among the most important questions to ask yourself when you plan your paper. In the following exercise I have given some sample subjects. Determine which are more or less appropriate for the kind of term paper you might have to write. Why would you select or not select any of the subjects?

Can you think of any good *thesis statements* for any of the topics?

SELECTING A TOPIC - WORKSHEET

Examine each of the following topics. Which ones do you feel would be too broad, too narrow, appropriate or inappropriate? What might be done to change the topic to fit your needs?

Come up with as many good *thesis statements* as you can.

The History of France

_____

_____

_____

Glassblowing

_____

_____

_____

The Short Stories of Ernest Hemingway

_____

_____

_____

The *Punk Rock* Lifestyle

_____

_____

_____

An Interview with Ronald Reagan

_____

_____

_____

Researching Your Work

Research means knowing <u>where</u> and <u>how</u> to get information.

For our purposes, the term *Research* means a serious inquiry into a subject, an *investigation* of available information. The tasks are:

- *Locating* the information. **What** are the sources? **Where** are they? How do you get to them?

- *Selecting* what you will use. This is the review and decision-making process.

- *Formatting* the information so that it is easy to use when writing your paper. This means taking notes, making cards, outlines, and anything else that gives you the best use of the information you have collected.

LOCATING THE INFORMATION

<u>Where</u> to find facts.

In addition to the textbook and other materials your teacher can give you, there are reference materials that are grouped according to the kind of information they contain. If you discuss your paper with one of the librarians, you should get all the help you might need as to which reference books to use. The following are examples of what you should be able to find at your school or community library.

- *Guides*. These give you titles of articles, books and other types of information by specific categories. For example, Constance M. Winchell's **_Guide To Reference Books_**. This contains about 7000 titles in five areas: General Reference, the Humanities, Social Sciences, History and Area Studies, Pure and Applied Sciences.

  There are many other *Guides* that you can use. The **_Reader's Guide To Periodical Literature_** will give you the author and subject index for all the magazine articles that have been published in specific subject areas, and between specific dates.

  If you don't know where to begin in your research, the *Guides* would be a good starting place.

- *General Indexes*. These are similar to the *Guides* mentioned above. The *Index* is usually very specific and very extensive. For example, **_The Cumulative Book Index_** is a list of books from all over the world that are written in the English language.

- *General Encyclopedias*. **_Brittanica_** and **_World Book_** are good examples. You may not necessarily get enough information from the encyclopedia article, but it may list other sources that you can use as a follow-up.

•*Dictionaries*.   You are most accustomed to using the dictionary to look up the meaning of words.   However, there are other types of dictionaries that you can use for reference purposes.   For example, a *Dictionary of American-English Usage* will help you use the correct expression when you write your paper.   A *Thesaurus* will help you avoid using the same word too many times when another word or expression might be better.   A *Dictionary of Synonyms* will also give you alternate words and expressions.

Biographical aids.   These books have information on many persons both living and dead that you may not find in most of the available encyclopedias.   For example, *Who's Who In America*, and in a broader sense, *World Biography*, which has a broad range of listings from all parts of the world.

•*Atlases and Gazetteers*.   These contain any type of map you might need as a reference.   For example, *World Atlases* and *Geographical Dictionaries*.

•*Handbooks and Yearbooks*.   These cover a variety of different subjects, for example, *Familiar Quotations*, *The Book of Days* which gives information about holidays, festivals, notable anniversaries, Christian and Jewish holidays, and *A Dictionary of American Proverbs and Proverbial Phrases*.   There are many others that might be helpful.

•*Bibliographies*.   These contain lists of materials that have been published or are scheduled for publication.   For example, *Publishers' Weekly* or the *Subject Guide to Books in Print*.   You might use this type of reference to locate a book in print that you could not find in your school or community library.

•*Government Publications*.   These can be very helpful if you know what they are, and how to get them.   Many are free, and others may have a nominal cost.   The *United States Government Publications* explains the nature, distribution, catalogs, and indexes of U. S. Government publications.

There is also a great deal of specialized information available in the major subject fields, including:

Fine Arts, Music, Painting, Sculpture, Architecture, Poetry, Literature, Myth and Folklore, Philosophy and Psychology, Religion, the Sciences (biological and physical), the Social Sciences, Education, Geography, and History.

SELECTING WHAT YOU WILL USE

Eliminating what you won't need.

After you have done the research, the next step is to review the information and select what you will need. Everything else should be put aside, but not necessarily discarded, at least not yet. You might want to refer to some of it later on. If you try to keep everything, you may drown in it. Don't become frustrated by having to deal with too much information. It is not at all necessary.

But, you ask, how do you decide what to keep, and what to set aside? This is the first really critical point. If you keep too much, you will not only waste time, but your paper could tend to be too long, and possibly boring. If you keep too little, your paper will be too "anemic." Develop a screening test that has two or three levels of rejection. For example, if I were writing a paper on "The Childhood of Sinclair Lewis," I would use the following questions as the first screening level:

- Is the information related to the place where Sinclair Lewis was born?

- To his parents and grandparents?

- To the school he attended?

- To his friends family and relatives?

- To incidents that helped shape his desire to write.

Any item that does not contribute significantly to any of these categories should be set aside. At this stage, it is not necessary to organize your material for your written first draft. The goal here is to reduce the amount of research to what you will eventually use when you begin to organize for the first draft.

After a first screening, if you still have too much material, repeat the process, but be more critical the second time. Add two or three more questions to the screening, if necessary. You want to end up with what you need. With practice you will be able to quickly pick out what is important, relevant, and appropriate for your use.

FORMATTING THE INFORMATION

Putting your information in a usable form.

This last step in the *research* category is to identify, label, and assemble all the material so you can use it effectively when you organize the paper. Think of *format* as a series of categories that you will use to make your material readily accessible and usable. For example, you will need a notebook, note cards, pictures, drawings, summaries, copies, etc. These must all be filed systematically. Once you have done this, you are ready to organize everything for writing the paper.

Organizing Your Work

You have chosen your topic, done your research, and formatted the information you will need. The proper organization of information and materials will greatly help you write a good first draft of your report. You will need to prepare the following:

- *Note Cards*

- An *Outline*

NOTE CARDS

You have collected and screened all the information you need for the report, but much of it may be uncategorized and unrelated. Put the information on note cards and arrange them to fit the pattern or flow of ideas you will use when writing your paper.

How to prepare Note Cards. See examples on page 84.

Condense your material. Summarize and rephrase the information you have collected so that you can put the main point on the card. Be as concise as possible. Copying large amounts of material from reference sources can be extremely tiring, as well as a bad habit. When you use a large amount of verbatim information in your report, you may forget that someone else wrote it; this becomes "plagiarism." Teachers tend to be very suspicious when they read a report that resembles the style of an encyclopedia or other reference source.

When you use a *direct quotation*, identify it as such, but try to avoid using too many quotations. Learn how to summarize and rephrase what you read or copy from other material.

Categorize your material. Identify each note card by a subject heading. This will help when you begin to prepare the outline of the report.

Summary: A well prepared note card should have the following:

- A *Subject Heading* that gives the main idea.

- *One Idea* only.

- A *Direct Quotation* when necessary.

- A reference to the *Author* and *Page Number(s)* from which the material has been taken.

On the following page you will see some sample note cards used for a report on the Discovery of Gold In California. Use them as models for your own work.

Direct Quote

Subject
Heading

> ### The Discovery of Gold in California
>
> "There, take a look at that, Captain. Tell me, is it gold? Do you think it could be? When I showed it to the men at the mill, they laughed at me. They said it must be iron pyrites--fool's gold. 'Looks like gold', they said, 'but fool's people.'"
>
> Bauer, p. 28

Body of the
quotation

Author/page #

To find the source, look up "Bauer" in your bibliography.

Rephrase

> ### The Discovery of Gold in California
>
> Marshall described exactly what happened on the morning he discovered the grains of gold at the millrace where he had been digging a ditch so the millwheel would have more room to turn. He was a carpenter and not a miner. He had never seen raw gold.
>
> Bauer, p. 29

Rephrase with a direct quote

> ### The Discovery of Gold in California
>
> The gold fever was spreading everywhere. "One hundred dollars a day--just imagine! I'll risk anything for that much!" People from all walks of life wanted to come where they thought they would get rich quickly.
>
> Bauer, pages 36-38

THE OUTLINE

While notes and note cards are used mainly for storage and recall of facts, comments, and observations, the **_outline is used to structure information_** in order to show the relationship and importance of topics and subtopics.   For example, if you were writing a paper on "The Decisive Battles of World War II," You would write an introductory section in order to explain your thesis and whatever else you might want the reader to know.   The two major divisions that follow would be:

The purpose of an <u>Outline</u>.

I. The War In The Pacific

II. The War In Europe

Under each of these headings you would list the battles, and under each of the battles, you would list any related topics.   The most common form is what is called indented "Alpha-Numeric."   This is a system that identifies the importance and the relationship of the topics by the use of a letter or number, successively indented.   For example, look at the following arrangement:

How to construct an <u>Outline</u>.

I.

    A.

        1.

           a.

              (1).

                 (a).

II.

    A.

Each indented section is related to the one above.   It is much more formal than notetaking.   The purpose of an **_outline_** is to provide you with a logical plan that you can follow as you write and edit your report.   If you would rather use a different form for your outline, that's fine.   The indented Alpha-Numeric form is not the only one, and for your purposes, another system might be better.

On the following page is a summary of the main differences between outlining and notetaking, and also the main characteristics of a good outline, regardless of what system you use.

DIFFERENCES BETWEEN OUTLINING AND NOTETAKING

A good Outline, plus good Notes help make a good Report.

Outline	Notes
1. Topics and subtopics in a logical sequence.	1. A series of individual related or unrelated facts.
2. Formal. Follows a specific format. May be copied by others.	2. Informal. Individually styled for personal use.
3. Objective.	3. Mixture of objective and subjective comments and observations.
4. Primary purposes are for structure and a view of relationships.	4. Primary purposes are for storage and recall of information.
5. Precedes many projects.	5. Notes are used to develop the outline.

What is a good Outline?

Seven Characteristics of A Good Outline

1. All the headings and subheadings relate to the theme or thesis of the report.

2. The sequence of the topics and subtopics follows a specific order.

3. The beginning, middle, and end are evident.

4. The Alpha-Numeric (or other system) relationships are evident and logical.

5. The outline has been developed with relative ease, once the research has been done and the thesis has been formulated.

6. The outline is functional and easy to use.

7. The outline serves as a guide in writing the report.

A Final Word About Outlines

Many students may think that the *outline* is an unnecessary amount of busy work which has to be done because the teacher insists on it. If possible, ask your teacher for an example of a model *outline*. Follow it carefully, and think of it as a "tool" (#6 above) that can save you a great deal of time and also help you do a better report.

Writing Your Report

THE FIRST DRAFT

You have chosen a subject (which I hope is interesting to you), you have done the necessary research, accumulated note cards, developed a clear thesis statement, and made a good working outline. You are now ready to begin writing the *first draft*.

The <u>first</u> <u>draft</u> means getting it down on paper.
Editing comes later.

Remember, the *first draft* is *not* the final form of the report. It is exactly what it is called: the *first draft*. The purpose is to get the ideas down on paper where you can see them, criticize them, change what needs to be changed, and edit what needs to be edited.

If you have a computer Word Processing program, *use it*. If you don't know how to type or do word processing, learn how *as soon as possible*. I cannot encourage you enough to *learn Word Processing*. Everything in this **MANUAL** was done on a Word Processor. I personally use *Spellbinder,* but there are many excellent programs. The purpose is twofold: *save* a great deal of *time* and *improve your work*. I won't dwell on this, but I hope I have made my point. Now back to the *first draft*.

A Word Processor is an invaluable tool.

Use your *outline* as a guide. Be certain that all of your note cards are properly categorized, and that they can be easily used.

Use your Outline and Note Cards.

Think of your *thesis statement* and write an opening   paragraph in which you present and support your *thesis*. Do not try to be too critical at this point. Your job is to get something down on paper. The critiquing and editing will come later. However, if you are using a Word Processor, you can begin editing immediately. It is one of the main advantages of using a Word Processor.

Continue the writing process by following your outline and using your notes. Do not be concerned about whether it all fits perfectly, or whether it all belongs in the report. The important thing about a *first draft* is to get as much down as possible -- without too much interference or reconsideration. You should know that professional writers write and re-write until they are absolutely satisfied.

After completing your *first draft*, (take a well earned break and then) read through it and answer the following:

First Draft Checklist Questions.

●Does your opening introductory paragraph support
 your thesis statement? Is the paragraph interesting?
 Do you think anyone would want to read on? This is
 the time to make corrections, additions, deletions, or
 even re-write the entire paragraph, if necessary.

●Have you followed your outline?

87

• Are all sub-headings related to headings?

• Is the progression of ideas logical?

• Is your evidence well founded?

• Is there a clear beginning, middle, and ending to the report?

• Are your major divisions well formed?

• Do your transitions provide good and logical continuity?

• Is the report too long? too short?

• Are there any obvious gaps? omissions?

• Are you satisfied that you are now ready for the second draft or revision?

RE-WRITING

Revising and editing techniques.

Many students resent re-writing. It seems like the most unnecessary thing to do. It takes a lot of time, and after taking all the trouble to write the report, what's the point of re-writing? How will it improve the report? How many times should it be re-written?

Think of *re-writing* as *editing for perfection*. What you want is a report that says what you want it to say, in the way you want it said, and with the impact that will keep the reader's attention and interest. Use the following guidelines:

• *Style*. How well do you express your thoughts and ideas? Is your use of language correct? It would help if you kept a copy of *Modern English Usage* at your desk for quick reference whenever you have any doubts about usage. For example, when is it correct to say "different from," and "different than?"

Another excellent and very concise book you will find very useful is the classic by William Strunk and E. B. White entitled *The Elements of Style*.

• *Position*. Are all the divisions of your paper in the right place? Are the thoughts and ideas expressed in a logical sequence?

• *Clarity*. Are your ideas edited and expressed clearly, intelligently, and forcefully?

• *Objectivity.* Unless you are writing an editorial, most reports should remain as objective as possible. In other words, your own opinions should be left out unless the topic specifically requires them.

Revising and editing techniques.

• *Ending.* Does the report come to a logical ending, or does it simply come to a halt? Most reports should end with a summary statement tying everything together and leaving the reader with a sense of completion.

• *Footnotes.* Have you identified every source and quotation with a numbered footnote which corresponds to a reference in the bibliography at the end of the report? Have you used the proper form for footnotes? Use the system your teacher expects.

• *Bibliography.* Your teacher should give you the form for the bibliography or explain how to list all the references and sources you use to write your report. If your teacher does not give you a model, use the Strunk *Elements of Style* or any other style manual as a guide.

Presenting Your Paper

As I pointed out earlier, if at all possible, type your paper on a Word Processor. If you have access to a "letter quality" printer, so much the better. Neatness and good form will almost always pay off in higher grades.

Make the presentation as attractive and readable as possible.

If you don't have access to a Word Processor, use a typewriter, and double space, using the correct width for all margins. If you don't know how to type, try and get someone else (parent, relative) to do it for you. If you can possibly avoid it, never turn in a handwritten paper. It is usually difficult and tiring to read, and it can affect your grade.

If it is a term paper, invest 50 cents in a cover with a label that gives the title of the paper and your name as author. When you consider all the time and energy it took to prepare the paper, it makes good sense to present it as attractively as possible in order to give yourself every advantage.

The following two pages are an example of the format most teachers expect for a written report or research paper. It is taken from an article I wrote which was published in the *Phi Delta Kappan* in June, 1972.

Use the example for comparison purposes and follow your teacher's directions for margins and footnotes.

Use the format required by your teacher. See example on pages 90-91.

2" MARGIN ON FIRST PAGE

NEEDED: EXPORTABLE MODELS OF SIGNIFICANT
CHANGES IN EDUCATION

Educators are barraged today with highly recommended programs, ranging from modest changes in structure or curriculum to a total re-ordering of all components in a system. Change resources range from single outside consultants to the expenditure of large sums from foundations and government sources. The results are sometimes real, more often hoped for; they are rarely if ever completely evaluated; they are described glowingly in prestigious journals and written up in textbooks. To read what is being done elsewhere is enough to make the

← 1" →

average overworked educator drool with envy and squirm with guilt about his own inadequate contribution. "Why can't things like the John Adams High School or the Parkway Program happen here?" he asks.

I intend to answer that question. The following are examples of present and recently past panaceas worth mentioning.

Melbourne High School

In its heyday several years ago, the Melbourne (Florida) High School became the most prominent model of the nongraded secondary school in the U. S. Its architect was the principal, B. Frank Brown. Ten of 11 chapters in Brown's book, **The Nongraded High School,**[1] deal with the historical basis, the rationale, and how the school was run.

5 SPACES

[1]B. Frank Brown, **The Nongraded High School.** Englewood Cliffs, New Jersey: Prentice-Hall, Inc., 1964.

90

It attracted countless visitors to the school. In the eleventh and final chapter, Brown instructs the educator on how to sell a nongraded secondary program to his community.[2] It is quite clear that he is not describing how **he** sold the program to **his** community (if indeed he did), but how others should do the job.

Nova High School

At about the same time that Melbourne became a Mecca for innovators, Nova High School in Ft. Lauderdale, Florida, was attempting similar breakthroughs. It was publicized as another link in the then current chain of panaceas. By 1970 the link had broken, at least as reported in the following account from **Newsweek:**

> Many of the school's experiments simply didn't work. "We got into real jams," says one Nova administrator. People got to this place Disneyland and they were often right."...
>
> Today rules and regulations have replaced Nova's initial freedom and individuality. A yellow poster on the door of an art room , "Dear God--how come you have only ten rules but Nova has a million?" Last month half a dozen students were suspended five days--and their grades lowered one point-- because they parked their cars in the faculty parking lot; they said the student parking lot was filled with broken glass.[3]

John Adams High School

Recently John Adams High School in Portland, Oregon, has received more favorable publicity than any other innovative high school program in over a decade. **Newsweek** called it the "best around."[4]

---

[2]Brown, op.cit., p. 209.

[3]**Newsweek.** February 16, 1970, p. 68.

[4]Ibid., p. 68.

Presenting An Oral Report

An oral report is similar to a written report in regard to the procedures for selecting a subject and doing the necessary research. The organization and writing are less formalized, but demanding in other ways. When presenting an oral report to a class, you have the advantage of using your persuasive and theatrical skills; you also have the disadvantage of having to work on those skills as well as doing all the necessary research and preparation.

ORGANIZATION

After you have selected your topic and gathered the information you need, make an outline for the proper arrangement and sequence of the issues and points you want to make. Each of these points should then be written on a note card.

The note card for the oral report is essentially a cue card. Information should be written in a form that will enable you to talk about the subject, item by item, as if you were working from an *agenda*. Use a 5 x 8 or similar type note card and include enough information on each card so you don't have to flip through too many. See the example below.

Gather information in the same way you would for a written report.

An oral report Note Card is like an Agenda. You discuss each of the items.

The Discovery of Gold in California

James Marshall's discovery:
  -Meeting with Captain Sutter

  -Marshall's story about digging the ditch and finding the gold

  -Pounding the pieces on a stone

  -How he tested the gold in Mrs. Wimmer's lye

  -Captain Sutter's reaction. What would become of Sutter's "kingdom in the wilderness?"

Bauer, pp. 28-31

PRESENTATION TIPS AND TECHNIQUES

1. Try to look at your presentation from the point of view of your audience. Try to imitate the speed of other speakers you find interesting and easy to follow. Talking too slowly will make your presentation boring, while going too fast may confuse your listeners.

   Interest your audience?

2. Consider how you will use visual aids. If they are mechanical, like an overhead projector, make sure **beforehand** that everything works. If you use pictures from a book, pass the book around instead of just holding up the picture. Mark the pictures you want students to look at.

   Use visual aids.

3. Plan to speak in natural, not too formal language. The words and sentences you use in your presentation will probably be more informal than when writing. Remember, talking and writing are **different forms** of communication.

   Speak naturally.

4. Should you sit or stand when you give your presentation? Decide according to what is most comfortable for you, or according to classroom standards.

5. Do not stare at your notes, or focus entirely on a high point in the back of the room. Make eye contact with your audience, without singling anyone out.

   Make eye contact with your audience, not with your notes.

6. Rehearse your presentation so that you avoid the "ers," and "ums."

7. If you still feel a little nervous, don't worry. It happens to nearly everyone, including actors and other professional speakers. Rehearse your speech privately, before a mirror, and in front of friends or parents.

   The more you rehearse, the more confident you will be.

8. If for some reason you have to talk without written notes, there is a way to help you remember what you want to say. It is a variation of the Memory Trip (See Chapter Eight on **MEMORY**). Go to the room where you are going to speak and look at some of the landmarks that you will see while talking. Starting from left to right, jot down the most visible ones. Then match points in your speech to the objects you have identified, being careful to keep the order correct. Memorize each point in your speech and match it with the corresponding object.

   Use memory techniques when notes are not permitted.

9. In short, prepare thoroughly, try to be relaxed and natural, and maintain good eye contact with your audience. The more you practice, the easier it becomes.

Report Preparation - Chapter Summary

The 5 Preparation and Presentation Steps are:

1 - CHOOSE

● **CHOOSING A SUBJECT.** It should be something:

> You would *enjoy* doing
> That is related to a *hobby* or *special interest*
> That is based on a *group* you happen to belong to
> That is based on a *personal experience*
> That is related to *another course* you are taking

Avoid subjects that are too:

> *recent*
> *specialized*
> *broad*
> *difficult*
> *complex*

Include in your selection a *Thesis Statement* which reflects your personal point of view on the subject you have chosen.

2 - RESEARCH

● **RESEARCH**

> *Locate* your information
> *Select* what you will use
> *Arrange* your facts for proper use

3 - ORGANIZE

● **ORGANIZATION**

> Prepare *Note Cards*
> An *Outline*

4 - WRITE

● **WRITING**

> First *draft*
> *Editing* procedures

5 - PRESENT

● **PRESENTATION**

> *Style*
> *Format*
> *Techniques*

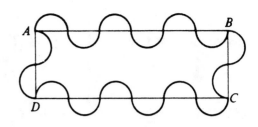

In the figure above, *ABCD* is a rectangle and the curved path is made up of 16 semicircles of equal diameter. If the total length of this curved path is 32π, then the <u>area</u> of rectangle *ABCD* is

(A) 24 (B) 32 (C) 48 (D) 64 (E) 192

6

TEST TAKING

"I don't think much of a man who is not wiser today than he was yesterday"
(Abraham Lincoln)

The mere mention of the word "test" arouses varying amounts of fear in the minds of most students. Check any of the following items that describe your feelings about test days.

Test days remind me of:

_____1. The day of reckoning.

_____2. The moment of truth.

_____3. Doomsday.

_____4. Confrontation with the inevitable.

_____5. All of the above.

_____6. None of the above.

If you checked #5, don't worry, you're normal. If you checked #6, you haven't been taking any tests. The purpose of this chapter is to help you relieve test taking stress and anxiety by telling you all you need to know about tests, and how to get the best results.

TYPES OF TESTS

There are essentially two different types of tests that you have taken and will continue to take for many years:

Tests are an important part of learning.

•**TEACHER CONSTRUCTED TESTS.** What are they, how do most teachers score them, and how can you get the best possible grade?

•**STANDARDIZED TESTS.** What are they, when and under what circumstances are they given? What is their importance to you, and how can you do your best?

There are three basic skills that you need:

1. How best to *prepare* for the test.

2. How to *remember* everything you need to know.

3. How to *take* the test.

I will begin with what you need to know about **TEACHER CONSTRUCTED TESTS**: their purposes, and how they differ from standardized tests. Then I will explain what you need to know about the three basic test taking skills.

Teacher Constructed Tests

Most of the tests you take are teacher made. The most important characteristic of this type of test is that it is *Criterion Referenced.* This means that the test attempts to measure how well you have achieved the goals that have been set for the class. The *criterion* or standard is set by the teacher, not some outside agency. What is on the test has probably been taught in class.

There is a glossary of test terms at the end of this chapter which will help you understand the technical aspects of test taking.

WHY TEACHERS GIVE TESTS

Most teachers give tests for two main reasons:

•To *motivate* you to learn.

•To determine *how much* you have *learned*.

These are two extremely important reasons. When you understand and accept them, anxiety about tests begins to diminish. Let's start with the first.

THE TEST AS MOTIVATION

A social studies teacher announced that there would be no tests, and that final grades would be based strictly on attendance. How would this affect you? How would it affect other students?

- Do you think the students would study very much?

- Do you think the students would learn very much?

- Would most students likely be in class every day?

- How much respect would the class have for the teacher?

- Would you choose this teacher over one who gave the usual number of tests during the year? (Be honest).

Except for the last question, your answers would be obvious. Why? Is it because though we all want to learn we still need to be prodded? Is it because when left to our own devices, we do as little as possible? Is it because we really don't like to learn, or there is no real pleasure in learning? Why would you and most of the other students possibly lose respect for the teacher?

By now you certainly get the point. You tend to be *motivated* when you know that you will be tested and graded on the work you must do in a specific class. But there is much more to *motivation* and test taking.

The key word here is *challenge*. It leads to that "sweet smell of success." It can be highly *motivating*. You can feel *challenge*. It is really a test of yourself. How much have you learned about a certain subject? How well *can* you perform? How *good* are you at solving problems? How good are you compared to the rest of the class? Are you learning up to your real potential? Does the test measure your ability, is it too easy, or too difficult? Do you really want to do well, do you want to succeed. Are you willing to *risk* giving it your "best shot?"

Challenge.

Remember, *nothing succeeds like success*. It is the best of all motivators. It makes all the hard work worthwhile, and you become more willing to take whatever risks are necessary to succeed.

If you have a bad day every so often (we all do) don't be discouraged. You know yourself better than anyone, and you can learn how to get beyond a bad day without letting it drag you down. Remember, there are too many good days ahead to enjoy.

THE TEST AS A MEASURE OF HOW MUCH YOU HAVE LEARNED

Most teachers see this as the main reason for giving tests. In order to give you a grade, they have to measure how much you have learned. The traditional way to do this is to give tests: written tests, oral tests, all kinds of tests. How many and how often will depend on the individual teacher and his or her particular philosophy. As a student, try to understand what that philosophy is.

Measure of learning.

For example, at one end of the spectrum are teachers who have a formal and traditional view of *the test*. It can only be given once, makeups are allowed only under the strictest of circumstances, cheating in any form is the worst crime imaginable, and the grade you get is absolutely "set in concrete." It can never be changed. When you have a teacher like this, follow the rules implicitly, as if they were handed down from above. Although you may disagree with this philosophy, it is not your mission in life to change it; besides, the teacher may be excellent in other ways. Follow the rules, and you will come out ahead.

At the other end of the spectrum is the teacher who could be described as non-traditional, and informal. The rules will usually be very flexible and this teacher would tend to put most of the emphasis on *learning*, rather than *testing*. In this type of class your attitude will be very important. You should impress the teacher with your desire, your interest, your curiosity, and your willingness to contribute to class discussions and class projects. The actual tests given will likely be less important than the impression you make as a participating class member. If you do poorly on a test, always ask to make it up. This teacher rarely sees any grade as "immutable." The fact that you would want to improve could be a strong point in your favor.

Most of your teachers will be somewhere in between these two extremes. Find out which end of the spectrum they tend to lean towards, and then use it to your advantage.

Incidentally, it was not my intention to characterize the two philosophies of testing described above as "good" and "bad." The purpose of this **MANUAL** is to prepare you to   do your best under all possible circumstances.

THE DIFFERENT VALUES OF TESTS

Teachers usually give *Quizzes*, *Tests*, and *Examinations*. Let's look at the characteristics of each form.

THE QUIZ

Quizzes are nearly always short, 10 to 15 minutes at most. Some teachers announce them in advance, others like to "pop" them (like a cork) often when you least expect it. When you understand the teacher's philosophy of testing, you should be able to predict who is most likely to "pop" the quiz, and who will announce it in advance. There are times when a "pop" quiz may be given in order to quiet a disruptive class, as a form of punishment. Once again, know your teacher's philosophy of testing.

The *content* of a quiz is usually taken from recent classwork. The *purpose* is to find out if you understand the material. It also gives the teacher something to put in the grade book.

The actual *value* of a quiz is usually small compared to the full period test or examination. However, quizzes do add up and can significantly affect your grade. Be sure you know the value, and the procedures for making up any quizzes you may have missed. If you do well on the quizzes, you will have an edge when you take the longer, more important tests. Think of it as insurance.

How much does the quiz count toward your grade?

Many teachers have well developed quiz styles, in the type of questions they ask, and also in their selection of content. Be alert in class, and look for these patterns and you will be able to predict quite a bit about what will most likely appear on the quiz. Remember, teachers are "creatures of habit" just like anyone else. Learn their habits and use the knowledge to your advantage.

THE TEST

Your teacher will usually consider a test to be from 30 minutes to a full period in length. Content is usually a full unit of the course, approximately 4 to 6 weeks of work. Suppose we look at the types of tests that are often associated with different subject areas.

Mathematics. This is the most straightforward as tests are composed of problems you have to solve: numerical problems and word problems. *Overlearn everything.* You won't have time to "think" things out. Knowledge has to be instinctive, like the times tables. Don't try to "cram" for a math exam. What you learn by "cramming" you will quickly forget which means double and triple cramming the next time. It's a trap you should avoid by doing your work daily and consistently.

Math test: <u>overlearn</u>.

Most teachers expect you to solve problems logically and show all the steps of the solution. Always come with scratch paper so you can try out solutions before putting final steps down on the test paper. Neatness will be important. Make it easy for the teacher to read and correct.

Foreign Language. In foreign language it will depend on which year you are in, and what the teacher's emphasis happens to be: conversation, composition, grammar, culture, literature, or a combination of all five. The key, as in mathematics, is *overlearning*. If you try to "cram" for a foreign language test, you may pass, but you could be in trouble later when you have forgotten what you learned through "cramming." Look at **SUPPLEMENT B** on Foreign Language and the Glossary of Grammatical Terms to help you prepare for these tests.

Foreign Language: <u>overlearn</u>.

Science. Science tests are usually designed to measure your understanding of concepts, and your ability to solve problems. What I have found to be most helpful is doing additional outside reading. For example, if you are doing a unit on Genetics, after you have gone through the material in your textbook, and taken notes on it, get

Science: <u>overlearn</u>.

another science text from the library and read the chapter(s) on Genetics. The more sources you use, the broader your knowledge will be, and it will pay off in greater confidence when you take the test. Your teacher relies on many sources for his or her knowledge of the subject. Try doing the same, and see how much it pays off.

English: know exactly what the teacher expects.

English. Tests will require knowledge of structure, usage, and communication. The following should be helpful:

● **Structure.** Think of the grammar rules. Why are certain forms and expressions correct and others not?

● **Usage.** Put rules into practice, orally and in writing. Vocabulary, spelling, composition, and correct speech are the most common divisions of usage.

● **Communication.** You listen, speak, read, and understand. Communication skills are more difficult to measure by conventional tests. The areas of structure (grammar) and usage (rules into practice) are precise. A noun is a noun. You will use "different from" and "different than" for specific reasons.

Be sure you know what your teacher's standards are for measuring your *communication* skills.

Social Studies: Same as English.

Social Studies. I left this for last because of the wide variety of approaches, and teaching methods used. Some social studies teachers *lecture* every day for practically the entire period. Others conduct lots of discussions; organize for group activities, and projects; emphasize issues and events; require research and term papers; relate everything to current events; stress politics, ecology, the constitution, social and economic problems, dates, names, and places. Find out as soon as possible how your teacher conducts the class and all you can about the tests that are given.

If you have been at the school for more than a year, your friends can give you information about most of the teachers. The information may be biased, but once you account for that you should end up with useful information.

THE EXAMINATION

Know how much the exam counts toward your grade.

When it's called an "examination" it's usually important. You rarely ever take a mid-term or final "test." It's invariably a mid-term *exam* (examination) or a final *exam*. It's because it counts a lot toward your final grade. Examinations usually cover large amounts of material. In math and foreign language, the examination may mean knowing practically everything that you learned from the first day. In other subjects how much you have to remember may vary according to the teacher.

Preparation for an examination includes going over all prior tests, quizzes, handouts, notes, and whatever else you have accumulated during the semester   Some teachers may just give mid-terms and final examinations. Although it may be pleasant not to have to worry about other tests and quizzes, be sure that you don't leave everything to the last minute.

Following are descriptions of some typical   teacher made tests with tips about what you should watch for.

Teacher made tests are often known as *criterion referenced*. This means that the questions or items are related directly to the subject matter of the course *as presented by the   teacher*. If the teacher tells you to skip a chapter in the history book, the test will not contain any questions on the chapter you skipped.

The advantage of the *criterion referenced* test is that you can be more assured that you have studied the right material.   Another type of test called *norm referenced* will be discussed in the section on Standardized Tests.

Following are examples of teacher constructed tests.

♦*Multiple Choice*.   Example:

Which of the following is not a river?

    a. The Potomac

    b. The Rhine

    c. The St. James

    d. The Rhone

    e. The Thames

Which of these do you recognize? Which can you eliminate?

There are two points about this question that could be helpful.

(1) The question is *negative*. Watch for this. It could be confusing if you overlook it.

(2) The correct answer is **c**. If you are in doubt about **the** answer, studies have shown that there tends to be a bias toward the third or **c**. choice. Professional test makers know this and they assign as many   **c**. answers as any other. But teachers are not professional test makers, and they could well follow the bias. If you can narrow the choices to two and one of them is **c**., pick **c**.

More on Multiple Choice in the section on Standardized Tests.

◆*Essay Questions*.   Example:

Select one of the following questions and support your position with as much evidence and reference as possible.   Keep your essay brief, to the point, and include important details.

1.   What parts of President Truman's Fair Deal that were turned down are now laws?

2.   Do you think the quota system set up in 1924 is a fair way to control immigration?

3.   What do you think of the techniques that Senator McCarthy used to get the communists and spies out of government?

These are questions from a U. S. History unit on post World War II in America.   You would obviously have had to read and take notes on the chapters involved.   None of the questions should come as a surprise to you if you have been attentive in class and if you have done all the assigned work.

If you selected the *first option*, you should identify the Fair Deal in your first paragraph, tell what it was, and explain why it was important.   You would next list the parts you remember that were not passed.   This should all be in your notes, both from the text and from discussions in class.

If you selected the *second option*, you would open with a paragraph on the 1924 law that was passed.   From the text and class discussions, you can state what the intent of the law was at the time, and whether the same intent can be justified today.   In giving your opinion, the more facts and figures you can bring in the better.   In other words, be as objective as possible even about controversial issues.

If you selected the *third option*, you took what I think is the most difficult of the three, although it is the one that most students would probably pick.   They would feel that they have a lot to say, which can be a problem.   It is not how much you say, but how much you stick to the point.   This happens to be a "black and white" issue with practically no shades of gray.   Senator McCarthy represents evil, and it is difficult to describe his techniques objectively and critically.

When you have a choice of essay questions, be careful.   Select the one that allows you to stay close to the subject, and also one in which the points can be numbered and elaborated on briefly.   The essay question that interests you the most could well be the one to stay away from, especially if you feel that most of the class will probably select it.   The competition becomes greater.   But, by all means, go for it if you really feel you have something to say and you can support your position.

♦Sentence Completion.   Example:

General Custer's Last Stand was fought at

_____ .

This question requires good recall of information.   You may get some clues from the item itself, but don't rely on that alone. Sentence Completion items usually test your knowledge of facts. Prepare by reviewing facts: dates, places, formulas, names, anything related to factual content.   Sentence Completion does not allow much chance for guessing.   You either know the answer or you don't.

Therefore, *know your facts!*   Go through all your notes, outlines, teacher handouts, and homework assignments.   Pay attention to *facts*.   It would help if you could look at a Sentence Completion test your teacher has given in the past.   Get an idea of how the teacher makes up the items.

Review and study for <u>facts</u>.

♦Short Answer.   Example:

Give three possible translations for the sentence:
"Elle donne le livre."

The answer is: (1) "She *gives* the book." (2) She *is giving* the book, and "She *does give* the book."

The teacher wants to know whether you understand the three possible ways to translate a simple present tense in French.

Get examples from the teacher, then study accordingly.

Short answers come in many forms   and levels of difficulty. They test your ability to recall facts, as well as your ability to think. For example, try the following:

"What are the main hazards of toxic waste materials?"

This type of question assumes that you know what toxic waste materials are, and how they affect different environments.   In other words, *think* before you answer this question.   It is not simply knowing facts and figures.

♦True/False.   Example:

H_2SO_4 is sulphuric acid.   T____F____

You can get half right by guessing, so <u>prepare</u>.

Although the True/False questions may seem easier than other types of tests because you have a 50-50 chance of getting the answer right, the teacher knows this.   It means that you have to get at least 70% or better to pass.   So prepare for a True/False test as diligently as you would for any other test.

♦ _Open Book._

You don't have as much time as you think to use the "open materials."

This is the most tricky of all. You think that because you can use your book, your notes and other materials that you won't have to spend too much time preparing for the exam. Right? Wrong! If you assume that you will have enough time to use all the materials, you are in for a rude surprise. The teacher knows that with an open book, you will have no trouble finding the answers, so guess what? The teacher will likely expect your answers to be much more detailed and informative. You won't have nearly as much time as you may think to look up answers in your book. And to make matters worse, teachers tend to be tougher on grading an open book exam.

All things considered, you should prepare for an open book exam expecting to use the book as little as possible. When you do use the book, have it referenced with markers that will get you the information you want. Do this with all your materials, and use any other reference aids that will save time.

Remember, in the open book exam, _time is the key factor_. You can't waste any of it fumbling and looking for answers. Be completely organized and ready to take the test. If you finish early, go back and check your answers with your reference sources.

♦ _The Departmental Examination._

Be sure you know whether your teacher has covered the material.

This occurs in a school where more than one instructor teaches a specific course. Suppose for example that there are three teachers teaching U. S. History classes. Ordinarily, each would prepare his or her tests, quizzes, and examinations. However, the three teachers could meet and decide to give the same mid-term or final examination to all of their U. S. History classes. There are two reasons why this can and often does happen:

(1) The teachers save time by preparing one examination instead of three.

(2) They insure that all students are accountable for the same amount of subject matter.

The problem that you face on a departmental exam has to do with which of the three teachers you have. What goes on in each of the classes can be quite different. One teacher could be very strict and demanding, another less so. One could "teach students to the exam," which means that he would prepare students for the departmental exam, while one or both of the other teachers could teach to a different set of objectives.

In which class do you think you would have the best chance for a good grade? Why? Would that ordinarily be the class taught by the best of the three teachers?

How should you prepare for a Departmental Exam? If you have the teacher who "taught to the exam," you will have a head start. Your teacher will have given you many clues about what to expect. Follow them closely, and review all of your material.

If your teacher digressed a lot, and demanded very little, then you could be in for a shock when you take the exam. As soon as you know that you will have a departmental exam, try to find out as precisely as possible what it will cover, and the types of questions that will be asked. Don't assume that the subject matter will have been taken up in class. That may not be true. More than likely, most if not all of the content will be taken from the textbook. Study your textbook carefully. I hope you took good notes on all of the chapters, and that you have made maps of each chapter from your notes. Review everything, assume that everything will be covered, and leave as little as possible to chance.

What does a Departmental Exam look like? It is usually an ***objective*** exam. All questions will have only one correct answer. The questions will probably be Multiple Choice, Short Answer, Sentence Completion, and True/False. This type of test tends to be close to the Standardized Test format which will be discussed later in this chapter.

♦*Problem Solving Examinations*

Examples are math problems, computer problems, and anything else that requires arriving at a solution in which there are a number of specific steps to be taken. The teacher will very likely expect you to show every step in the solution. No matter how simple you may think the step is, write it down. You can't lose anything, and with some instructors, you could have points taken off for omitting any steps.

Neatness counts. Make it as easy as possible for the teacher to see at a glance exactly how you reached the solution.

See Chapter Nine, **CRITICAL THINKING**, for more detailed information on *Problem Solving*.

♦*Oral Examinations*

The most frequent use of the Oral Examination is in foreign language classes. In the first and second year it will require memorizing dialogues, vocabulary, verb conjugations, grammar, idiomatic expressions and relevant cultural facts. Practice beforehand with the intent of "overlearning" as much as possible.

Try to be spontaneous and enthusiastic. Language tends to lower your grade on an oral exam when you hesitate too much and too often. It is sometimes better to say something even if it may be wrong than to grope around and say nothing.

Use all your notes, handouts, and prior exams. Try to get past year departmental exams.

Practice step by step procedures.

Prepare and practice.

In more advanced classes, the oral examination will more likely be conversation and discussion on topics that you are studying. These could be literary, cultural, and personal. The purpose is to determine how well you can use the language as a means of communication.

You may also have oral exams in English and Social Studies classes. The questions could test your knowledge of facts, or sample your opinion on issues. The following are some tips:

Use these as a Checklist before the exam.

- Know well in advance what the oral examination will cover.

- Listen very carefully when classmates are questioned. Take some notes during the process that might help you when you are called on.

- Be sure you understand the question you are asked. If you have any doubts, get a clarification.

- Don't be in too much of a rush to answer. Take a few seconds to think about what you will say.

- Try not to show complete lack of knowledge about a subject. Find something you know and try to elaborate. Be careful not to go too far.

- Don't bluff your way through. It won't do you any good and it shows disrespect for the examiner's intelligence. It also can create a negative atmosphere which could have a bad effect on the entire exam.

- Don't go beyond the point of a sensible response. Padding will only get you into trouble.

- Make sure that when you give an opinion, you identify it as an opinion. The same with a guess.

- Be polite, and show some enthusiasm.

- Make eye contact with the questioner. Be confident.

TEACHER CONSTRUCTED TESTS - SUMMARY

Teachers give tests to:
1. Motivate and
2. Measure.

There are 2 principal reasons why teachers give tests:

MOTIVATION. If there were no tests, you would probably study less.

MEASURE ACHIEVEMENT. Determine how much you have learned in order to give you a grade.

There are *9 basic types* of teacher constructed tests:

1. *Multiple Choice.*

2. *Essay Questions.*

3. *Sentence Completion.*

4. *Short Answer.*

5. *True/False.*

6. *Open Book.*

7. *Departmental Examination.*

8. *Problem Solving.*

9. *Oral Examination.*

Become familiar with all of these.

Ask yourself these *questions* as you prepare.

● How well do you *understand* the subject matter?

● How well can you *use* what you have learned?

● Are there any *gaps* in your knowledge?

● How should you *organize* for the test?

● How can you conquer the *fear* of taking the test?

The following is a *preparation check list* that will help you get ready for the test. Read the items and don't overlook any details.

Preparation Checklist.

● What *kind* of a test will it be? Review the 9 types listed above.

● How much *time* will you have? Is it a timed test? Are you expected to finish? Do you have a watch? If speed is important, then be sure you know your material backward and forward. Get in the habit of timing yourself during a test. It will help when you have a "time crunch."

Time.

● How will the test be *answered*? Will it be on a data card? On notepaper? On an answer sheet? Will you need scratch paper? What other materials should you bring? Bring more than you think you will need. Remember the scout motto: *"Be Prepared."*

Answer Sheet.

● Is the Multiple Choice test graded by the teacher or a machine? The machine *demands* that you follow directions.

Grading.

When should you guess?

•Is there a penalty for *guessing*? In other words is it better to leave the item blank or to guess? Be sure you ask. If there is a penalty, know what the formula is, and you will know when to guess. This is discussed in the section on Standardized Tests. Teacher don't usually penalize for guessing on the tests they make.

Can you take a makeup?

•Will there be a chance for a *make-up*? If you are sick, or you have to miss the test for any reason whatsoever, what are the chances for a make-up? Find out beforehand. If you get a poor grade, is there a chance for a re-test? Some teachers are very liberal in this matter. They see the test as a "learning tool." Others may be more strict. Get to know what kind of teachers you have.

Getting Ready To Take The Test

Are you ready?

In addition to the preparation steps listed above, there are some important ways to improve your *readiness* for the test. Once again, my advice is not to leave anything to chance. Check the items below carefully.

Content.

•Identify the *content*. Which chapters, units, grammar sections, mathematical concepts, stories, principles of physics or chemistry...? Have you been studying all of this regularly? Try not to make a habit of "cramming."

References.

•Collect all important *references* to the content. This includes past tests, teacher handouts, homework assignments, the notes you took in class and from the textbook. Organize everything so that it is easy to get at and includes all that you need. Be sure you save all past tests.

Review.

•Decide what to *review*. Now you can see how important it is that you know what kind of test you will have. For Multiple Choice, you need to know your facts, but memorizing them is not so important. This would not be true for an essay, sentence completion or short answer test.

Preparation time.

•Set the stage. Set aside *enough time* for the review session or sessions. Work where it is quiet and where there are few distractions such as the telephone or TV. Study at the times when you know you do your best work.

• Have a *purpose*. Set a goal for yourself and decide that you want to do your very best. Don't sabotage your effort by procrastinating, losing confidence, or allowing yourself to be distracted. Get actively involved in the process, and think of how great you are going to feel when it is all over and you know you did your best.

• Prepare yourself <u>physically</u>. Get a good night's sleep before the exam. Get up early and do some exercise, if possible.

• Eat *breakfast*. Studies show that protein helps you remember. Try it, but don't overdo it. Nothing can replace a good notetaking and recall system. *Don't drink too much fluid!*

Just Before and During the Test

• Arrive a little <u>early</u>, and be sure you have all the necessary equipment. Relax, get comfortable, think positive thoughts, and remember: There is life after the exam!

• Read all test *directions* carefully. Make sure you understand exactly what to do. Underline key direction words such as:

<u>Analyze.</u>   State all sides or main ideas; show how they are related; state why the whole is important.

<u>Comment on</u>. Clarify the main idea. Offer your opinion give reason(s) for it.

<u>Compare</u>. List similarities and differences. What is more alike or unlike?

<u>Contrast</u>. List and identify main differences.

<u>Criticize</u>. List good and bad points plus your opinion or judgment, but do not "attack."

<u>Define</u>. List the formal meanings, usually what you memorized.

<u>Demonstrate.</u>   State the main point and give an example.

<u>Describe.</u>   List all points or steps in a logical sequence.

Know what your purpose is.

Be physically ready.

Before the test.

Be sure you understand all of these.

<u>Discuss</u>. State the main details. Give pros and cons.

<u>Evaluate</u>. Identify the main issues and state advantages, disadvantages, and your opinion.

<u>Explain</u>. Summarize the main ideas and state how they follow each other logically.

<u>Illustrate</u>. State the ideas; give examples and make comparisons.

<u>Interpret</u>. State the idea; suggest a meaning with examples of personal opinion or judgment.

<u>Justify</u>. State the idea, suggest reasons and support them.

Note: All direction words can be broken down to 4 steps:

1. Clearly state main parts of the idea(s).

2. Give examples.

3. Give pros and cons, advantages and disadvantages, good and bad parts.

4. Give your opinion and reasons for it.

• Glance through the test and make a *time plan*. Use a watch and be sure to pace yourself so you can finish the test, or do as much as possible.

• Check to see whether some questions are *worth more* than others. Gauge your time accordingly.

• Bring *scratch paper* to jot down anything that might be helpful during the exam.

• Don't spend *too much time* on any one item. Skip it if necessary, and go back to it later.

• Be absolutely certain when you *change an answer*. Studies have shown that you will tend to change twice as many right answers as wrong ones.

How much time?

Importance.

Scratch paper.

Don't get hung up.

Be <u>careful</u> when you change an answer.

What To Do On An Essay Examination

For many students the essay exam is very difficult. You must know the subject matter, organize your thoughts, and express yourself in a logical, concise, convincing manner. Grading an essay exam is another unknown quantity because each teacher does it individually.

If you know that you will have an essay exam, find out all you can about it. Ask for a sample format if possible. Does the teacher like quotations as support for ideas? If so, memorize some and use them. What format does the teacher prefer? Outline? Separate headings? Numerical, meaning a series of numbered points relating to the topic or sub-topic? Long essay? Short, concise essay? Creativity, lots of your own ideas? Objectivity, strictly facts? Subjectivity, your own opinions?

Be sure you know exactly what your teacher expects.

Following are general tips and techniques that could be helpful. Read them carefully.

Tips. Read these carefully.

- Use *one side of the paper* only. Skip lines between questions so you can include additional material if necessary.

- Take time to *organize* your answer. Put a few key words by the questions or make brief outline on your scratch paper. Ask yourself **Who, What, When, Where**, and **Why**? This can help you organize your answer.

- Answer as much of the question as possible in your *opening statement*. Then support that statement as you complete your answer. You might find it helpful to turn the question around and use it in your answer. For example:

Question: What Are the Causes of the Civil War?

Answer: The causes of the Civil War are:

- Underline the *direction words* and do exactly what you are asked. See the definitions of direction words in #2. under the heading, **What To Do Just Before and During the Test** on page 109.

- If you have a choice, use a *pencil* so you can erase if necessary.

- Remember *neatness*. Leave margins, and write carefully and legibly.

- If you run short of time, list the *points* you were intending to make to show the teacher that you know the material. It may help. It won't hurt.

- If you finish early, *polish* your essay. It's best to get it right the first time. Think ahead, then you won't have to do too much revising.

•If you have a choice of essays, select the one you feel you have the *most knowledge* about, not the one that you have the strongest opinions about.

•Get to the *point*. Give a direct, specific answer to the question if you can. Try to give an answer in your first sentence and then elaborate with supportive information.

•Stay *calm* while writing. Remember, the quality of what you write is more important than the quantity.

•If you are permitted an open book during the exam, do your research ahead of time, not during the exam. Use reference markers, and index cards with information summaries that you can use easily during the exam.

So much for teacher constructed tests. They represent most of the tests you will take on a regular basis. The other major test division is called the Standardized Test. It has its own format and specific purposes which will be discussed in the next section.

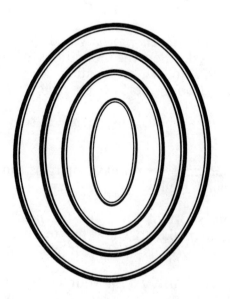

Standardized Tests

There are times when you will be given a Standardized Test to measure your skills, performance, abilities or knowledge. The reason the test is called "Standardized" is because each item on the test has been prepared by experts and given to large numbers of students to determine as precisely as possible what the response patterns are. For example, I ask 10,000 high school students to answer the following Multiple Choice question:

What is the capital city of Pennsylvania?

____A. Pittsburgh   ____B. Harrisburg

____C. Philadelphia   ____D. State College

____E. Wilkes Barre

The correct answer is B. Harrisburg. Suppose that 6300 students (63%) answered the question correctly, and when I asked another similar group of 10,000 students the same question, 6200 answered it correctly. I could then reach a conclusion about the level of difficulty of the item when asked to a cross section of typical American high school students.

If I then ask the same question to a social studies class at a local high school and 97% answer it correctly, what comparison might I make between the social studies students at the local high school and the typical American high school student?

If I have the results of how 10,000 typical American high school students answer all the questions on the test, how can I use the information when I compare the scores of the social studies class?

The 10,000 typical American student sample was used to give me the standard by which I could compare the students in the social studies class, or any other class. The 10,000 student sample gives us what we call the *National Norms* of the test. Since these norms are the standards for comparing other scores, the test has been what is called "*standardized.*"

Most of the *standardized tests* you will take have norms that are based on the general population, however, other standards may also be used. For example, entering college freshmen would be a very selective group for establishing standards. Your own school or community could be very different from the group that established the standards for the tests you may take. In many instances, your score may be reported according to national norms (standards), and also local norms--your own community. The differences can be quite varied, depending upon where you live.

Standardized tests give accurate results.

113

Another important aspect of the standardized test is in regard to the content. When you take a teacher constructed test, you can be reasonably certain that the test will be based on what you have been studying in class. It will be taken from your textbook, lectures, discussions, and other assigned work. In other words, no surprises.

Standardized tests are usually much more generalized. Consequently, it is more difficult to study for them. In fact, some of the testing companies, the Scholastic Aptitude Test (SAT) is a good example, will tell you that you will waste your time trying to prepare. Although that may not be completely true, it is a characteristic of the standardized test that you should be aware of.

THE PURPOSE OF STANDARDIZED TESTS

The main purpose of a standardized test is to get the most "scientifically" possible measurement. The comparison of scores provides that type of reliable and valid information. For example, a student in Alabama who scores 640 on the Mathematics Section of the Scholastic Aptitude Test (SAT) demonstrates the same level of knowledge as any other student in the country who scores 640.

Would the same be true for a student who got an A in Mr. Clark's Algebra class. Would that student automatically get an A in any other Algebra class in the country?

Would the same student definitely get an A if Mr. Clark gave a Standardized First Year Algebra Test?

Admission requirements for many universities include standardized test scores (SAT or ACT) in addition to a high school grade point average. It is interesting to note that the University of California considers the GPA to be twice as good a predictor of success in college as the SAT. The reason is that GPA tells them how *hard* you work; the SAT tells them how much natural ability you have. It seems that *hard work* is the real key to success.

SOME COMMON TYPES OF STANDARDIZED TESTS

There are five basic categories of standardized tests:

- Learning Ability tests

- Aptitude and Interest tests

- Achievement tests

- Competency tests

- Personality tests

114

LEARNING ABILITY TESTS

These are best known as Intelligence tests (IQ) because they measure your mental abilities and how well you can *use* those abilities (knowledge and skills) at the time of the test. The result is an Intelligence Quotient (IQ) which is more appropriately known as a *Deviation IQ*. Turn to page 121 and look at the diagram of a "Normal Bell Shaped Curve."

Notice the bottom line labeled *Deviation IQ*. Without going into an involved and complicated statistical explanation, think of the term *deviation* as a certain number of points--15 in the case of the most frequently used IQ tests. The middle of the curve is 100. Each vertical line to the right or left of the mid-point is either plus or minus 15 points. The numbers inside the area under the curve are the percents of the (normal) population that fall into that category.

For example, 68% of the population fall between IQ scores of 85 and 115. This group can also be expressed as plus or minus one *standard deviation* from the mean. The mean is 100. Minus one deviation is 85; plus one deviation is 115.

Notice also how small the population becomes as you get farther from the mean, either to the right or the left. Less than .02% of the population has an IQ below 55 or above 145.

The significant thing to remember about ability or IQ tests is that the scores are not likely to change very much from year to year. *Intelligence* tends to be a constant. However, don't be overly impressed or discouraged by whatever your score happens to be. The score is only an index. It does not indicate how motivated you are, how hard you work, or how determined you happen to be. Most of your teachers have no idea what your IQ is. All they know is the quality and quantity of the work you do.

APTITUDE AND INTEREST TESTS

These tests are designed to assess your interests and your capabilities or aptitudes in order to predict what occupation(s) you would most likely succeed in. The aptitude section deals with your skills, knowledge and experience in a wide variety of occupational clusters. The interest section is essentially an inventory or check list of the different areas that seem attractive to you. By combining interest and aptitude, it is possible to make reasonably accurate predictions of success in what are considered occupation clusters.

Many schools use 15 or so of these clusters to classify jobs with similar work activities. For example, the *Communications and Media* cluster includes: film projectionists, braille translators, camera operators, photographers, radio and television announcers, journalists, scriptwriters, and telephone engineers.

Intelligence.

Skills, knowledge, and experience.

Examples of the other clusters are:

- Agribusiness

- Business and Office

- Construction

- Environment

- Fine Arts and Humanities

- Health and Home Economics

- Hospitality and Recreation

- Manufacturing

- Marine Science

- Marketing and Distribution

- Personal and Public Services

- Transportation

There are not many careers, vocations, professions or occupations that would not be included in the above "clusters." If you have not already done so, take advantage of your first opportunity to take an aptitude-interest test battery.

ACHIEVEMENT TESTS

The most common test given during your school years is the Achievement Test. This test measures how much you have learned in a given subject, or in a group of subjects. For example, mathematics, reading, history, science, etc.

A good example of a well known Achievement Test Battery is the Iowa Test of Basic Skills. The battery includes:

- Vocabulary

- Reading Comprehension

- Language Skills
  Spelling
  Capitalization
  Punctuation
  Usage

116

- Work-Study Skills
    Visual Materials
    (maps, graphs, tables)
    Reference Materials

- Math Skills
    Concepts
    Problem Solving
    Computation

The *Iowa Tests of Basic Skills* are given to groups of students. In the past they were taken once in the elementary school and twice between grades 7-12.

Other examples of achievement tests are the *readiness tests*. These tests help the teacher know when to start certain subjects on the theory that it makes no sense to start teaching something until the child is "ready" to begin learning. As an extreme example, you would not try to teach a six year old how to drive a car. Some students are "ready" to learn how to read at age 3, others at age 6 or 7. The Readiness Test provides this kind of information.

COMPETENCY TESTS

This is another form of an Achievement Test. In California and other states, students must demonstrate at least the equivalent of 8th grade competency in language arts and mathematics in order to graduate from high school. Each school district is required to construct their own competency tests and give them to all students. They are not as "standardized" as the professionally made tests mentioned above, but they are "standardized" for the students in that district.

<u>Demonstrate</u> how much you have learned.

Some school districts have developed competency tests for each grade level from 1-12 in all academic subjects. A student's promotion to the next grade depends on passing these tests.

The theory behind the use of competency tests is that it tends to guarantee that students will learn what would be considered the minimum expectations for promotion to a higher grade, or for graduation from high school. It is an attempt to make both teachers and students accountable for what they do.

PERSONAL PROFILE TESTS

These tests tell you about yourself, usually with a Profile, and at times with a score. There are two types:

- Personality

- Performance

What makes you different from other persons?

Personality measurement generally deals with such things as what you think about yourself, how well you get along with other people, how happy you are, how responsible you are, how well you communicate with others, how well you get along in a group, your leadership qualities, and anything else that characterizes you as a person.

These characteristics are usually described in the form of a *Profile.* which gives information in the form of a graphic or visual outline. For example, each of the items below have a range from 1 to ten, with 1 being low and 10 being high. You would be asked to rate yourself on the following character traits:

Honesty
1   2   3   4   5   6   7   8   9   10

Dependability
1   2   3   4   5   6   7   8   9   10

Neatness
1   2   3   4   5   6   7   8   9   10

Frugality
1   2   3   4   5   6   7   8   9   10

You can see at a glance that when you connect the numbers of each of the items you begin to get a *profile* of your qualities. The *profile* provides information about you, your personality traits, and also where you excel or where you might need to improve.

The rating scale can vary according to the type of *profile*. Ten points gives you lots of positions, which can at times be confusing. Five points could be easier. Some of the tests identify each point on the scale with a brief definition. See the examples of Performance Profiles in Chapter Twelve.

As an exercise, construct your own Personality Profile, then measure yourself in the categories you selected. Have your friends take it, and make comparisons. Try it with any or all of the following traits on a five point scale. Start with, "My concern for *health*," "my attitude toward *school*," etc.

Health, religion, politics, school, happiness, friendliness, compassion, money matters, fairness, laziness, respect, punctuality, honesty, intuition, communication, and personal appearance

Have a friend do your profile and you do your friend's. It will be interesting to compare how you see each other.

Performance Profiles

This is another way to look at yourself to see how well you are performing in school and in what specific areas you can improve. The best examples of this are described for you in **SUPPLEMENT A** to this **MANUAL**. I have also included the means to arrive at a *Performance Quotient* in addition to the *Profile*.

How well do you perform?

A Performance Profile can be constructed for any type of performance. A high school baseball coach looked at the profiles in **SUPPLEMENT A** and decided to construct a Performance Profile for his players. He wanted them to see themselves in ways that could give them the information they might need to improve.

Different types of performance.

The same could be applied to music, drama, used car selling, class presidency, or anything else that involves progress, growth and improved performance.

★　　★　　★　　★　　★　　★　　★　　★

The final section of this chapter is a Glossary of most test terms that you should understand when taking tests during your years in school.

Glossary of Test Taking Terms

The following terms describe tests and the meaning of test results. Be sure you understand everything you need to know about any test you take. Most of the terms are associated with standardized tests.

Ability Test

A test of general mental ability or intelligence. The score indicates what you are capable of doing, not necessarily what you actually do. You may at one time have been told that "You can do better." In other words, you have the *ability* to do better.

Achievement Test

This test measures your skills and the knowledge you have acquired. In many ways this is more important than the Ability Test, because it is based upon your actual performance, rather than what you are capable of doing.

Admission Test

This may be required for acceptance to various private and parochial schools. It usually measures both ability and achievement. If possible, find out what test is used by the school you plan to attend. Get as much information as possible about the test from the school, a local book store, or the library.

Analogy Item

Analogy items are found on most aptitude and ability tests, and are a measure of your ability to think at some level of abstraction. You have to compare similar sets of terms, ideas, or objects. For example, how are a marble and a ball alike?

Antonym Item

Antonym means opposite. You have to select a response which means the opposite of the term given in the item.

Aptitude Test

This is a form of ability test which measures skills in areas such as clerical, mechanical, academic, business, sales, etc. The purpose of an aptitude test is to predict how well you will do on a job, or in a training program. It also indicates to you what your aptitudes are.

Battery

A group of tests administered with a similar purpose. For example, an Achievement Test Battery would contain a number of different achievement tests; an aptitude test battery would contain different aptitude tests.

Intelligence.

Skills and knowledge.

Specific purpose.

Skills in specific areas.

A group of tests.

120

Bell Curve

This is the term used to describe the distribution of scores for a "normal population." You will see it when you get an explanation of your scores on a standardized ability (IQ) or achievement (College Board) test. The curve is perfectly symmetrical.

Look at the example below. The first two terms are common test measurements. "Percentile" indicates the percentage of the population above and below you, while "Stanine" is a *range* classification from 1 to 9.

The Normal Bell Shaped Curve

Visual and comparative display of test results.

	-4	-3	-2	-1		+1	+2	+3	+4
	less than .02%	2%	14%	34%	34%	14%	2%	less than .02%	
Test Scores									
Percentile	1	5	10	20 30 40 50 60 70 80		90	95	99	
Stanine	1		2	3 4	5	6 7	8	9	
College Board (SAT)	200	300	400	500	600	700	800		
Deviation IQ	55	70	85	100	115	130	145		

Use this Bell Curve when you get the results of any of the standardized tests you take. The results will nearly always include "percentiles." By extending the vertical lines, you can compare any of the score categories to each other. For example, an IQ score of 115 is equivalent to approximately the 80th percentile.

A definition of each of the terms is also included in this **Glossary**.

Demonstrate how much you know.

Classification.

Type of test.

Classification.

Score.

For vocational purposes.

IQ.

Competency Test
> This test is given to determine how much skill or knowledge you have in specific subjects. Many schools require that you pass Competency Tests for promotion to higher grade levels and/or for high school graduation.

Completion Item
> You supply the missing part of the question or statement. See pages 100-101 for an example and explanation of this type of test item.

Criterion-Referenced Test
> These are teacher made tests covering material that you have been using in class every day. "Criterion" means "test." You prepare for Criterion-Referenced tests by using all the information and sources your teacher has given you. The opposite is Norm-Referenced.

Essay Test
> A test in which you answer questions with information and supporting evidence, usually written in paragraphs or a point by point structured response. See the section on Essay Tests on pages 99-100 for a more detailed explanation.

Intelligence Test
> A measure of your intellectual ability which yields an IQ score. In many states Intelligence Tests must be administered to one student at a time. There is usually a special reason for the school to give you an Intelligence (IQ) Test. It is most often done for placement in special programs: gifted and talented, and special education classes. Look at the Bell Shaped Curve on page 119 for the distribution of IQ scores.

IQ

> The Intelligence Quotient is the score you get from an Intelligence Test.

Interest Inventory
> Usually given in connection with vocational testing. Your interests have a lot to do with the decisions you make about a job, profession, or school program.

Matching Item
> A Multiple Choice in which you select the term or concept that is similar to (matches) the test question.

Mental Ability
> Another name for Intelligence.

Multiple Choice Item

Your task is to choose from four or five answers to a test question. See page 101 for an example and explanation.

Norms

The average or mid-point score on a test. You can be above or below the norm. Look at the Bell Curve on page 121.

Standards.

Open Book Test

A test in which you can use your textbook and other reference materials. The goal is to be well prepared so you will not have to waste valuable time looking up information. See the Open Book Tests information on page 102 for a more complete explanation.

Type of test.

Percentile Rank

The percentage of students above and below the score you made on a test. For example, if your score on the Reading Comprehension section of the California Achievement Test is equivalent to the 80th Percentile, then 20% of the students who take the same test have higher scores than you, and 80% had scores that were lower than yours. Look at the Percentile line in the diagram on page 121. Notice how close the numbers are to each other in the middle, but far apart at the ends.

A position between 1 and 99.

Performance

Any measure of what you can do. It may be in a classroom, on a stage, the field, or in a laboratory. See **SUPPLEMENT A** of this **MANUAL** for examples of academic Performance Profiles.

What you can do.

Personality Test

This test gives information about you, your attitudes, opinions, beliefs, social relationships, and other aspects of your personal makeup.

Classification.

Proficiency Test

This is a type of achievement test that measures how much skill and knowledge you have in specific or general areas. In California, the High School Proficiency Test measures the *equivalent* of what you should know in order to earn a high school diploma.

Classification.

Profile

This is a visual interpretation of a series of subtests within a test. The Profile enables you to see at a glance what the results are. The Performance Profiles in **SUPPLEMENT A** of this **MANUAL** are good examples.

A visual method of reporting results.

Numerical position in a group.	**Rank** Your numerical position in the group. If 100 students take a test and you place 70th, that would be your Rank. Percentiles indicate Rank.
Number of correct answers.	**Raw Score** The actual number of correct answers on a test. The Raw Score is the only score you get on nearly all teacher made tests. On Standardized Tests (pages 113-119) the Raw Score is primarily used in a formula to arrive at a "standardized" or final score which is different from the Raw Score.
The "accuracy" of test results.	**Standard Error of Measurement** Testing is not always as "scientific" as we would like it to be. If you run 100 yards, your time can be measured to a fraction of a second. The tests discussed in this chapter cannot be so precisely measured. The score you get may be so many points above or below your actual knowledge. These points "above or below" are called the "error of measurement." For example, an IQ test could have a "standard error" of plus or minus 10 points. If your score turned out to be 125, it could actually be as high as 135, or or as low as 115. Most standardized tests have a specific Standard Error of Measurement. Be sure you know what the Standard Error is.
Provides uniform results.	**Standardized Test** A test that is given to a large population for the purpose of developing "norms" or standards which are used to interpret scores uniformly, regardless of where, or when you may take the test.
Scale of results.	**Stanine** A score reported on a scale of 1 to 9. Look at the Bell Curve on page 121 and compare the Stanine scores to Percentiles.
	Synonym Item A test item in which you select a word or term whose meaning is similar to another word or term.
Type of test.	**Take Home Test** A test that your teacher allows you to complete at home. You must follow the directions, but you can take as much time as you like.
Type of test.	**True-False Test** Questions or statements that are answered either true or false, right or wrong. See page 103 for a fuller explanation.

124

Test Taking - Chapter Summary

There are two basic types of tests: **TEACHER CONSTRUCTED** and **STANDARDIZED**.

•TEACHER CONSTRUCTED

Teachers give tests to motivate you and also to find out how much you have learned. The tests may be:

Multiple Choice
Essay Question
Sentence Completion
Short Answer
True/False
Open Book
Departmental
Problem Solving
Oral

•STANDARDIZED

Standardized tests are "scientifically" made so that the results will be the same for any given level of knowledge or ability. They are used most often to measure:

Learning Ability
Aptitude and Interest
Achievement
Competency
Personality Traits

USE THE SPECIAL PENCIL. MAKE GLOSSY BLACK MARKS.

7

READING

"Reading is to the mind what exercise is to the body"
(Sir Richard Steele)

In your opinion, are the following statements True or False?

●Words must be read one at a time.

●Reading more than 500 words per minute is impossible.

●Fast readers do not appreciate what they read.

●Higher reading speeds give lower comprehension.

●Average reading speeds are natural, and therefore best.

All the statements are False. After you complete this chapter, you should know why. Now to the heart of the matter. Check any of the following statements that refer to your experience with reading:

●I read too slowly.

●I don't understand what I read.

●I don't remember what I read.

●I don't like what I have to read.

●I want to read more than I do.

●Sometimes, I really enjoy reading.

●I like to go to libraries and bookstores.

If you really want to become a good reader, you can, but you will have to work at it. Practice alone will not do the job. You have to learn *how* to improve your reading skill. Start with the directions in this chapter, then if necessary, investigate more on your own.

READING SKILLS

The single most important skill that will lead to your academic success is *Reading*! When I use the term "reading," I also include "comprehension." You not only have to be able to read well, but you have to understand and remember what you read.

What is a good reader? What is a good reading speed? What is good comprehension?

In this chapter, I will show you how to do a brief analysis of your reading speed and comprehension. I will also give you some techniques that will help you improve, according to the type of material you are required or desire to read. For example, you would obviously not read a chapter in your Biology text at the same speed you read a mystery novel.

Also, review the chapter on Notetaking. Reading and remembering are two related but often very separate skills. Much of the information on Notetaking will help you remember what you read, particularly when reading textbooks.

HOW FAST DO YOU READ?

The average student in grades 7-12 reads about 200 words per minute of normal fiction or newspaper articles. You need to do much better in order to succeed at higher academic levels, unless you want to spend every waking hour in the attempt. A reasonable goal would be 600 - 700 words per minute, with no loss of comprehension. The first step is to find out what your reading speed is, plus some important facts about your comprehension.

SPEED TEST

All you need is a watch with a second hand. You are going to read an 800 word selection from a book on the discovery of gold in California. Before you start, be sure you are comfortable and in a place where there are no distractions. When you are ready, read the passage at your normal speed. I will give you the formula for calculating your speed in words per minute at the end of the selection.

Relax, and when you are ready, turn the page and begin.

Reading is a skill.

Comprehension is a skill.

Average speed of most students is about 200 wpm.

Get ready for a speed test.

Gold Is Where You Find It

The FORTY-NINERS came with picks, shovels, and pans. Fortunes could be made with just these tools, they were told. The new gold hunter could hardly wait to begin. He would never forget the first day he found gold!

He walked quickly along the bank of the river. His eyes searched the edge of the stream. "Plenty of water here. 'Wet diggings,' I guess they call it. Well I'll just stop here and try my luck." A second bar had formed where the river made a turn. Placer, or loose gold, was often found in such places. Down went his pan, pick, and shovel.

First he dug away the sand and gravel with his pick. Into his tin pan he scooped some of the sand, gravel, and water. He soon found it was best to fill the pan half full of gravel. Then he placed it under water. With both hands he broke up the larger lumps. Swirling the gravel round and round, he saw golden bits in the gravel. Getting them out was the hard part. With each turn of the pan, some of the water and gravel spilled out. When most of the water was gone, he did the same thing, adding some water again. This was called "panning" for gold. Any trace of gold was called "color." He could hardly wait to get to the bottom of the first pan. If he was lucky, the gravel left at the bottom would have gold dust or gold flakes in it. It might even have one or more nuggets of gold.

If the gravel had much gold in it, it was called "pay dirt." A miner learned to tell very soon whether the gravel was "pay dirt" or not. If little or no "color" showed, he moved on. He counted on every pan to bring him luck. Each pan might have from ten cents to a dollar in gold in it. Nuggets might be worth even hundreds of dollars! It was all a chance, but it was worth it-sometimes!

It was not long before miners found gold hidden between rocks. "Dry diggings," they called this. As the water had swirled around the rocks, bits of gold had caught in the cracks. The same was true in dry gulches, where water had once been. Only a knife was needed to dig the gold out. Miners even cut horns in half lengthwise and used them to scoop it out.

Panning was done not only on the riverbanks. Miners had to wade out into the icy cold streams too. There they stood knee deep for hours. Pan after pan of gravel and sand was taken from the river bed. This was "wet diggings." The hot sun blazed down on the miner's back. His muscles grew tired from bending all the time. His back and legs ached. But this was the kind of life the miner expected. One miner wrote to his family, "A miner's life is the hardest in the world. Luck or not, it's plain hard work!" Men who had sailed to California were not ready for the new, rough life at the diggings. It was a little easier for those who had traveled overland.

Once in a while the silence of the mountains would be broken. A shout of "Boys, I've found it!" could be heard from an excited man. Then those near him rushed to the spot. "It's gold all right enough," they would agree. "Worth plenty, too--maybe five hundred dollars. It's not as big as the nugget found over at Auburn. That one was over a hundred pounds. But I guess your little gold lump will do!" Cheered on by one man's luck, they all worked a little harder than usual. Where there was gold like that, there must be more. Sometimes a man would make a find and keep it a secret for a while. But it wasn't easy to keep something like that a secret.

Bending, swirling the water, the miners tried to find gold again and again. Hour after hour, day after day passed in this way. Some days hundreds of dollars of gold were found. If not, they had to decide where to go next. That's the way it was--the next place, the next pan. Would luck be just ahead--or just behind? Miners always thought, "Our luck will change. It's bound to get better." Some were willing to give up. Others had the courage to go on. Most of them had not panned enough gold to get back home again. But they had to find enough gold to do it. No one wanted to go home empty-handed. So he kept working and trying. The next day, the next pan--and the next. **(800 Words)**

Selection from: Bauer, Helen, *California Gold Days.*
Sacramento: California State Department
of Education, 1957. pp.66-73.

READING SPEED IN WORDS PER MINUTE (W.P.M.)

Divide the number of words in the selection (800) by the number of minutes it took you to read it. Round off the minutes to the nearest quarter. For example, if it took 3 minutes, 42 seconds, divide 800 by 3 3/4 or 3.75. Your answer should be 213 Words Per Minute. Now calculate your own **Word Per Minute** score.

$$\frac{800}{\text{Minutes}} = \textbf{Your Score}$$

COMPREHENSION TEST

Answer as many of the following questions as you can without referring to the selection. If the question is Multiple Choice, circle the correct letter. For True-False questions, circle **T** or **F**. The correct answers are on page 131.

1. The title of the selection is:

    A *The Forty-Niners*
    B *Gold Is Where You Find It*
    C *Gold Days*
    D *California Gold Mining*

2. The word *placer* means:

    A Wet diggings
    B The place where nuggets are found
    C Loose gold
    D The miner's pan, pick, and shovel

3. When *panning* for gold, the miners used:

    A Water
    B Gravel
    C Color
    D Water and Gravel

4. If the gravel had much gold in it, it was called:

    A Pay dirt
    B Color
    C Pan gold
    D None of the above

5. What did the miners call the gold they found hidden between rocks?

    A Dry gulch gold
    B Dry diggings
    C Dry rock
    D Dry scoops

6. T - F   Panning was done only on the riverbanks.

7. T - F   The men who sailed to California were ready for the rough life.

8. T - F   The biggest nugget around was found at Auburn.

9. T - F   Most of the miners got rich.

10. T - F   Whether they found gold or not, the miners liked to stay in one place.

ANALYSIS

The correct answers to the **COMPREHENSION TEST** are:

1-**B**, 2-**C**, 3-**D**, 4-**A**, 5-**B**, 6-**F**, 7-**F**, 8-**T**, 9-**F**, 10-**F**

List the number of each question you answered correctly.

_____

What was there was about the particular question that made it possible for you to answer it correctly.   For example, you are good at remembering titles, or you made a visual association, or there was a special point of interest.

What helped me answer questions correctly?

_____

_____

_____

List the questions you skipped or answered incorrectly.

_____

Why did I skip questions or answer them incorrectly?

For example,

#1-I seldom bother to remember the title of a book.

#2-I thought it had something to do with "place."

#4-I must have read that too fast. I can't remember.

#8-I have trouble remembering numbers and details.

Now some of your own reasons:

#

_____

#

_____

#

_____

Use the information on questions answered correctly or incorrectly to help you improve your reading comprehension. For example,

1. Be sure to remember the author's name and the title of the book, article or selection.

2. Try to notice significant details such as the meaning of technical terms like "placer," "color," or "golden bits." These will very likely come up on a quiz or exam.

3. Relate the title to what you read. "Gold Is Where You Find It" should keep your mind on the different places the miners dug or panned for gold.

4. Don't neglect human interest. What made the miners work harder than usual?

Analyze your tendencies.

List any other points that you think you should be more aware of as you read this or any other selection. What should you be more conscious of in order to improve your reading comprehension?

_____

_____

_____

_____

_____

What do you think would help you improve? Do you have any habits such as skipping over lengthy descriptions or other types of writing? Do you concentrate too much on dialogue because it's more interesting? What causes your mind to wander when you read? What do you do when you don't know the meaning of a word, term or expression?

What do you think might help you improve?

_____

_____

_____

_____

_____

Techniques To Improve Reading Speed

EYE MOVEMENT

Use your index finger as a pacing guide and keep your eyes moving swiftly across the printed page. This should help prevent your eyes from wandering, and establish a consistent reading pace.

Try this until you can do it without using your finger.

This may seem awkward at first, but stick with it until you are reading at a consistent and more rapid speed.

PURPOSE

Always read with a purpose in mind. You will read better, faster, and with greater comprehension if you know precisely why you are reading something. It is not enough for you to simply read because you are told to do so. Fit the reading assignment into the overall scope of the course you are taking. If necessary, ask the teacher what the purpose of the reading assignment is. It could certainly help improve your concentration and reading comprehension.

Be sure you know <u>why</u> you read something.

SKIMMING

There are times when it is helpful to get a general impression of the material without reading every word. One technique for doing this is to "skim" over the material. Read the first two or three paragraphs word for word. Then quickly read the first sentence of each paragraph, looking for any key words, terms, concepts, or meaningful clues. Then read the last two or three paragraphs word for word. This should give you enough of an impression so that when you go back to read more carefully you will be able to recall information more easily. (Review Chapter Four on Notetaking and Recall Systems).

Do this to get a <u>general impression</u> of the material.

If there is a summary section at the end of the chapter, be sure to read it word for word.

SCANNING

This is sometimes confused with "skimming," however, they are not the same. You "skim" to get a general impression of the material. You "scan" when you are looking for something specific. For example, when you are looking for a word in the dictionary, you may have to "scan" one or more pages before you find the word. You would never "skim" through the dictionary to look for a word. If you are doing research on a specific author, you would "scan" various sources for information about the author's life. You would "skim" through some of the author's works in order to get a general impression of the author's writing.

Do this to find <u>something specific</u>.

You need to be "motivated" to improve.

You may have heard the expression, "Practice makes perfect." It is not generally true. The correct expression is, "Practice makes permanent." It applies to reading. If you read a lot, you will not necessarily improve your speed, comprehension, or vocabulary. In fact, if you have poor reading habits, they will become "permanent." You have to *want to improve*. This means using proper techniques, combined with lots of practice. It is no different in reading than in sports, drama, or any serious learning exercise. Intent comes first; then proper technique, followed by lots of

P R A C T I C E

★　　★　　★　　★　　★

Reading - Chapter Summary

Reading skills include both *speed* and *comprehension*.

Reading speed and comprehension can be measured, and improved. Comprehension is improved through analysis, attention to specific areas, and lots of *practice* in:

- Proper *eye movement*.

- Reading with a *purpose*.

- *Skimming*.

- *Scanning*.

- Reading with *intent*.

8

MEMORY

"Memory is the essence of being"
(Anonymous)

In **CHAPTER 4** on **NOTETAKING**, we examined what was necessary to develop a good "recall system." *Memory* will certainly be an important part of that recall system. In this chapter we will help you develop techniques to strengthen and improve your memory. First, understand three basic facts:

> •*Always* know *why* you are reading something, and *what* you want to remember.

Purpose.

> This may seem simple but many students read without knowing why or how the assignment fits into the overall makeup of the course. When that is the case, it is difficult to know what to remember.

> •*Forgetting occurs mostly within a very short time* after learning has taken place.

> After you have taken notes, look them over almost immediately afterwards. Don't trust anything to remain in you memory after you have read it. Written notes, outlines, summaries, synopses, and re-reading are an absolute must.

> •Failure to use or *practice what you have learned* causes forgetting to take place at a faster pace.

> You have to cement it into your mind with repeated practice and constant repetition. Remember, in subjects like math and foreign language, you have to "overlearn." so that the knowledge can be used "instinctively."

Repetition and practice will help you remember.

SEVEN PRINCIPLES FOR IMPROVING YOUR MEMORY

Apply these principles to your current assignments.

● *Motivated Interest.* You need to have a reason for wanting to remember.

● *Selectivity.* You should be able to pick out what is most important to remember.

● *Intent.* You have to consciously <u>want</u> to remember something.

● *Basic Background.* You need a certain amount of specific knowledge about a subject.

● *Logical Organization.* You should be able to arrange facts and concepts in categories for quicker recall, recognition, and memorization.

● *Consolidation.* Temporary learning becomes permanent learning with consistent and repeated practice.

● *Distributed Practice.* Your best results will come from repeated short practice sessions, followed by short intervals.

MEMORY TECHNIQUES

The following are three very effective memory devices. Learn how to use them for your own purposes. Create others for yourself. This will help you develop a good memory support system, in addition to the recall methods you learned to use in **CHAPTER 4.**

● *Association.* This is a technique for remembering any number of items in a series. The first step is to memorize a list of ten "peg" words that rhyme with the numbers one through ten:

Use these "pegs," or invent your own.

Try to *visualize* each of the "peg" words as you recite them. Make the *association* between number and word as strong and as vivid as possible.

1	sun	6	tricks
2	stew	7	heaven
3	bee	8	slate
4	store	9	sign
5	hive	10	den

By associating each of the "peg" rhyme words with a specific list of words, you will find that you will be able to remember the items more easily and you will retain the information longer. The important thing is to form a visual association with the "peg" word and the item you need to memorize. The more ridiculous, silly, or dramatic the association, the more likely you are to remember it. Try it with the following list of words:

Try this experience until you think you remember each word.

1   chair

2   fly

3   button

4   milk

5   rock

6   fence

7   car

8   table

9   apple

10   ball

Try it again a week later. Did you forget anything?

This technique can help you with much more than the simple list of words above. You can use it for more complicated series that include concepts, ideas, parts of an argument, or as in the example on the next page, the first ten amendments to the United States Constitution, otherwise known as the Bill Of Rights.

Remember, make your associations as visual and sensory as possible. The Bill of Rights is as difficult a list as you will likely have to remember. Most of what you get in the future should be much easier. Now try the exercise on the next page.

THE BILL OF RIGHTS

1) Freedom of Religion, Speech, Press, Assembly, and Petition. (R S P A P)

2) Right to bear arms.

3) Privacy (no one allowed in your home without consent).

4) No unreasonable search or seizure.

5) Due process of law for persons accused of a crime.

6) Right to a fair and speedy trial.

7) Right to a trial by jury in civil cases.

8) No cruel or unusual punishment.

9) Other rights of the people

10) Powers that belong to the states.

Exercise.

Use the space below to describe some of the associations you make for any or all of the ten amendments listed above. For example, the First Amendment contains five freedoms: Religion, Speech, Press, Assembly, and Petition. A numerical association could be as follows:

1 - *sun*: I associate **Religion** with Sun Worshippers.

2 - *stew*: **Speak** about your fabulous stew!

3 - *bee*: The Killer Bees were written up in the **Press**.

4 - *store*: There is a big **Assembly** at the local store.

5 - *hive*: The neighbors signed a **Petition** to remove the hive.

You can form other associations. In the space below, Try whatever works best for you with the above Amendments.

_____

_____

_____

_____

_____

•**Mnemonics.** This is a rhyming or visual device that helps you remember certain concepts and spelling combinations. For example, "Thirty days has September..." "i before e except after c."

It can be used visually as well. For example, you want to remember that Mr. Sanders is a big real estate broker. You might visualize Mr. Sanders building a big sand castle with a FOR SALE sign stuck in front of it. Try creating your own mnemonic device for something you need to remember. Use the following examples, or make up your own.

Miss Josephine Hanratty, Librarian

Be as imaginative and creative as possible.

_____

_____

Andrew Johnson, 17th President of the United States

_____

_____

$E=MC^2$

_____

_____

•**Mapping.** This was discussed in Chapter Four (pages 67-68) in relation to textbooks. The technique can be used with many other materials: magazines, brochures, etc.

Refer to the diagram on page 68.

The purpose of mapping the material is to enable you to see at a glance how ideas, concepts,, topics, and subtopics relate to each other. It is a quick visual reference that you can use just before an exam or oral presentation to help you remember information.

When you map information that contains a series of items under a particular heading, you should number the items and use the association technique (page 136) to remember as many as possible.

★　　　★　　　★　　　★　　　★

After you have used these memory techniques, you will begin to develop your own. This plus everything discussed in Chapter Four will give you a real advantage when acquiring and remembering information.

Memory - Chapter Summary

THREE BASIC FACTS OF MEMORY:

- Know why you read and **what** you intend to remember.

- **Forgetting** occurs soon after you acquire information.

- Repeated **practice** prevents forgetting.

SEVEN PRINCIPLES FOR IMPROVING MEMORY:

- Motivated interest

- Selectivity

- Intent

- Basic Background

- Logical Organization

- Consolidation

- Distributed Practice

MEMORY TECHNIQUES:

- Association

- Mnemonics

- Mapping

9
CRITICAL THINKING

"I think, therefore I am"
(Rene Descartes)

$E = MC^2$

What Is Critical Thinking?

For our purposes, **CRITICAL THINKING** means two things: *Problem Solving* and *Creative Process*.

PROBLEM SOLVING

You have to *think* in order to *solve problems*. We all can think and solve problems. We do it every day. For example, if I told you that your favorite band was giving a concert in two weeks at a place about fifty miles from where you live, you would have to think (problem solve) about how you could get to the concert, and also how you would get the money for the ticket. If you had a car, and a generous allowance from your parents, the problem would be solved very easily. But if not, the problem would be more difficult. If you wanted to go (were motivated) with all your heart and soul, you would probably find a way. If not, you would forget it. This is typical of the kind of problems you encounter.

How you solve problems has a lot to do with your critical thinking ability, and the degree of interest you may or may not have in a subject or activity. Your answers to the following questions should give you a good indication of your problem solving ability. Explain your answers as much as possible in the space below. The purpose of this exercise is to analyze your problem solving ability. Circle **Y** for Yes; **N** for No.

How do <u>you</u> solve problems?

141

Statement: I am often frustrated by problems I cannot solve quickly, and I tend to give up.   Y   N

Explain_____

_____

_____

_____

My Comment

Analyze your tendencies.

If you are in the habit of throwing up your hands as soon as you come face to face with a difficult problem:

- What keeps you from trying harder to solve the problem?

- Have you really tried?

- Do you have all the facts or figures that you need?

- Do you know where to get help when you need it?

- Do you have enough interest in the subject?

- Do you care enough about solving the problem?

Statement: I use a *system* to solve difficult problems.   Y   N

Explain_____

_____

_____

_____

My Comment

Develop a <u>system</u> for problem solving.

Good problem solvers use systems. Some even invent their own. Most systems have common characteristics such as:

- *Reorganize* the problem in order to understand it better. For example, you have to locate the cause of some sort of mechanical failure. You turn on the switch, and nothing works. What do you do? The first step is to reorganize. Find out where the power source is. Is that working? Why not? What parts of the mechanical apparatus are not functioning? Identify them. Isolate them. Can they be repaired? Do you have the tools to repair them? Do you understand how the parts work, by themselves, and as a unit?

- Make use of *hypotheses*. This means coming up with trial solutions. In the case of the mechanical failure, could it be possible that a bearing has worn out? What would lead you to believe that was the problem? Test it out. If there is nothing wrong with the bearing, what else could be wrong? Test that possibility. Keep repeating the process until you begin to "strike pay dirt." Don't give up, and don't become discouraged.

Trial solution.

- Rule out the *irrelevant*. As you continue to test each new "hypothesis," you should gradually get closer to the solution. As you do, you will be able to discard what doesn't work.

Eliminate the obvious.

- Set up *criteria* which the solution must meet. This happens as you rule out possibilities that have little or nothing to do with the solution. Each new possibility suggests something that gives you a clue to the solution.

Test your ideas.

- Give as much *time* as possible to the solution of the problem. In other words, don't be in too much of a hurry. Relax. Let your mental and creative processes do their work. Forget about time. You will be amazed how fast it goes by when you are really involved in solving the problem.

- *Recall* and relate other solutions to similar problems.

- Proceed from the *simple to the complex*. If the problem seems too complicated, start with the simplest part. Be sure you understand it, and then go on from there. By the time you understand all the parts, the problem itself will not be so complex. This process is known as Cartesian Thinking, after the seventeenth century French philosopher and mathematician, Rene Descartes. From the simple statement, "I think, therefore I am," ("Je pense donc je suis" in French, or "Cogito ergo sum" in Latin) he constructed his entire method of philosophy.

Separate the parts.
Start with the simplest.

- Be as *orderly* as possible. Avoid too much impulsive jumping around. In other words, don't let your frustration take over.

- *Be persistent*. Follow a system, and stay with the problem until you begin to get signs of a solution.

143

Statement: My problem solving attitude could be better.   Y   N

Explain_____

_____

_____

_____

My Comments

Attitude is important.

Attitudes are extremely important.   Some students look at problems as a challenge.   They are willing to take risks, make mistakes, and push themselves to the limits of their ability.   The following could help improve your attitude.

Don't be afraid to take risks or make mistakes.

- *Reasoning* or "thinking" is the key to solving problems. Get in the habit of thinking.   After a while your mind will become more "fertile," and you will get many good ideas about whatever problem you are trying to solve.

- *Consider all problems*, not just those that seem easy enough to solve, or those that are backed up by large amounts of information.

That is all part of problem solving.

- *Make assumptions* when you have to fill in gaps where you have little information.   It is like figuring out the meaning of a word you don't understand from the context of a sentence.   An assumption is like an hypothesis.   It helps give you direction toward a solution.   For example, if you heard a strange noise, you would immediately assume what it might be: thunder, a plane breaking the sound barrier, an auto crash, a fire cracker, or something that fell outside your house.   The fact that you didn't know what it was would do two things: arouse your curiosity, and start you thinking and making assumptions about the noise. Next you would test those assumptions as you would test an hypothesis.   If you didn't know where Iran was, what assumption(s) would help you find it on a map?   What part of the world might it be in?   What other knowledge or news reports might be helpful to recall?   That is an example of the process.

- *Objectivity* is a must.   In problem solving, don't let any personal biases or feelings interfere with the process.   Stay with facts, details, and information that can be proven.

144

CREATIVE THOUGHT PROCESS

The best problem solvers are usually creative thinkers. Their thinking goes beyond the obvious and they do not limit their thinking by preconceived notions or other barriers. Creativity means doing what hasn't been done before. Nearly everyone has some degree of creativity. The important thing is to bring it out and use it to solve problems. Invent things, write, draw, build, rearrange, decorate, explore--in short, anything else that demands or challenges the mind or intellect. To illustrate, try the following exercises:

List as many uses that you can think of for a toothpick. Give your mind all the freedom you can.

_____

_____

_____

_____

_____

What would you do?

You have an appointment for a job that you want very much. You are to meet the employer at 10:00 AM about 20 miles from where you live. You have no car, and you can't afford to take a cab for 20 miles. You also have to be well dressed, and you need to bring certain papers with you, which means that you will have to carry a brief case. The buses are often ten or twenty minutes late, and are very crowded between 8:00 and 10:00 in the morning. Think of as many possible ways as you can to be at the interview on time, and in a good psychological state of mind.

Remember, be creative.

_____

_____

_____

_____

_____

Creativity is a higher level of problem solving.

Try these exercises.

Creative problem solving.

145

You leave home one morning to go to school. An English Report you have been working on for three weeks is due to be handed in. The stakes are high: if you get a good grade on the Report, you get an A in the course and your parents have also promised you something you really want. If you don't turn the Report in, or turn it in late, you will probably fail the course. You have worked long and hard on this Report, and you have it in a very attractive binder. You arrive at school just in time. But when you go to your first class, you suddenly realize that you left the Report at home. There is a school rule that you cannot leave before the end of the day. You don't have a gun, so you can't shoot yourself. What do you do? Be creative!

_____

_____

_____

_____

_____

These exercises should give you an idea of the nature of creative thinking. Answers are not sometimes immediately evident or available. You have to move outside of what you may have been accustomed to consider as the usual limitations. Most of us hardly realize the extent of those limitations. The following puzzle is a good example. Look at the nine dots.

$$\bullet \quad \bullet \quad \bullet$$
$$\bullet \quad \bullet \quad \bullet$$
$$\bullet \quad \bullet \quad \bullet$$

Can you connect all nine dots by drawing four straight lines, **without lifting your pencil from the paper**? Try two or three times before turning the page to see the answer.

If you are still puzzled, before you turn the page, be creative. What I mean is don't limit yourself to what you believe are boundaries of the figure or the exercise.

146

Remember, creative thinking means going beyond usual boundaries. Most people see the nine dots as a fixed area which they can't break out of. Why? Because that is what they are used to. The shape of a figure usually represents the area of the figure and you tend to want to stay within that area.

Nonsense! There are no laws that require you to limit yourself. Create new boundaries if necessary to solve problems. Look at the dot exercise. The solution is very simple as soon as you realize that there are no boundary restrictions.

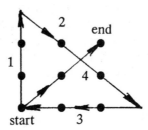

What are some good ways to further develop your creativity? Following are some suggestions. Remember, try not to restrict yourself.

● *Be original.* Look for interesting avenues and let your mind be free. Originality cannot be restricted. When you get your first ideas, do not, I repeat, *Do Not* be critical. That will come later. The important thing is to get your mind working. Think of it as a vehicle; it works better on the open highway than on crowded city streets.

Originality is habit forming. Develop the habit of looking for unusual and effective solutions to difficult problems. You will be training your mind to work harder and to explore farther than ever before. Once you acquire this habit, you will be amazed at how "creative" you become. Your friends and teachers will also be amazed.

● *Trust your instincts.* Open the mental faucet and let ideas pour forth. Let them be as wild and bizarre as ever. Don't worry. You can weed them out later. The important thing is to reduce interference as much as possible. This means trusting your instincts, enjoying your mind and how remarkable it can be as a producer of ideas.

This is what creative thinking is all about.

•*Develop a healthy disrespect for conventionality.*
The dot exercise above is an example of this. Look
for the conventional approach to solving a problem,
then think of what might happen if you reject that
approach. Try whatever comes to mind and originate
your own conventions. By now you should realize
how much creativity depends on unrestricted mental
activity. Many conventional limitations, either
real or imagined, inhibit free outpouring of ideas.
I encourage you to have a <u>healthy</u> disrespect for
such conventions. I emphasize the word "healthy,"
or you could get in the habit of almost always
rejecting every convention, even the ones you might
want to use for your own creative purposes.

•*Be willing to accept change.* Change is a constant.
It happens continually in many ways: your body is
changing, science continues to advance, nature is
constantly going through cycles of change, and
institutions change. Most people, however, tend to
resist change. There are many reasons for this,
but the most important consequence for you is that
resistance to change tends to erode and diminish creativity.

I do not advocate change for the sake of change.
That is foolish. But habitual and consistent
resistance to change prevents progress. In order
to develop your creativity, you need to see change
as a necessary part of growth. You are growing,
your mind is growing, and you can contribute to
this growth by being receptive to change. When you
are convinced that a change is necessary, go for it
with all of the creativity, persistence and tact
that you can muster.

•*Look for creativity in every type of activity.* Just as
there should be no limits or boundaries in creative
response to a problem, there are no limitations or
boundaries to where or how you can be creative. For
example, I've admired creative typists, carpenters, cooks
musicians, actors, businesspersons, cleaners, artists,
athletes, or anyone else who puts extra determination and
pride in what is to be done. I call these people
"creative" because they try to go beyond their own personal
limits and the usual expectations. That takes creativity.

Critical Thinking - Chapter Summary

Critical Thinking is a combination of Problem Solving and Creativity.

Good **PROBLEM SOLVERS** know how to:

- **Reorganize** the problem.

- Make use of *hypotheses*.

- Rule out the *irrelevant*.

- Arrange for enough *time* to find a solution.

- **Recall** and *relate* solutions to similar problems.

- Work in an *orderly manner*.

- Be *persistent* in the search for a solution.

CREATIVE THINKERS tend to:

- Be *original*.

- Trust their *instincts*.

- Develop a *healthy disrespect* for conventionality.

- Be willing to *accept change*.

- Look for creativity in a great many *activities*.

10

MOTIVATION

"Get what you like, or like what you get"
(George Bernard Shaw)

Three parts to Motivation.

MOTIVATION is a power source that helps you find or make the "circumstances" you want. It fires you up. It gets you going and keeps you going until you reach your goal. Where does that power or energy come from? How do you get it? How do you use it? How do you hold on to it so that you always have it when you need it? Why do some people have so much more than others? Do only smart people get motivated? If people are smart, do they have to be motivated?

Suppose we look at **MOTIVATION** in relation to what you do every day in school, and how you can become *motivated* in order to get what you want out of school, and out of life.

There are three basic parts to **MOTIVATION**:

1. Goal Setting.

•*GOAL SETTING.* *What* do you want to achieve? This is the end point, but unless you have some idea of *what* you want, there is little you can do to become motivated. Before you start out on a trip, you have to know where you want to go, or what the end point will be.

2. Purpose.

•*PURPOSE.* Now that you know what you want, you will have a greater chance of getting it if you know *why* you want it. While the goal was the "end point," the *purpose* is the reason. Goals without a clearly defined *purpose* are seldom fulfilled. For example, suppose your goal is "to become a millionaire" before you reach the age of 21. A lot of people have goals to "get rich." There is nothing wrong with wanting to "get rich." It is a legitimate goal, provided that there is a purpose. Why become a millionaire before the age of 21? Without sitting in judgment about whether the reason is right or wrong, the goal will remain a fantasy if it has no purpose and is not connected to the goal.

•*SELF INITIATION.* You have a goal; you know the reason (purpose) for the goal; now all you need is the "fuel" or energy to reach the goal. What do you do to reach your goal? How do you get started and keep going? You can certainly understand that simply "putting fuel in the tank" won't necessarily get you anywhere. But once you know where and why you are going, it then is up to you to arrange to get there. More on this later.

3. Self Initiation.

The three parts of **MOTIVATION** are like the legs of a three-legged stool: take any one away and the stool falls. Each is equally important. It does no good to have goals without a purpose, and even with a goal and the best reason in the world, if you can't get yourself going, you might as well forget the whole thing. Let's look at the three parts of **MOTIVATION** in greater detail.

Goals and Goal Setting

Goals are best described in terms of **RANGE**, the length of time it takes to reach the goal; and **CLASSIFICATION**, the priority or importance of each of your goals.

RANGE

There are three:

• *Short*, concerns the here and now.

• *Intermediate*, is several months to several years.

• *Long*, usually deals with lifetime and career.

Three ranges for goals:
Short
Intermediate
Long

Review the following information on goal characteristics, and think of where you would place most of your goals.

Short. The most significant characteristic here is the need for some sort of *immediate gratification*. You want results *now*, not next week or next month. Students whose goals are mostly in this range would have few plans for what they intend to do after they graduate from high school. They also may respond in extremes to the way they feel about a teacher, or the way they think a teacher feels about them. When I ask about an occasional high grade among mostly poor grades, they are inclined to say that they happened to like that particular teacher. Conversely, there are many teachers they did not like, or who they feel did not like them. These students are unmotivated in terms of goal setting, and they are on a perpetually moving carousel of short range needs that require immediate gratification.

Results <u>now</u>!

I hope you don't get the notion that *short range* goals are bad. Not true!   We all have them. The point I would stress is that when a student's goals are practically all limited to short range, then what I have stated in the previous paragraph tends to be valid.   But how do you begin to reverse this pattern?

The first step is to become more *realistic* when setting short range goals.   The key word is "realistic."   It removes goal setting from the world of immediate gratification and fantasy.   There are two *"musts"* for making short range goals realistic and effective:

 • Goals *must* be *achievable*.

 • *Outcomes* must be clearly stated and understood.

An achievable realistic short range goal should be accomplished without interference or unnecessary delay.   These goals should be task-oriented which means "doing" rather than thought-oriented which means "thinking" or "fantasizing" about doing.   Following are examples of task oriented short range goals:

 • *Complete* a homework assignment due the following day

 • *Prepare* for a spelling test

 • *Memorize* ten Spanish vocabulary words

Each of these can be done in a short time.   Each is "achievable," clearly stated, and most important of all, each is associated with a "realistic" outcome that will soon occur.   The homework assignment is due the following day; the spelling test will likely take place on the next day; the Spanish vocabulary words are in the daily lesson.

I am certain you have noted that these goals are all connected with school work.   Why would a student who rarely ever does any school work decide to do a homework assignment, prepare for a spelling test, or memorize Spanish vocabulary words?

Here is where the "achievable" notion becomes all important. Start with whatever piece of the task you might be willing to undertake.   Something is better than nothing.   If the homework assignment is eight pages of United States History, even two pages would be better than nothing.   Half the spelling words would be better than none, and the same for half or any part of the Spanish vocabulary words.

You wonder how a piecemeal approach can accomplish anything.   You will still be unprepared.   Your grades will still be low.   Your performance will be below minimum standards.   What good will it do?

Remember, we are trying to move beyond "immediate gratification" to some sort of realistic goal setting. It is almost impossible to make the jump in one leap. It will have to happen gradually, in short steps.

The value of the small first step is that the step has been made. It should set the stage for the next step. If good notes are taken on the two pages of United States History, then you will retain something, and hopefully a new pattern of goal setting performance will have begun.

I also suggest that when moving from "immediate gratification" to short range realistic goals, you speak with your teachers about what you are doing. You will need their cooperation and assistance.

Intermediate. For these goals the time span is from a few months to several years. It requires a longer period of waiting for results or gratification. Students who set goals in this range are more concerned about the quality of their work than whether the teacher likes them, or if they like the teacher.

Intermediate: a few months to a few years.

These require planning and preparation. Nothing is left to chance. There are specific activities, tasks, problems to be solved and things to be accomplished if these goals are to be achieved. When you can set intermediate range goals and follow through, with everything required, you are a candidate for success. You know what you want, and are willing to do what it takes to get it.

Long. These are the big ones. What do you want to do with your life? Do you want to be the president of a large corporation? A professional tennis player? Write a great (best seller) novel?

Long: career, life goals.

Although this type of goal may not be too important to you at this time, you should be able to give some thought to any possible long range goals you may think of. As you get older, your goals will undoubtedly change. That is quite natural.

CLASSIFICATION OF GOALS

All goals are not the same. Some are more important than others. Earning a varsity letter is not in the same category as getting into a "good" college. (Are there any "bad" colleges?) Goals are best ranked as follows:

A - *Most Important;* B - *Important;* C - *Least Important*

Setting priorities for goals: A, B, C.

On the following page are examples of *short, intermediate,* and *long range* goals, and the priorities given them by three different students. What can you assume about these students from the priorities they set?

SHORT RANGE GOALS	Priority For Student #1	#2	#3
Go on a ski trip next weekend	A	B	B
Read a good book	C	B	A
Receive a good grade on a test in Algebra	B	A	A
Get a new outfit for the prom	B	B	C
Go to a party on the weekend	A	B	C

INTERMEDIATE RANGE GOALS

	#1	#2	#3
Get into a good college	B	A	A
Save enough money to buy a bicycle or a car	A	A	B
Earn a varsity letter	C	B	B
Spend the summer in Mexico	C	B	C
Become an Eagle Scout	C	B	A
Get a summer apprenticeship at IBM	C	C	A

LONG RANGE GOALS

	#1	#2	#3
Become an airline pilot	C	B	C
Do "life saving" research	C	C	A
Make lots of money	A	A	B
Own a yacht	B	C	C
Become a senator	C	C	C
Retire by age 40	A	B	C
Create something new and original	C	C	A

Notice where the higher priorities are. Next, eliminate all the C GOALS, and examine what remains. See the following page.

Notice the configuration of priorities after eliminating the <u>C</u> GOALS.

SHORT RANGE GOALS	Priority For Student #1	#2	#3
Go on a ski trip next weekend	A	B	B
Read a good book		B	A
Receive a good grade on a test in Algebra	B	A	A
Get a new outfit for the prom	B	B	
Go to a party on the weekend	A	B	

INTERMEDIATE RANGE GOALS	#1	#2	#3
Get into a good college	B	A	A
Save enough money to buy a bicycle or a car	A	A	B
Earn a varsity letter		B	B
Spend the summer in Mexico		B	
Become an Eagle Scout		B	A
Get a summer apprenticeship at IBM			A

LONG RANGE GOALS	#1	#2	#3
Become an airline pilot		B	
Do "life saving" research			A
Make lots of money	A	A	B
Own a yacht	B		
Become a senator			
Retire by age 40	A	B	
Create something new and original			A

Read the analysis of these students on the next page and see if you agree with the interpretation.

Student #1 has a cluster of short range goals that provide clues about what he thinks is most important and also how he prefers to spend his time. His intermediate range goals show a type of "lip service" regarding his going to college. His long range goals have an element of fantasy about them when we see the inconsistency with his short and intermediate range goals.

Student #2 has fairly well balanced short and intermediate range goals. He wants to enjoy himself, but he also thinks beyond the immediate present. His long range goals have little substance. Viewed alone, they would be cause for concern, but not so when we look at his other priorities.

Student #3 is the serious member of the group. His priorities at every range are consistent with what I would consider strong purpose and dedication. In my opinion, there is a hint of potential anxiety. I would want to look more deeply at his background and former records to determine if this is true. He doesn't seem to have much fun. He seems highly driven to perform and prepare for the future. I would wonder how much of this is for himself, or how much is an effort to please others.

What we don't know from examining the priorities is how much effort the students will put forth to achieve their **A** goals.

★   ★   ★   ★   ★

It is now time for you to look at your own goals and priorities. On the next page, write down as many of your short, intermediate, and long range goals as possible. List the first ones that come to mind; don't edit them. You can do that later. Use more paper if necessary. Then classify all the goals as <u>A</u>, <u>B</u>, or <u>C</u>. After you finish, look over what you have done and take out whatever you feel does not belong. Keep the list and edit it from time to time. Think of what you need to do to achieve your <u>A</u> and <u>B</u> goals.

GOAL SETTING EXERCISE

SHORT RANGE   **PRIORITY**

1._____A__B__C__

_____

2._____A__B__C__

_____

3._____A__B__C__

_____

4._____A__B__C__

_____

INTERMEDIATE RANGE

1._____A__B__C__

_____

2._____A__B__C__

_____

3._____A__B__C__

_____

4._____A__B__C__

_____

LONG RANGE

1._____A__B__C__

_____

2._____A__B__C__

_____

3._____A__B__C__

_____

4._____A__B__C__

_____

Purpose

The 2nd part of Motivation.

It is not enough to simply **want** something (goal). You have to know **why (purpose)** you want it. You have to have a reason, and the reason has to be "legitimate." Otherwise you are living in a world of fantasy. For example, suppose your goal (in this case - long range) is "to be rich and famous." It already sounds like a fantasy! If I ask you what the possible reasons are, you might say that:

- You could then have everything you want.

- Everyone would want your autograph.

- You could help the poor people.

- You would't have to work.

Ridiculous, you say. But how many people do you know who think that way? Why are lotteries and other types of gambling so popular? What chance is there to be a winner? Why do they keep trying? Is it "human nature?"

You need good reasons to achieve your goals.

Whatever it is, it may **not** be an attainable goal. The reason is because the **purpose** is unrealistic. It doesn't stand up well even as a fantasy. Let's look at some other examples.

You want to be admitted to the University of California at Los Angeles. This would be an intermediate range goal, with undoubtedly an <u>A</u> priority. **Why** do you want to go to the University of California (or a comparable university)?

The reason is that U. C. L. A. has an excellent program in Biology, and one of your long range goals is to become a biologist. Note how the reason to attend U. C. L. A. applies to both of your goals. You definitely have a "legitimate" purpose in wanting to go to U. C. L. A.

Your intermediate range goals require a lot of short range goals to help you get where you want to go. Once you have set the University of California goal, then your day to day work at school becomes more **purposeful**. Why? Because it will all help you achieve your University of California goal.

Suppose, however, you had a goal of being admitted to the University of California, Santa Barbara. When I ask you why, your answer is that you want to be near the ocean because you like to surf. What do you think I would say? If this is your only reason for going there, what do you think your chances for admission would be? If you were admitted, what would have to happen for you to succeed there?

158

THE PERSONAL VALUES INVENTORY

As you think about your beliefs and values, you get closer to what *purpose* is all about. It is not my intent to be the judge of those values. That is for you to decide. However, it is important to clarify your values, your beliefs, and how they relate to your goals. Use the following check list as a starting point, and make your own additions, or modifications as you see fit. The Inventory consists of three parts: **Family**, **School**, and **Vocation**. Answer True, False, or Not Applicable to each of the statements.

Analyze yourself.

Family

T F NA   1. I enjoy spending time with my parents.

T F NA   2. I enjoy spending time with my brother(s) and sister(s).

T F NA   3. I feel I take more than my share of the responsibilities at home.

T F NA   4. I ought to help make the decisions that affect me or our family.

T F NA   5. I usually agree with what my parents expect.

T F NA   6. I often disagree with my parents "old fashioned" ideas, but I don't argue about it.

T F NA   7. I don't expect to make the same mistakes my parents made when I become an adult.

T F NA   8. My parents ideas don't ever seem to change.

T F NA   9. I am proud of my parents accomplishments.

T F NA 10. I value the advice I get from my parents.

School

T F NA   1. The main reason I go to school is to learn.

T F NA   2. I would transfer to any school that my friends attended.

T F NA   3. I work harder for teachers I like.

T F NA   4. I respect teachers who have high standards.

T F NA   5. Whenever possible, I select teachers who have the highest standards.

T F NA 6. The grade I get is the most important part of the course.

T F NA 7. I have good reasons to be proud of my school.

T F NA 8. I am actively involved in my school.

T F NA 9. Most of my teachers care a lot about me.

T F NA 10. Most of my friends work hard at school and get good grades.

Vocation

T F NA 1. I think a lot about what I would like to do after I leave school.

T F NA 2. I am interested in jobs that pay a lot.

T F NA 3. I like working with people.

T F NA 4. I expect the work I do to be more important than how much I earn.

T F NA 5. I have some general ideas about what I would like to do, but I think it's too early to be specific.

T F NA 6. I would like to take a year off after I graduate from high school so I can get a better idea of what I would like to do with my life.

T F NA 7. The most important thing about school or college is the diploma.

T F NA 8. "The harder I work, the luckier I get." (Quote by John Wooden, former basketball coach at U. C. L. A.)

T F NA 9. The more I learn, the more confident I become.

T F NA 10. My ambition is to be #1 when I do something I really like.

After you respond to these statements, you should have a fairly good view of your personal values as they relate to your idea of *purpose*.

160

Self Initiation

How do you get yourself started, and once started, how do you keep going and maintain momentum. Obviously, you start with a goal and a purpose for having the goal. *Plan* what you have to <u>do</u> to achieve the goal. First you *plan,* then you *implement* the plan--a fancy way to say "get the job done."

The 3rd part of Motivation: getting the job done.

PLANNING

Planning to achieve intermediate or longer range goal involves *strategy*. Look for the most direct routes or means to reach your goal. It has to be done long enough in advance to avoid any type of potential problem. For example, your goal is to attend an Ivy League college such as Stanford, or Princeton. That goal should be set no later than your first year in high school. The strategy (strategic plan) is to acquire broad knowledge, get outstanding grades, develop any other skills that interest you such as sports, music, drama, journalism, or student government. At the same time, you will need to develop good relationships with your counselor, school administrators, and teachers. They are the ones who can give you the recommendations you will need to compete with other outstanding students from all over the country.

Does this sound hypocritical, phoney, or what some people call "opportunistic?" Maybe so, especially if your purpose is a bit foggy. But if you want to go to a University like Stanford because you believe that the preparation at Stanford will be the most challenging and thorough, then there is nothing, in my opinion, "opportunistic" about your strategic plannning. If you want to go to Stanford because you expect to meet and marry someone rich and socially prominent, then your efforts (which may get you there) are, in my opinion, "opportunistic," (phoney).

You can apply the same strategic planning to almost any of your goals. It is the starting point, and the closer you adhere to the plan, the more likely you will be to reach the goal. Next, however, is the most difficult part: making the plan work.

IMPLEMENTING YOUR PLAN

Once you decide where you are going and how you plan to get there, then everything you do must get you closer to that goal. With a goal like getting into a University such as Stanford, start early, and monitor yourself all the way. It means studying, participating, building skills, and developing, confidence, good relationships, and good insight into yourself. It is a difficult goal and one with a certain amount of risk. Remember this: the harder you work the more confident you become, and the lower the risk becomes.

Motivation - Chapter Summary

There are three parts to **MOTIVATION**:

- *Goal* Setting.
- *Purpose*.
- *Self Initiation*.

GOALS have *RANGE*, and *CLASSIFICATION*. The *RANGES* are:

- *Short*: up to a few months.
- *Intermediate*: up to a few years.
- *Long*: career and life.

    CLASSIFICATION or *PRIORITY* has three levels:

    <u>A</u> - *Most Important*

    <u>B</u> - *Important*

    <u>C</u> - *Least Important*

PURPOSE is your *reason* for having a goal.

SELF INITIATION is the *energy* needed to achieve your goals.

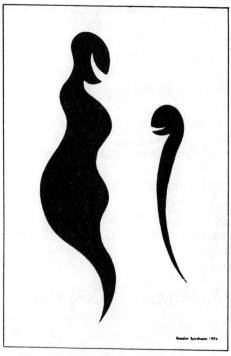

"Mabel, I just can't stick to a diet the way you do!"

SUPPLEMENT A
The Performance Profile

T he information in this **SUPPLEMENT** will make it possible for you to collect and analyze information on your performance in order to know exactly where you need to improve. This can be done in a single subject or in all subjects as a whole. There is a separate **PROFILE** for Foreign Language (page A3).

The **PERFORMANCE PROFILE** will show you the LEVEL of school performance in the following Divisions and sub-categories. Complete **PROFILES** are on pages A2 and A3.

MOTIVATION - Well directed energy and the incentive to use it

Goal Setting
Purpose
Self Initiation

SELF MANAGEMENT - The ability to organize

Time
Place
Use of Resources

ESSENTIAL SKILLS - The abilities needed for success in school

Listening
Reading/Comprehension
Computation
Communication (Speaking and Writing)
Concentration (Staying On Task)
Research
Note Taking
Test Taking

CRITICAL THINKING - Correct judgments

Problem Solving
Analytical Reasoning

ACCOUNTABILITY - Basic responsibilities for all students

Behavior
Participation
Homework
Classwork

Look at the **PROFILES** on the next two pages.

STUDENT PERFORMANCE PROFILE

Name_____Grade Level____Subject_____Teacher_____PQ_____

INSTRUCTIONS: Check box of **Category Item** at **LEVEL** or **Mid-LEVEL** of Performance

NA* ✓ CATEGORY	LEVEL I Minimum or Below 1 1.5	LEVEL II Satisfactory 2 2.5	LEVEL III Above Average 3 3.5	LEVEL IV Consistent Excellence 4

MOTIVATION, Definition: A combination of well directed energy and the incentive to use it

	□	□	□	
□ Goal Setting	□ Needs immediate gratification	□ Sets realistic short range goals	□ Sets intermediate range goals	□ Sets goals and priorities at all levels
		□	□	
□ Purpose	□ Sees little reason for doing school work	□ Accepts that school-work has a purpose	□ Can identify importance of purpose	□ Relates purpose to success in school
			□	
□ Self Initiation	□ Does only what is absolutely necessary	□ Self initiates when interested and confident	□ Enjoys the challenge of self initiation	□ Self initiation is part of learning

SELF MANAGEMENT, Definition: The ability to organize efficiently and effectively for the best possible results

	□	□	□	
□ Time	□ Makes little connection between time and task	□ Knows the importance of completing work on time	□ Good use of time both in and out of class	□ Plans use of time and anticipates needs
		□	□	
□ Place	□ Tends to avoid proper study places	□ Usually finds proper place when necessary	□ Has a permanent well organized study area	□ Has a personal well equipped study area
		□		
□ Use of Resources	□ Does not use any outside resources	□ Uses what is readily available	□ Uses many resources in and out of class	□ Selects most appropriate resources available

ESSENTIAL SKILLS, Definition: The abilities that must be developed in order to succeed in school

	□	□	□	
□ Listening	□ Has very short attention span	□ Tends to get the important facts	□ Actively involved in the process	□ Uses critical approach while listening
		□	□	
□ Reading/ Comprehension	□ Reads only what is absolutely essential	□ Reads and understands most assigned material	□ Enjoys reading and has good comprehension	□ Regularly reads a wide variety of material
□ Computation	□ Lacks arithmetic skills	□ Does most assignments with moderate interest	□ Shows keen interest and ability	□ Enjoys the challenge of problem solving
		□		
□ Communication (Speak, Write)	□ Has difficulty expressing ideas	□ Needs mild coercion and encouragement	□ Is very articulate and understandable	□ Demonstrates creativity in self expression
		□	□	
□ Concentration (On Task)	□ Disinterest is a barrier to concentration	□ Attempts to control the main distractions	□ Actively eliminates all distractions	□ Is motivated by the purpose of assignments
			□	
□ Research	□ Dislikes and avoids reference work	□ Knows how to use reference materials	□ Has good investigation skills	□ Identifies research with discovery
		□		
□ Note Taking	□ Takes few notes and rarely uses them	□ Takes notes mainly during lectures	□ Has good discriminatory notetaking ability	□ Note taking is part of a total recall system
		□	□	
□ Test Taking	□ Dislikes taking most types of tests	□ Prepares adequately for most tests	□ Prepares well for all types of tests	□ Views test as learning index and a challenge

CRITICAL THINKING, Definition: The ability to make correct judgments about written or symbolic materials

	□	□	□	
□ Problem Solving	□ Becomes easily frustrated by problems	□ Tries to solve most of the difficult problems	□ Tries a variety of solutions to solve problems	□ Uses scientific method to solve problems
	□	□	□	
□ Analytical Reasoning	□ Deals only with easily understood facts	□ Can use basic data to reach conclusions	□ Can differentiate, sort and classify effectively	□ Uses logic to develop functional systems

ACCOUNTABILITY, Definition: Basic responsibilities for all students

	□	□	□	
□ Behavior	□ Can be disruptive or overly passive	□ Abides by all rules and school regulations	□ Demonstrates high standards of behavior	□ Behavior is an asset to teacher and school
			□	
□ Participation	□ Participates rarely or not at all	□ Participates mainly when interested	□ Is a regular participant and contributor	□ Participation enriches classroom activities
	□	□	□	
□ Homework	□ Resents doing work outside of class time	□ Completes most home-work assignments	□ Recognizes purpose and importance of homework	□ Works independently & effectively on projects
		□	□	
□ Classwork	□ Has difficulty completing assigned work	□ Completes most class work assignments	□ Completes all work with high quality	□ Work frequently merits extra credit

NA* Not Applicable

A 2

FOREIGN LANGUAGE STUDENT PERFORMANCE PROFILE

Name_____Grade Level____Subject_____Teacher_____PQ_____

INSTRUCTIONS: Check box of **Category** Item at **LEVEL** or **Mid-LEVEL** of Performance

NA* ✓ CATEGORY	LEVEL I Minimum or Below 1 1.5	LEVEL II Satisfactory 2 2.5	LEVEL III Above Average 3 3.5	LEVEL IV Consistent Excellence 4

MOTIVATION, Definition: A combination of well directed energy and the incentive to use it

□ Goal Setting	□ Needs immediate gratification	□ Sets realistic short range goals	□ Sets intermediate range goals	□ Sets goals and priorities at all levels
□ Purpose	□ Sees little reason for doing school work	□ Accepts that school-work has a purpose	□ Can identify importance of purpose	□ Relates purpose to success in school
□ Self Initiation	□ Does only what is absolutely necessary	□ Self initiates when interested and confident	□ Enjoys the challenge of self initiation	□ Self initiation is part of learning

SELF MANAGEMENT, Definition: The ability to organize efficiently and effectively for the best possible results

□ Time	□ Makes little connection between time and task	□ Knows the importance of completing work on time	□ Good use of time both in and out of class	□ Plans use of time and anticipates needs
□ Place	□ Tends to avoid proper study places	□ Usually finds proper place when necessary	□ Has a permanent well organized study area	□ Has a personal well equipped study area
□ Use of Resources	□ Does not use any outside resources	□ Uses what is readily available	□ Uses many resources in and out of class	□ Selects most appropriate resources available

ESSENTIAL SKILLS, Definition: The abilities that must be developed for success in learning a foreign language

□ Speaking	□ Is highly inhibited most of the time	□ Attempts to respond when requested to do so	□ Frequently volunteers to speak or respond	□ Responds quickly; can think in the language
□ Listening/ Hearing	□ Has auditory difficulties	□ Is attentive and can differentiate sounds	□ Is well tuned in to all sounds and gestures	□ Seeks outside of class enrichment
□ Understanding	□ Lacks the ability to translate	□ Usually gets the meaning of most material	□ Has quick grasp of nearly all meanings	□ Attempts to understand without translating
□ Reading/ Comprehension	□ Gets little meaning from written materials	□ Can translate most written material	□ Has good speed and ease in comprehension	□ Enjoys reading and has extensive vocabulary
□ Writing	□ Cannot express thoughts or ideas	□ Can translate single thoughts and ideas	□ Can express main and subordinate ideas	□ Writes with advanced style and substance
□ Knowledge of grammar	□ Does not understand grammatical concepts	□ Knows enough grammar to "get by"	□ Has good background and understands concepts	□ Has strong linguistic capabilities
□ Recall/ Retention	□ Takes few notes and rarely uses them	□ Makes determined effort to remember	□ Overlearns nearly everything for good retention	□ Uses a variety of effective recall systems
□ Test Taking	□ Dislikes taking most types of tests	□ Prepares adequately for most tests	□ Prepares well for all types of tests	□ Views test as learning index and a challenge

CRITICAL THINKING, Definition: The ability to make correct judgments about written or symbolic materials

| □ Problem Solving | □ Becomes easily frustrated by problems | □ Tries to solve most of the difficult problems | □ Tries a variety of solutions to solve problems | □ Uses scientific method to solve problems |
| □ Analytical Reasoning | □ Deals only with easily understood facts | □ Can use basic data to reach conclusions | □ Can differentiate, sort and classify effectively | □ Uses logic to develop functional systems |

ACCOUNTABILITY, Definition: Basic responsibilities for all students

□ Behavior	□ Can be disruptive or overly passive	□ Abides by all rules and school regulations	□ Demonstrates high standards of behavior	□ Behavior is an asset to teacher and school
□ Participation	□ Participates rarely or not at all	□ Participates mainly when interested	□ Is a regular participant and contributor	□ Participation enriches classroom activities
□ Homework	□ Resents doing work outside of class time	□ Completes most homework assignments	□ Recognizes purpose and importance of homework	□ Works independently & effectively on projects
□ Classwork	□ Has difficulty completing assigned work	□ Completes most class work assignments	□ Completes all work with high quality	□ Work frequently merits extra credit

NA* Not Applicable

A 3

Each Performance Category is described on 4 **LEVELS** of classroom performance: By checking the **LEVEL** (or between the **LEVELS**) of performance for each Category, you will get a Profile of overall student performance in each subject. You can use this as a blueprint and at a glance you will be able to pinpoint exactly where improvement is most needed. Later on in the chapter I will give suggestions, examples and strategies of how you can bring this about.

Below is a brief description of performance standards at each of the four **PROFILE LEVELS**. Remember, if your performance is between two **LEVELS**, you check the box that is located at the mid-point between the **LEVELS**. The numbers just beneath the **LEVEL** Headings (1, 1.5, 2, 2.5, 3, 3.5, and 4) are used to arrive at the *Performance Quotient*, which will be explained later.

LEVEL I - Minimum Or Below

I - The bottom of the Ladder.

Any checks at this **LEVEL** indicate immediate need for intervention. Many of you, however, do not know exactly what the minimum performance standards are in some of your classes. For example, tardies, absenteeism, tests, participation, required standards. Once you identify the "minimums," then you at least have the "bottom line."

The key words in the descriptions at this **LEVEL** are: *needs, avoids, lacks, dislikes, has difficulty, rarely,* and *resents.*

LEVEL II - Satisfactory

II - Moving up.

This is the real beginning of the performance ladder. It describes students who do what is required, but do not make any great effort to reach higher ground. They tend to be satisfied with moderate attempts that keep them out of difficulty with the teacher and with parents. The key to performance improvement at this **LEVEL** is *MOTIVATION.*

The key words here are: *when interested, usually, tends to, most,* and *adequately.*

LEVEL III - Above Average

III - Getting higher.

Students at this **LEVEL** are not satisfied with just getting by. They want to succeed and make a mark for themselves. They recognize the importance of school in relation to success in later years. These students are more likely to be risk takers. They are not afraid to make mistakes, because they learn from them. They can also be motivated more easily to try for more success and to move up to higher **LEVELS** in some categories.

The key words in the behavioral descriptions at this **LEVEL** are *enjoys, good, many, keen interest, high standards, high quality,* and *regular participant.*

LEVEL IV - Consistent Excellence

This is the top of the ladder. This type of performance indicates perseverance, motivation, goals, achievement orientation, and great desire to excel and succeed. When students reach this **LEVEL**, the strategy is to stay there. These students know how to study, and how to learn. They can get more done in less time. They compete mainly against their own potential, and work beyond usual classroom expectations.

The key words are: *consistent, plans, anticipates, most appropriate, regularly, challenge, creativity, purpose, asset, enriches,* and *works independently.*

★   ★   ★   ★   ★

Try filling out the **Profile** on page A 2 for what you would consider to be your "worst" subject. The reason for starting with the "worst" is that you should quickly see the categories where improvement is most needed.

The next step will be for you to practice analyzing several examples of performance given in the next section in different subjects and at different grade levels. This will help you to arrive at your own **Performance Profile**.

Remember. The purpose of all this is to help you gather performance information and then use that information in order to improve your school performance.

IV - The top of the ladder.

Analyze your performance.

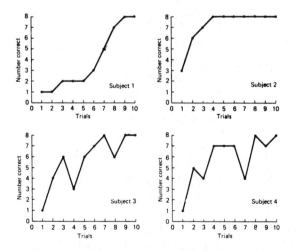

A 5

How To Analyze Your Own Performance

In this section, I will describe the two main parts of a performance analysis: *collecting* and then *using* the information to make plans for improvement. In the next section, I will explain how to derive a Performance Quotient or score which will give you a general indication of your performance range either overall or in a given subject.

WHAT IS A LEARNING ANALYST?

A **LEARNING ANALYST** for our purposes:

- **Collects** information on learning skills in each of the school subjects.

- Makes plans to **improve performance** in the specific areas where improvement is needed.

You can analyze your performance.

This section will show you how to become a Learning Analyst. It is a new role, and one that will help you improve your school performance in ways that will be lasting and permanent. The role deals with the "how" of learning as well as the "what."

WHAT KIND OF EXPERIENCE DO YOU NEED?

You have enough experience.

Your best experience is what you have been doing every day for years: going to school. You already know a great deal about your capabilities, likes, dislikes, desires, sociability, goals, perseverance, attitudes, fears, physical and mental stress threshholds, risk taking, and much more that only you can really understand.

In addition to going to school every day, any experience teaching or supervising persons young or old would be very helpful. Think of what you did at those times when you feel you were successful, and also when you "bombed." You can get lots of insight from both success as well as failure. Remember, no one bats 1000.

The most important thing to keep in mind is that with your experience, and what you learn from this book, you can gather information about your performance, and then use that information in constructive ways to improve your school performance.

WHAT SPECIFIC SKILLS DO YOU NEED?

You can acquire the skills.

The first skill is collecting information. You will need to go through the categories in the **Performance Profile** and decide which **LEVELS** represent the most accurate description of your performance in the various school subjects. In order to do this you will need to examine the **PROFILE** Categories carefully and refer to the detailed information on the exact meaning of the Categories. If you have any questions about the different **LEVELS** of performance for each of the Categories, refer to the appropriate section for an explanation. That should clear up the difficulty.

After you have collected the information and filled out the **Profile**, the next step (in addition to computing the score) is to make good use of the information. This is the *Analytical* part. It is important to know how to collect the right information and make the best possible use of it. This results in planning for improvement where needed. Examine the sample **Profiles** on pages A11, A12, and A13. Even without experience, you can reach some conclusions about each of the students, the nature of their performance, and what some strategies for improvement might be.

STUDENT #1, Male, Eighth Grade Science -- S.P.Q. Score: 135

Sample analysis.

You will notice immediately the predominance of **LEVEL I** checks. Since this is an 8th grade student, if his performance in other subjects is in any way similar to his performance in Science, he is in serious difficulty. If he continues this pattern, it is unlikely that he will be promoted to the 9th grade. If he is, he will surely have a great deal of difficulty in high school. Out of 20 categories, his performance is satisfactory in only 7, and 2 of those are between **LEVELS I** and **II**. His highest point is halfway between **LEVELS II** and **III** in **Computation**. His **Science Performance Quotient** is 135, which indicates a need for immediate attention.

There are some definite indications in this **Profile** that suggest some workable strategies for improvement. Suppose we look at each of the Divisions:

MOTIVATION. One possible sign of hope is a slight recognition of Purpose. It is probably too slight to make a difference since he has only short range goals, and does not initiate anything by himself. I would begin by trying to extend the gratification range. There are many suggestions for how to do this in the chapter on **MOTIVATION**.

SELF MANAGEMENT. This is the only Division where he scored higher than **LEVEL I** in all (3) Categories. He received 5 of his 30 points, or 1/6th of the total. It's not much, but since the Division is **SELF MANAGEMENT**, it could be a starting point for improvement.

ESSENTIAL SKILLS. For the most part this is a disaster area. The improvement strategy should utilize Reading, Computation, and Communication, his best Categories, as the point of departure. Satisfactory performance in Reading, Computation, and Communication, particularly writing would lead me to believe that there is no serious concern about the possibility of learning disability.

CRITICAL THINKING. The low **LEVEL** of performance here is predictable. This student has much to do in other Categories before he can begin to raise his **CRITICAL THINKING** capability. I recommend leaving any intervention in this Category until a later date.

ACCOUNTABILITY. The Behavior Category tells us something positive about this student: he "abides by all rules and school regulations." It is likely that he would be receptive to a series of carefully planned steps and expectations.

SUMMARY

If we find that he performs in other subjects as he does in Science, then we may assume that his past record would also indicate lack of adaptation to school work requirements. I would want to get a history of what has already been tried, or not tried to help this student. I would want to know something about his capability (Intelligence), and clues to any success he might have had in the past.

The plans for improvement should begin with his strengths, and include continual feedback and adjustment to what works best. This young man needs a lot of help, and he needs it as soon as possible.

STUDENT #2, Female, 6th Grade, All Subjects -- **S.P.Q. Score: 300**

Sample analysis.

At first glance, this is a student whose performance is well above average. Her S.P.Q. score of 300 is at the upper limit of the Talented Range of performance. She has only 3 checks at **LEVEL II**, and **I** combination of **LEVELS II** and **III**. All indications are that she is a diligent, hard working student who shows signs of continued success. Let's examine some of the specifics in each of the Divisions:

MOTIVATION. The key to her overall excellent performance lies in her **LEVEL IV** mark in the **Purpose** Category. This is a highly motivated individual who has an advanced understanding of **Purpose**. She knows *why* it is important to study, get good grades, and spend all the time necessary on school work. She has a finely tuned set of intermediate range goals that keep her on the right track. As I look at the rest of the **Profile**, I get the impression that this student is very likely what we call an "over achiever." This means that she works hard and long and has a strong desire to succeed. This **Profile** suggests that she will do just that, no matter how great the barriers.

SELF MANAGEMENT. Notice the well organized use of time. This is the last thing in the world she can waste. She knows it, and she knows the importance of being well organized.

ESSENTIAL SKILLS. If I had looked at this Category first, without seeing any of the others, I would tend to conclude that this student's performance needed more stability to remain solidly "above average." I would prefer to see more than one mark at **LEVEL IV**. The Communication Category between **LEVELS II** and **III** would also give me cause for concern. But when I look at her higher performance in **MOTIVATION** and **SELF MANAGEMENT**, I reach another conclusion. This student's **Communication** skills can and should be improved; her scores in other Categories convince me that she will be receptive and cooperative.

CRITICAL THINKING. The evidence here would suggest that she is not inclined to risk-taking and that hard work is more likely to get the results she wants. Careful guidance here could have very dramatic results, as well as a very positive effect on movement up to higher **LEVELS** of performance in other Categories and subjects.

ACCOUNTABILITY. Here she is very predictable and consistent. I would not be surprised to see her score several points higher after some significant improvement in the **Communication** Category.

SUMMARY

This is a good student. She works hard, she has goals, and her performance reflects seriousness, dedication and diligence. She is also likely to be very responsive to any improvement strategies that are well planned and logical. Her **Performance Quotient Score** of **300** is excellent. She seems to be the type of student who will continually strive for higher performance **LEVELS**.

STUDENT #3, Male, 11th Grade English -- **S.P.Q. Score: 211**

The overall impression I get from analyzing this **Profile** is that this is a very average English student. Overall improvement might occur if he could be substantially motivated, but it would have to happen quickly since he is already a high school junior. If this **Profile** is consistent with his performance in other subjects, changes can be made, but it will take combined and concerted effort. Fortunately, there are some clues that indicate possibilities for higher **LEVELS** of performance.

MOTIVATION. There is a slight clue in the **Purpose** Category. He seems to have some understanding of the importance of **Purpose**. It would be worth exploring how he might be influenced to set longer range goals to reach. It seems to me that this is the kind of leverage that could be used to improve his overall **LEVEL** of **MOTIVATION**.

SELF MANAGEMENT. His performance here indicates very average organization skills. If improvement occurs in **MOTIVATION**, he might begin to appreciate the benefits of a higher **LEVEL** of performance in the **Use of Resources** Category. Organization skills are difficult to improve without a push from some other source. In this case, the source should most likely be **MOTIVATION**.

ESSENTIAL SKILLS. This is the brightest light in the **Profile**. There is clearly "above average" performance in **Reading/Comprehension** and **Communication**. The fact that he is between **LEVELS I** and **II** in **Research** is consistent with his similar mark in the **Use of Resources** Category above. I would use **Reading** and **Communication** in whatever ways possible to improve the **MOTIVATION LEVEL**.

CRITICAL THINKING. Performance is predictably low in this area. Improvement here may take place only *after* it occurs elsewhere.

Sample analysis.

A 9

ACCOUNTABILITY. Another bright light, and a real clue. His behavior "demonstrates high standards." To me, this means he could be receptive to most efforts to motivate him.

SUMMARY

This supposedly very average English **Profile** represents how important it is to get *all* the information possible about your performance. At first glance, it would seem that this student's Profile is consistently average. More detailed investigation, however, provides us with a somewhat different impression, a more hopeful impression. He could well respond positively to an improvement plan that was prepared with his involvement. If he plans to continue his education after he graduates from high school, he will need to find ways to perform at higher **LEVELS** in order to be successful in later years. This type of analysis could help him along the path to that success.

STUDENT PERFORMANCE PROFILE

Name _MALE_   Grade Level _8_ Subject _SCIENCE_   Teacher   _–_   PQ _135_

INSTRUCTIONS: Check box of **Category Item** at **LEVEL or Mid-LEVEL of Performance**

NA* CATEGORY	LEVEL I Minimum or Below 1 1.5	LEVEL II Satisfactory 2 2.5	LEVEL III Above Average 3 3.5	LEVEL IV Consistent Excellence 4

MOTIVATION, Definition: A combination of well directed energy and the incentive to use it

☐ Goal Setting	☑ Needs immediate gratification	☐ Sets realistic short range goals	☐ Sets intermediate range goals	☐ Sets goals and priorities at all levels
☐ Purpose	☐ Sees little reason for doing school work	☐ Accepts that school-work has a purpose	☐ Can identify importance of purpose	☐ Relates purpose to success in school
☐ Self Initiation	☑ Does only what is absolutely necessary	☐ Self initiates when interested and confident	☐ Enjoys the challenge of self initiation	☐ Self initiation is part of learning

SELF MANAGEMENT, Definition: The ability to organize efficiently and effectively for the best possible results

☐ Time	☐ Makes little connection between time and task	☐ Knows the importance of completing work on time	☐ Good use of time both in and out of class	☐ Plans use of time and anticipates needs
☐ Place	☐ Tends to avoid proper study places	☐ Usually finds proper place when necessary	☐ Has a permanent well organized study area	☐ Has a personal well equipped study area
☐ Use of Resources	☐ Does not use any outside resources	☑ Uses what is readily available	☐ Uses many resources in and out of class	☐ Selects most appropriate resources available

ESSENTIAL SKILLS, Definition: The abilities that must be developed in order to succeed in school

☐ Listening	☑ Has very short attention span	☐ Tends to get the important facts	☐ Actively involved in the process	☐ Uses critical approach while listening
☐ Reading/ Comprehension	☐ Reads only what is absolutely essential	☑ Reads and understands most assigned material	☐ Enjoys reading and has good comprehension	☐ Regularly reads a wide variety of material
☐ Computation	☐ Lacks arithmetic skills	☐ Does most assignments with moderate interest	☐ Shows keen interest and ability	☐ Enjoys the challenge of problem solving
☐ Communication (Speak, Write)	☐ Has difficulty expressing ideas	☑ Needs mild coercion and encouragement	☐ Is very articulate and understandable	☐ Demonstrates creativity in self expression
☐ Concentration (On Task)	☑ Disinterest is a barrier to concentration	☐ Attempts to control the main distractions	☐ Actively eliminates all distractions	☐ Is motivated by the purpose of assignments
☐ Research	☑ Dislikes and avoids reference work	☐ Knows how to use reference materials	☐ Has good investigation skills	☐ Identifies research with discovery
☐ Note Taking	☑ Takes few notes and rarely uses them	☐ Takes notes mainly during lectures	☐ Has good discriminatory notetaking ability	☐ Note taking is part of a total recall system
☐ Test Taking	☑ Dislikes taking most types of tests	☐ Prepares adequately for most tests	☐ Prepares well for all types of tests	☐ Views test as learning index and a challenge

CRITICAL THINKING, Definition: The ability to make correct judgments about written or symbolic materials

☐ Problem Solving	☑ Becomes easily frustrated by problems	☐ Tries to solve most of the difficult problems	☐ Tries a variety of solutions to solve problems	☐ Uses scientific method to solve problems
☐ Analytical Reasoning	☑ Deals only with easily understood facts	☐ Can use basic data to reach conclusions	☐ Can differentiate, sort and classify effectively	☐ Uses logic to develop functional systems

ACCOUNTABILITY, Definition: Basic responsibilities for all students

☐ Behavior	☐ Can be disruptive or overly passive	☑ Abides by all rules and school regulations	☐ Demonstrates high standards of behavior	☐ Behavior is an asset to teacher and school
☐ Participation	☑ Participates rarely or not at all	☐ Participates mainly when interested	☐ Is a regular participant and contributor	☐ Participation enriches classroom activities
☐ Homework	☑ Resents doing work outside of class time	☐ Completes most homework assignments	☐ Recognizes purpose and importance of homework	☐ Works independently & effectively on projects
☐ Classwork	☑ Has difficulty completing assigned work	☐ Completes most class work assignments	☐ Completes all work with high quality	☐ Work frequently merits extra credit

NA* Not Applicable

A 11

STUDENT PERFORMANCE PROFILE

Name **FEMALE**   Grade Level **6**   Subject **ALL**   Teacher   —   PQ **300**

INSTRUCTIONS: Check box of **Category Item** at **LEVEL** or **Mid-LEVEL** of Performance

NA* ✓ CATEGORY	LEVEL I Minimum or Below 1 1.5	LEVEL II Satisfactory 2 2.5	LEVEL III Above Average 3 3.5	LEVEL IV Consistent Excellence 4

MOTIVATION, Definition: A combination of well directed energy and the incentive to use it

☐ Goal Setting	☐ Needs immediate gratification	☐ Sets realistic short range goals	☒ Sets intermediate range goals	☐ Sets goals and priorities at all levels
☐ Purpose	☐ Sees little reason for doing school work	☐ Accepts that school-work has a purpose	☐ Can identify importance of purpose	☒ Relates purpose to success in school
☐ Self Initiation	☐ Does only what is absolutely necessary	☐ Self initiates when interested and confident	☒ Enjoys the challenge of self initiation	☐ Self initiation is part of learning

SELF MANAGEMENT, Definition: The ability to organize efficiently and effectively for the best possible results

☐ Time	☐ Makes little connection between time and task	☐ Knows the importance of completing work on time	☐ Good use of time both in and out of class	☐ Plans use of time and anticipates needs
☐ Place	☐ Tends to avoid proper study places	☐ Usually finds proper place when necessary	☐ Has a permanent well organized study area	☐ Has a personal well equipped study area
☐ Use of Resources	☐ Does not use any outside resources	☐ Uses what is readily available	☒ Uses many resources in and out of class	☐ Selects most appropriate resources available

ESSENTIAL SKILLS, Definition: The abilities that must be developed in order to succeed in school

☐ Listening	☐ Has very short attention span	☐ Tends to get the important facts	☐ Actively involved in the process	☐ Uses critical approach while listening
☐ Reading/ Comprehension	☐ Reads only what is absolutely essential	☐ Reads and understands most assigned material	☒ Enjoys reading and has good comprehension	☐ Regularly reads a wide variety of material
☐ Computation	☐ Lacks arithmetic skills	☐ Does most assignments with moderate interest	☒ Shows keen interest and ability	☐ Enjoys the challenge of problem solving
☐ Communication (Speak, Write)	☐ Has difficulty expressing ideas	☐ Needs mild coercion and encouragement	☐ Is very articulate and understandable	☐ Demonstrates creativity in self expression
☐ Concentration (On Task)	☐ Disinterest is a barrier to concentration	☐ Attempts to control the main distractions	☒ Actively eliminates all distractions	☐ Is motivated by the purpose of assignments
☐ Research	☐ Dislikes and avoids reference work	☐ Knows how to use reference materials	☒ Has good investigation skills	☐ Identifies research with discovery
☐ Note Taking	☐ Takes few notes and rarely uses them	☒ Takes notes mainly during lectures	☐ Has good discriminatory notetaking ability	☐ Note taking is part of a total recall system
☐ Test Taking	☐ Dislikes taking most types of tests	☐ Prepares adequately for most tests	☒ Prepares well for all types of tests	☐ Views test as learning index and a challenge

CRITICAL THINKING, Definition: The ability to make correct judgments about written or symbolic materials

☐ Problem Solving	☐ Becomes easily frustrated by problems	☒ Tries to solve most of the difficult problems	☐ Tries a variety of solutions to solve problems	☐ Uses scientific method to solve problems
☐ Analytical Reasoning	☐ Deals only with easily understood facts	☒ Can use basic data to reach conclusions	☐ Can differentiate, sort and classify effectively	☐ Uses logic to develop functional systems

ACCOUNTABILITY, Definition: Basic responsibilities for all students

☐ Behavior	☐ Can be disruptive or overly passive	☐ Abides by all rules and school regulations	☒ Demonstrates high standards of behavior	☐ Behavior is an asset to teacher and school
☐ Participation	☐ Participates rarely or not at all	☐ Participates mainly when interested	☒ Is a regular participant and contributor	☐ Participation enriches classroom activities
☐ Homework	☐ Resents doing work outside of class time	☐ Completes most home-work assignments	☐ Recognizes purpose and importance of homework	☐ Works independently & effectively on projects
☐ Classwork	☐ Has difficulty completing assigned work	☐ Completes most class work assignments	☒ Completes all work with high quality	☐ Work frequently merits extra credit

NA* Not Applicable

A 12

STUDENT PERFORMANCE PROFILE

Name __MALE__   Grade Level __11__ Subject __ENGLISH__   Teacher ___–___   PQ __211__

INSTRUCTIONS: Check box of Category Item at LEVEL or Mid-LEVEL of Performance

NA* / CATEGORY	LEVEL I Minimum or Below 1 1.5	LEVEL II Satisfactory 2 2.5	LEVEL III Above Average 3 3.5	LEVEL IV Consistent Excellence 4
MOTIVATION, Definition: A combination of well directed energy and the incentive to use it				
☐ Goal Setting	☐ Needs immediate gratification	☑ Sets realistic short range goals	☐ Sets intermediate range goals	☐ Sets goals and priorities at all levels
☐ Purpose	☐ Sees little reason for doing school work	☐ Accepts that school-work has a purpose	☐ Can identify importance of purpose	☐ Relates purpose to success in school
☐ Self Initiation	☐ Does only what is absolutely necessary	☑ Self initiates when interested and confident	☐ Enjoys the challenge of self initiation	☐ Self initiation is part of learning
SELF MANAGEMENT, Definition: The ability to organize efficiently and effectively for the best possoble results				
☐ Time	☐ Makes little connection between time and task	☑ Knows the importance of completing work on time	☐ Good use of time both in and out of class	☐ Plans use of time and anticipates needs
☐ Place	☐ Tends to avoid proper study places	☑ Usually finds proper place when necessary	☐ Has a permanent well organized study area	☐ Has a personal well equipped study area
☐ Use of Resources	☐ Does not use any outside resources	☐ Uses what is readily available	☐ Uses many resources in and out of class	☐ Selects most appropriate resources available
ESSENTIAL SKILLS, Definition: The abilities that must be developed in order to succeed in school				
☐ Listening	☐ Has very short attention span	☑ Tends to get the important facts	☐ Actively involved in the process	☐ Uses critical approach while listening
☐ Reading/ Comprehension	☐ Reads only what is absolutely essential	☐ Reads and understands most assigned material	☑ Enjoys reading and has good comprehension	☐ Regularly reads a wide variety of material
☑ Computation	☐ Lacks arithmetic skills	☐ Does most assignments with moderate interest	☐ Shows keen interest and ability	☐ Enjoys the challenge of problem solving
☐ Communication (Speak, Write)	☐ Has difficulty expressing ideas	☐ Needs mild coercion and encouragement	☑ Is very articulate and understandable	☐ Demonstrates creativity in self expression
☐ Concentration (On Task)	☐ Disinterest is a barrier to concentration	☑ Attempts to control the main distractions	☐ Actively eliminates all distractions	☐ Is motivated by the purpose of assignments
☐ Research	☑ Dislikes and avoids reference work	☐ Knows how to use reference materials	☐ Has good investigation skills	☐ Identifies research with discovery
☐ Note Taking	☐ Takes few notes and rarely uses them	☑ Takes notes mainly during lectures	☐ Has good discriminatory notetaking ability	☐ Note taking is part of a total recall system
☐ Test Taking	☐ Dislikes taking most types of tests	☑ Prepares adequately for most tests	☐ Prepares well for all types of tests	☐ Views test as learning index and a challenge
CRITICAL THINKING, Definition: The ability to make correct judgments about written or symbolic materials				
☑ Problem Solving	☐ Becomes easily frustrated by problems	☐ Tries to solve most of the difficult problems	☐ Tries a variety of solutions to solve problems	☐ Uses scientific method to solve problems
☐ Analytical Reasoning	☐ Deals only with easily understood facts	☐ Can use basic data to reach conclusions	☐ Can differentiate, sort and classify effectively	☐ Uses logic to develop functional systems
ACCOUNTABILITY, Definition: Basic responsibilities for all students				
☐ Behavior	☐ Can be disruptive or overly passive	☐ Abides by all rules and school regulations	☑ Demonstrates high standards of behavior	☐ Behavior is an asset to teacher and school
☐ Participation	☐ Participates rarely or not at all	☑ Participates mainly when interested	☐ Is a regular participant and contributor	☐ Participation enriches classroom activities
☐ Homework	☐ Resents doing work outside of class time	☑ Completes most home-work assignments	☐ Recognizes purpose and importance of homework	☐ Works independently & effectively on projects
☐ Classwork	☐ Has difficulty completing assigned work	☑ Completes most class work assignments	☐ Completes all work with high quality	☐ Work frequently merits extra credit

NA* Not Applicable

A 13

Computing and Interpreeting
the S.P.Q. Score

You are now ready to compute the **PERFORMANCE QUOTIENT**. The score indicates a performance range. I will discuss the significance of the ranges after you have learned how to compute the **P.Q.** score.

COMPUTING THE S.P.Q. SCORE

The **S.P.Q.** or **SCHOOL PERFORMANCE QUOTIENT** is a numerical score that summarizes a student's **LEVEL** of performance in each subject. The minimum or poorest possible score is **100**; the highest or best possible score is **400**. Unlike the **I.Q.** or **INTELLIGENCE QUOTIENT**, the **S.P.Q.** *can be raised*.

Examine the **PERFORMANCE PROFILE** on page A15. The Score of **226** in the top right hand corner was computed in two steps:

Step 1: Look at the Table on page A16. Enter and count the total number of points checked at each Category **LEVEL** and **Mid-LEVEL** from the **PROFILE** on page A15.

Note: **Step 2** continues on the bottom of page A 17.

FOREIGN LANGUAGE STUDENT PERFORMANCE PROFILE

Name _FEMALE_   Grade Level _9_ Subject _SPANISH 2_   Teacher ___–___   PQ _226_

INSTRUCTIONS: Check box of **Category Item** at **LEVEL** or **Mid-LEVEL** of Performance

NA* ✓ CATEGORY	LEVEL I Minimum or Below 1 1.5	LEVEL II Satisfactory 2 2.5	LEVEL III Above Average 3 3.5	LEVEL IV Consistent Excellence 4

MOTIVATION, Definition: A combination of well directed energy and the incentive to use it

		☐		☐	
☐ Goal Setting	☐ Needs immediate gratification	☑ Sets realistic short range goals	☐ Sets intermediate range goals	☐ Sets goals and priorities at all levels
☐ Purpose	☐ Sees little reason for doing school work	☐ Accepts that school-work has a purpose	☐ Can identify importance of purpose	☐ Relates purpose to success in school
☐ Self Initiation	☐ Does only what is absolutely necessary	☑ Self initiates when interested and confident	☐ Enjoys the challenge of self initiation	☐ Self initiation is part of learning

SELF MANAGEMENT, Definition: The ability to organize efficiently and effectively for the best possible results

	☐	☐	☐	
☐ Time	☐ Makes little connection between time and task	☐ Knows the importance of completing work on time	☑ Good use of time both in and out of class	☐ Plans use of time and anticipates needs
☐ Place	☐ Tends to avoid proper study places	☑ Usually finds proper place when necessary	☐ Has a permanent well organized study area	☐ Has a personal well equipped study area
☐ Use of Resources	☐ Does not use any outside resources	☐ Uses what is readily available	☑ Uses many resources in and out of class	☐ Selects most appropriate resources available

ESSENTIAL SKILLS, Definition: The abilities that must be developed for success in learning a foreign language

	☐	☑	☐	
☐ Speaking	☐ Is highly inhibited most of the time	☐ Attempts to respond when requested to do so	☐ Frequently volunteers to speak or respond	☐ Responds quickly; can think in the language
☐ Listening/ Hearing	☐ Has auditory difficulties	☑ Is attentive and can differentiate sounds	☐ Is well tuned in to all sounds and gestures	☐ Seeks outside of class enrichment
☐ Understanding	☐ Lacks the ability to translate	☑ Usually gets the meaning of most material	☐ Has quick grasp of nearly all meanings	☐ Attempts to understand without translating
☐ Reading/ Comprehension	☐ Gets little meaning from written materials	☐ Can translate most written material	☐ Has good speed and ease in comprehension	☐ Enjoys reading and has extensive vocabulary
☐ Writing	☐ Cannot express thoughts or ideas	☑ Can translate single thoughts and ideas	☐ Can express main and subordinate ideas	☐ Writes with advanced style and substance
☐ Knowledge of grammar	☐ Does not understand grammatical concepts	☑ Knows enough grammar to "get by"	☐ Has good background and understands concepts	☐ Has strong linguistic capabilities
☐ Recall/ Retention	☐ Takes few notes and rarely uses them	☐ Makes determined effort to remember	☐ Overlearns nearly everything for good retention	☐ Uses a variety of effective recall systems
☐ Test Taking	☐ Dislikes taking most types of tests	☐ Prepares adequately for most tests	☐ Prepares well for all types of tests	☐ Views test as learning index and a challenge

CRITICAL THINKING, Definition: The ability to make correct judgments about written or symbolic materials

	☐	☐	☐	
☐ Problem Solving	☐ Becomes easily frustrated by problems	☑ Tries to solve most of the difficult problems	☐ Tries a variety of solutions to solve problems	☐ Uses scientific method to solve problems
☑ Analytical Reasoning	☐ Deals only with easily understood facts	☐ Can use basic data to reach conclusions	☐ Can differentiate, sort and classify effectively	☐ Uses logic to develop functional systems

ACCOUNTABILITY, Definition: Basic responsibilities for all students

	☐	☐	☐	
☐ Behavior	☐ Can be disruptive or overly passive	☑ Abides by all rules and school regulations	☐ Demonstrates high standards of behavior	☐ Behavior is an asset to teacher and school
☐ Participation	☐ Participates rarely or not at all	☐ Participates mainly when interested	☐ Is a regular participant and contributor	☐ Participation enriches classroom activities
☐ Homework	☐ Resents doing work outside of class time	☑ Completes most homework assignments	☐ Recognizes purpose and importance of homework	☐ Works independently & effectively on projects
☐ Classwork	☐ Has difficulty completing assigned work	☑ Completes most class work assignments	☐ Completes all work with high quality	☐ Work frequently merits extra credit

NA* Not Applicable

A 15

LEVELS	NUMBER OF CHECKS	MULTIPLY BY	TOTAL
LEVEL I		1 point	
Mid-LEVEL (Between I & II)		1.5 points	
LEVEL II		2 points	
Mid-LEVEL (Between II & III)		2.5 points	
LEVEL III		3 points	
Mid-LEVEL (Between III & IV)		3.5 points	
LEVEL IV		4 points	
TOTALS			

Compare your figures with the completed version on page A17.

The following information is from the **PROFILE** on page A16.

Female, 9th Grade, Spanish II.   S.P.Q. Score: 226

LEVELS	NUMBER OF CHECKS	MULTIPLY BY	TOTAL
LEVEL I	0	1 point	0
Mid-LEVEL (Between I & II)	0	1.5 points	0
LEVEL II	11	2 points	22
Mid-LEVEL (Between II & III)	6	2.5 points	15
LEVEL III	2	3 points	6
Mid-LEVEL (Between III & IV)	0	3.5 points	0
LEVEL IV	0	4 points	0
TOTALS	19		43

Step 2: Divide the total number of points (43) by the total number of checks (19), then multiply the quotient by 100.

$$\frac{43}{19} = 2.26 \times 100 = 226 \text{ (Performance Quotient)}$$

Compute the **Performance Quotients** for the **PROFILES** on pages A11, 12 and 13. Compare your results with the completed versions on pages A19, 21, and 23.

Examine the **PROFILE** on page A11

Male, 8th Grade, Science. S.P.Q. Score: _____

LEVELS	NUMBER OF CHECKS	MULTIPLY BY	TOTAL
LEVEL I		1 point	
Mid-LEVEL (Between **I & II**)		1.5 points	
LEVEL II		2 points	
Mid-LEVEL (Between **II & III**)		2.5 points	
LEVEL III		3 points	
Mid-LEVEL (Between **III & IV**)		3.5 points	
LEVEL IV		4 points	
TOTALS			

$$\frac{\text{Total Points}}{\text{Total Checks}} = \underline{\quad\quad} \times 100 = \textbf{S.P.Q. Score}$$

Compare your figures with the completed version on page A19.

Examine the **PROFILE** on page A11

Male, 8th Grade, Science. S.P.Q. Score: _135_

LEVELS	NUMBER OF CHECKS	MULTIPLY BY	TOTAL
LEVEL I	12	1 point	12
Mid-LEVEL (Between I & II)	3	1.5 points	4.5
LEVEL II	4	2 points	8
Mid-LEVEL (Between II & III)	1	2.5 points	2.5
LEVEL III	0	3 points	0
Mid-LEVEL (Between III & IV)	0	3.5 points	0
LEVEL IV	0	4 points	0
TOTALS	20		27

$$\frac{\text{Total Points - 27}}{\text{Total Checks - 20}} = 1.35 \times 100 = 135 \text{ (S.P.Q.) Score}$$

Examine the **PROFILE** on page A12

Female, 6th Grade, All Subjects.   S.P.Q. Score_____

LEVELS	NUMBER OF CHECKS	MULTIPLY BY	TOTAL
LEVEL I		1 point	
Mid-LEVEL (Between **I & II**)		1.5 points	
LEVEL II		2 points	
Mid-LEVEL (Between **II & III**)		2.5 points	
LEVEL III		3 points	
Mid-LEVEL (Between **III & IV**)		3.5 points	
LEVEL IV		4 points	
TOTALS			

$$\frac{\text{Total Points}}{\text{Total Checks}} = \underline{\qquad} \times 100 = \textbf{S.P.Q. Score}$$

Compare your figures with the completed version on page A21.

Examine the **PROFILE** on page A12

Female, 6th Grade, All Subjects.   S.P.Q. Score _300_

LEVELS	NUMBER OF CHECKS	MULTIPLY BY	TOTAL
LEVEL I	0	1 point	0
Mid-LEVEL (Between **I** & **II**)	0	1.5 points	0
LEVEL II	3	2 points	6
Mid-LEVEL (Between **II** & **III**)	1	2.5 points	2.5
LEVEL III	10	3 points	30
Mid-LEVEL (Between **III** & **IV**)	5	3.5 points	17.5
LEVEL IV	1	4 points	4
TOTALS	20		60

$$\frac{\text{Total Points} \ - \ 60}{\text{Total Checks} \ - \ 20} = 3.0 \ \times \ 100 = 300 \ \textbf{(S.P.Q.) Score}$$

Examine the **PROFILE** on page A13

Male, 11th Grade, English. S.P.Q. Score_____

LEVELS	NUMBER OF CHECKS	MULTIPLY BY	TOTAL
LEVEL I		1 point	
Mid-LEVEL (Between I & II)		1.5 points	
LEVEL II		2 points	
Mid-LEVEL (Between II & III)		2.5 points	
LEVEL III		3 points	
Mid-LEVEL (Between III & IV)		3.5 points	
LEVEL IV		4 points	
TOTALS			

$$\frac{\text{Total Points}}{\text{Total Checks}} = \underline{\qquad} \times 100 = \textbf{S.P.Q. Score}$$

Compare your figures with the completed version on page A23.

Examine the **PROFILE** on page A13

Male, 11th Grade, English. S.P.Q. Score _211_

LEVELS	NUMBER OF CHECKS	MULTIPLY BY	TOTAL
LEVEL I	0	1 point	0
Mid-LEVEL (Between I & II)	3	1.5 points	4.5
LEVEL II	11	2 points	22
Mid-LEVEL (Between II & III)	1	2.5 points	2.5
LEVEL III	3	3 points	9
Mid-LEVEL (Between III & IV)	0	3.5 points	0
LEVEL IV	0	4 points	0
TOTALS	18		38

$$\frac{\text{Total Points} - 38}{\text{Total Checks} - 18} = 2.11 \times 100 = 211 \text{ (S.P.Q.) Score}$$

Notice the Not Applicable checks in the sample **PROFILES**?

> Page A11:   0
>
> Page A12:   1 (Computation)
>
> Page A13:   1 (Problem Solving)
>
> Page A15:   1 (Analytical Reasoning)

There are 20 Categories in the **PROFILE**. Be sure that the **Not Applicable** plus the checked Categories add up to 20.

On page A28 you will find the **INFORMATION SUMMARY** form you should use to tabulate **PROFILE** information. Make all the copies you need.

Interpreting the S.P.Q. Score

The SPQ <u>can</u> be raised.

The beauty of the **S.P.Q. Score** is that it can be raised when the proper steps for improvement are taken. The score itself gives you a general impression of performance either in an overall sense or in a specific subject. How much improvement is possible and necessary should be determined from an analysis of the **PROFILE** information. The first step, however, is to understand the different ranges of **Scores**.

SPQ ranges.

The full range is from 100 (poorest) to 400 (best). The scores are divided into six range groups:

RANGE	CATEGORY	EQUIVALENT TO
100 to 150 - **Marginal:**		Scores between 1 and 1.5
151 to 200 - **Acceptable:**		Scores between 1.5 and 2
201 to 250 - **Promising:**		Scores between 2 and 2.5
251 to 300 - **Talented:**		Scores between 2.5 and 3
301 to 350 - **Gifted:**		Scores between 3 and 3.5
351 to 400 - **Exceptional:**		Scores between 3.5 and 4

100 to 150 - MARGINAL PERFORMANCE

Description of Performance range.

An **S.P.Q. Score** in this range reflects performance at a **LEVEL** that is *less than satisfactory*. In the elementary grades it can also indicate a performance pattern that will likely become permanent if steps are not taken to make changes. For junior and senior high school students, performance in this range can be more serious.

The lower part of the range, from 100 to approximately 130, reflects a critical need for immediate intervention. In order to reach an **S.P.Q. Score** this low, over half of all performance would be at **LEVEL I**, and the balance between **LEVELS I** and **II**. It indicates that there is no **Satisfactory** performance in any Category. The questions I would have with this type of **PROFILE** would be as follows:

Pertinent questions.

●Is the student properly placed?

●What has been done, both past and present, to help this student?

●What is the student's educational and psychological background?

●What immediate attention and services can be provided to begin a program of remediation?

The important thing to understand here is the immediate need for definitive action. Something has to be done, and quickly. Otherwise, it will be too late.

An **S.P.Q. Score** in the 140's would likely have three or four Satisfactory performance Categories, with the others mostly between **LEVELS I** and **II**. This still indicates very marginal performance, but it should be possible to devise some workable plans for gradual improvement. I would also want information about the student's educational and psychological background, as well as any attempts that have been made in the past to provide help. Depending upon the time of the year, I would also be concerned about whether the student were properly placed.

To summarize, students whose performance falls in the Marginal Range, should be given some degree of immediate assistance. Decisions should be made with careful consideration of past educational and psychological history.

151 TO 200 - ACCEPTABLE PERFORMANCE

Performance in this range is above the minimum standards and moving upward. It would be safe to say that the major portion of student performance in this range is Satisfactory. This type of student "gets by," sometimes with little effort, and at other times with a great deal of effort. There is no real problem with the students who work diligently and perform at a Satisfactory **LEVEL**. They try, and they can often be motivated to move up to a higher **LEVEL** in some of the Categories, even though the movement may only be slight.

It is the "little effort" producers that deserve much more concern. They can obviously do better, and information on the **PROFILE** should provide the clues needed to begin the improvement process.

Description of Performance range.

Experience has shown that one of the best strategies is to plan for improvement in one or more of the stronger areas of performance especially those that can serve as leverage to move the weaker Categories to higher **LEVELS**. For example, if a student in the Acceptable Range is at 2.0 in the **Time** Category, "Knows the importance of completing work on time," it could be helpful to discuss what the student can do to move closer to the 2.5 **LEVEL** which is between the current position and 3.0, "Makes good use of time both in and out of class."

Making better use of time could have a good effect on some of the **ESSENTIAL SKILLS** and **ACCOUNTABILITY** Categories. The result could be a significantly higher **PERFORMANCE QUOTIENT**.

Make every effort to develop strength in the **MOTIVATION** and **SELF MANAGEMENT** Categories. These are the critical "effectors" that are directly related to improved performance in other Categories. You will find more information on this in the chapters on **MOTIVATION** and **SELF MANAGEMENT**.

201 TO 250 - PROMISING PERFORMANCE

Performance in this range is better than **Satisfactory**, and moving toward the Above Average **LEVEL**. It is considered to be "Promising" because of what it might become, not necessarily what it is. Students with performance in this range should be counseled about what choices they have, and the difference that a commitment by them could make. "Promising" is largely "transitional." The student is in "transit" from one place to another. The real decision to make is what direction to take. With proper encouragement and assistance, the result could be a move into the **Above Average LEVEL**.

251 TO 300 TALENTED PERFORMANCE

Performance in this range is, for the most part, Above Average. The "Talented" designation means good use of abilities. It also means dedication and seriousness about school work. These students tend to be reliable and they are willing to assume responsibilities that become part of the commitment and involvement in their success in school.

301 TO 350 - GIFTED PERFORMANCE

Performance in this range is well Above Average, and moving toward **Consistent Excellence**. The designation "Gifted" means not only superior capability, but also working up to that capability. These students have well established work study patterns that are efficient, effective and highly productive.

351 TO 400 - EXCEPTIONAL PERFORMANCE

Description of Performance range.

Performance in this range is of the highest caliber. The designation **Exceptional** means consistently above and beyond usual expectations. These students are not only superbly endowed with intellect and abilities, but they have unique understanding and insight into what learning is all about.

Although it would seem that this type of performance would not be subject to improvement strategies, this is not the case. Students who perform in this range are interested in discovering new frontiers and extending the boundaries of their knowledge. It is most important for teachers and parents to do everything possible to keep these students challenged.

SUMMARY

At this point you should be able to collect enough pertinent information on a student's performance to prepare a **PROFILE** and compute a **PERFORMANCE QUOTIENT**. This is the first step in the analytical process that leads to improvement.

The next step is to interpret the information you have collected and make appropriate plans for improvement where improvement is needed. Chapters 1 - 10 of this **MANUAL** will give you detailed and specific information on the nature of all the performance categories, and suggestions for what you can do to make your plans for improvement as effective as possible.

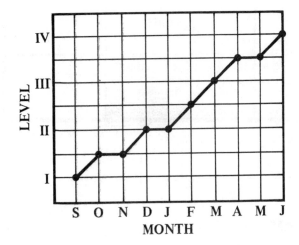

STUDENT PERFORMANCE QUOTIENT (S.P.Q.)
INFORMATION SUMMARY

Name_____Subject_____S.P.Q. Score_____

LEVELS	NUMBER OF CHECKS	MULTIPLY BY	TOTAL
LEVEL I		1 point	
Mid-LEVEL (Between **I & II**)		1.5 points	
LEVEL II		2 points	
Mid-LEVEL (Between **II & III**)		2.5 points	
LEVEL III		3 points	
Mid-LEVEL (Between **III & IV**)		3.5 points	
LEVEL IV		4 points	
TOTALS			

$$\frac{\text{Total Points}}{\text{Total Checks}} = \underline{\quad\quad} \times 100 = \textbf{S.P.Q. Score}$$

PERFORMANCE RANGE

100-150 Marginal   251-300 Talented
151-200 Acceptable   301-350 Gifted
201-250 Promising   351-400 Exceptional

SUPPLEMENT B
Foreign Language Learning Skills and Grammatical Glossary

You *can* learn a Foreign Language, any Foreign Language you choose. The basic skills are described below, followed by a **GLOSSARY OF GRAMMATICAL TERMS** that will help you understand nearly everything you need to know about the differences between English grammar and the grammar of the foreign language you are studying.

LANGUAGE LEARNING SKILLS

I refer to those languages taught most often in the public and private schools: Spanish, French, German, and Latin. Spanish, French, and German are "modern" (spoken) languages. The Latin that you study is "classical" Latin, which does not mean that it is "dead." It was the language used by the Romans at the height of their civilization when the greatest Latin "classics" were written.

Learning a modern foreign language involves 5 basic skills:

- *Speaking*
- *Listening*
- *Understanding*
- *Reading*
- *Writing*

If you are taking Latin, omit *Speaking.*

SPEAKING. The key to acquiring good speaking skills is constant *repetition*. Repeat over and over again words, phrases, conjugations, until you can say things instinctively -- almost without thinking. It is like learning the multiplication tables. If you have to think for longer than a split second that 6 x 9 = 54, then you really haven't "learned" it. The same thing applies to a modern foreign language. Practice, most preferably "aloud," what you have learned in the Vocabulary, Dialogue, or Verb Tense. Do this often enough to learn the material well enough so that you do not have to think in English first and then translate into the foreign language. This requires a great deal of effort, and for some it will be easier than for others. Try to lose your inhibition. Don't worry what others may think.

The important thing in speaking is to *say* something. Say it with words, say it with gestures, say it any way you can, *but get the words out*. Get in the habit of getting words to flow. This will become easier when you acquire the skill of careful, attentive, participatory Listening.

LISTENING.   Speaking and Listening go hand in hand.   The more carefully you learn how to listen, the better speaker you will become.   In the beginning, as you listen to your teacher, or to a native speaker, look at the person, as you listen to what is being said.   Observe and imitate as much as you possibly can.   Watch the gestures; imitate the gestures; look at the speaker's hands, face, body movements, anything that gives clues to what is being said.   Try repeating with the speaker exactly what he or she is saying.   This may sound silly, but it is far from it.   It gets you "tuned in."   When you want the speaker to repeat something, ask.   Avoid, at all costs, being simply a "passive" listener.   It is also important to lose as much of your inhibition as possible.   Inhibition is the "enemy" of learning to speak, to listen to, and to understand a foreign language.

UNDERSTANDING.   Understanding, or comprehension, relates to the skills of both Listening and Reading.   You have to know what the words mean.   You have to acquire a good Vocabulary, as well as a knowledge of idiomatic (not translatable word for word) expressions.   The goal is to understand in the language itself, without translating.   You have to consciously set this as a goal or it will not likely occur.   You also must continue to build your "usable" vocabulary.   By "usable" I refer to words and expressions that you have "indelibly" learned.   Simple recognition is good enough for reading, but not for speaking.

READING.   We now get into more of the "structural" part of language learning.   In addition to building a good vocabulary, you have to understand the grammatical makeup of the language -- how the words relate to each other within a sentence.   The Glossary of Grammatical Terms on the following pages will help you.   The goal is to be able to read without having to translate into English.   As I pointed out above in the section on Understanding, you have to set a goal of reading more and more while you translate less and less.   It won't happen overnight, however, it won't very likely happen at all, if you don't set it as a goal.

WRITING.   This is the most demanding skill of all.   You must understand not only the basic principles of composition, but you must also have a good working knowledge of grammatical concepts.   Beginning students should carefully plan what the content will be then attempt to express the ideas in a simple, direct manner.   Avoid long sentences with subordinate clauses.   After you have a first draft, examine it carefully and make corrections for both content and grammatical accuracy.   Re-write as many times as necessary.

At the more advanced levels of foreign language learning, use the same principles for writing a composition that you use in English.   The difference is that you will be thinking as much as possible in the foreign language as you compose your composition.   Remember, good writing skill requires what most all skills require -- lots of analysis, critique, and continued practice.

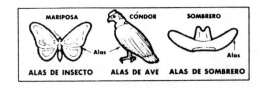

MARIPOSA   CÓNDOR   SOMBRERO
Alas   Alas
ALAS DE INSECTO   ALAS DE AVE   ALAS DE SOMBRERO

GLOSSARY OF GRAMMATICAL TERMS

HOW TO USE THE GLOSSARY

The Glossary is essentially a reference tool. It will help you overcome one of the most frustrating barriers associated with learning a foreign language: understanding the grammar. As a result, you will be able to avoid the unfortunate cumulative effect of an increasing gap in your knowledge of the essential grammar you need to succeed in your foreign language class.

The grammatical terms defined in this **GLOSSARY** are primarily those that are used in the four languages taught most often in the public schools: Spanish, French, German and Latin. When you come across an unfamiliar grammatical term in your language textbook, look it up in the **INDEX** and then refer to the appropriate section or sections in the **GLOSSARY**. Be absolutely certain that you understand it completely before going on. If the definition has terms that you don't understand, look them up also. It may be difficult and involved at first, but as your knowledge expands, your need for the **GLOSSARY** will diminish. You will also be more successful, and you should enjoy what you are learning.

ALPHABETICAL LISTING OF GRAMMATICAL TERMS

A

ABLATIVE CASE (See **CASE**)

ABSOLUTE
Grammatically the term Absolute is a relatively independent part of a sentence, but it is related to the rest of the sentence in meaning. For example, "Having eaten, he went to bed." "Having eaten" has no grammatical relationship to the sentence, but it does contribute to the meaning of the sentence. Think of "absolute" as being connected to the meaning of the sentence, but with no real grammatical connection.

ABLATIVE ABSOLUTE (Latin)
This is a separate part of a sentence consisting of a noun and a participle, a noun and an adjective, or two nouns -- always in the Ablative Case. For example, "Viis factis," "The roads having been made."

ABSTRACT NOUN (See **NOUN**)

ACCENT MARKS
The accent marks indicate *Stress* and *Pronunciation,* and they may also have linguistic significance. We will concentrate on *Stress* and *Pronunciation*. The most common marks are:

Stress: "aquí" in Spanish

ACCENT MARKS (Continued)

Pronunciation (See your text for the correct pronunciation)

(´) *Acute Accent*: école (French)

(¸) *Cedilla*: garçon (French)

(^) *Circumflex*: être (French)

(¨) *Dieresis*: naïve (French). Separates (divides)
   the pronunciation of two adjacent vowels.

(`) *Grave Accent*: élève (French)

(~) *Tilde*: año (Spanish)

(¨) *Umlaut*: über (German) Looks like the dieresis
   but used strictly for pronunciation.

ACCUSATIVE CASE (See **CASE**)

ACTIVE VOICE (See **VOICE**)

ADDRESS, DIRECT (also called **DIRECT DISCOURSE**)

A quotation or statement written exactly as it was stated.
Example, My mother said, *"Come home immediately!"*

ADDRESS, INDIRECT (also called **INDIRECT DISCOURSE**)
This is a version of the speaker's words rather than
the direct or actual statement. The version is
included in a larger sentence. The two examples above
of Direct Address would become Indirect as follows: *My
mother told me* (that) *I had to come home immediately.*
The speaker is reporting what his mother said, rather
than quoting her actual words. *John asked me if I were
going to the game this afternoon*, or *I told John that I
would go to the game this afternoon.* In Indirect
Address, the original words are replaced by a version
or summary of what was actually stated.

ADJECTIVE
A word that modifies a Noun or Pronoun. Examples: a
large stone, a *new* suit, she is *good*. In addition to this simple
definition, there are types of ADJECTIVES and ADJECTIVAL
functions. The following are the most important.

Abstract **ADJECTIVE**
An Abstract Adjective modifies an Abstract Noun
which is either expressed or understood. It describes
a quality or idea, rather than a specific substance.
For example, a *good* law, a *beautiful* thought, a *just* cause.

ADJECTIVE, (Continued)

Cardinal ADJECTIVE
A numerical modifier. It answers the question, "How many?" The number is specific: "two," "ten." The number is an Adjective, a Cardinal Adjective.

ADJECTIVE Clause (See CLAUSE)

Comparison of ADJECTIVES (See COMPARISON)

Concrete ADJECTIVE
Used with a concrete noun following it that is either expressed or clearly understood. (The Abstract Adjective was used with an abstract noun.) Examples: the *beautiful* people, the *happy* crowd. The adjectives are modifying concrete nouns.

DEFINITE ARTICLE (See also ARTICLE)
The is the Definite Article. It points to something or someone, singular or plural, that can be clearly distinguished from anything or anyone else. Examples: I want *the* book. Not just any book. If I wanted any book I would say that I want *a* (indefinite) book. He bought *the* car. Not just any car. In English there is only one form of the Definite Article -- *the*. How many are there in the language you are studying?

Demonstrative ADJECTIVE
This, *that*, *these* and *those*, followed by a noun are the most common of the Demonstrative Adjectives. They are called "demonstrative" because they "point" to specific things or to a specific person or persons. Examples: *this* book, *that* teacher, *these* boys, *those* papers. When the noun is omitted, the Demonstrative Adjective becomes a Demonstrative Pronoun (See PRONOUN).

Descriptive ADJECTIVE
An Adjective describes or limits the meaning of a Noun or Pronoun. The *green* grass, or the *beautiful* woman are examples of Descriptive Adjectives.

Indefinite ADJECTIVE (See also ARTICLE)
A, *an* are Indefinite Articles. They indicate something indefinite or non-specific. Examples: *a* book means *any* book, *an* engine can mean *any* engine. The plural of "*a*" or "*an*" is "*some*"or "*any*." I have "*some*" friends, or (in a negative statement) "I don't have *any* friends." Notice how all of the examples are non-specific, while the Definite Article, described above, points to specific things or persons, singular or plural.

Interrogative ADJECTIVE
The Interrogative Adjectives are *which*, or *what*, followed by a Noun. Example, "*Which* books did you buy?"

ADJECTIVE (Continued)

Limiting ADJECTIVE
The Limiting (as opposed to Descriptive) Adjective limits the application or idea represented by the noun or pronoun which the adjective modifies. Examples: *this* chapter, *ten* candles, or *my* car.

Ordinal ADJECTIVE
The Ordinal Adjective is a Numerical Adjective which denotes position or place in a series. *First, second, third,* etc. The other Numerical Adjective is called a Cardinal Adjective (one, two, three, etc.)

Participial ADJECTIVE (See also **PARTICIPLE**)
The Present Participle (ending in *-ing*) or Past Participle (ending usually in -<u>ed</u>, or *-en*) used to modify a noun or pronoun. Examples: the *singing* nun, or the *chosen* people.

Partitive ADJECTIVE
This is a *part* of the whole. Usually represented in English by *some, any,* or *no*. Examples: I have *some* candy, or *some* candies. In negative statements, I have *no* candy, or I don't have *any* candy. How is this expressed in the language you are studying?

Possessive ADJECTIVE
The Possessive Adjective indicates possession (what else?). The adjective is formed according to the appropriate person and number.

	Singular	Plural
First Person	my	our
Second Person	your	your
Third Person	his, her, its	their

Examples: *my* book(s), *their* toys, *its* price.

Predicate ADJECTIVE
The adjective or modifier appears in the predicate part of the sentence. In these cases you need to be careful about the "agreement" of the adjective according to the rules of the language you are studying. Examples: The roses look *red*. *Red* describes the roses. The Predicate Adjective is separated from the noun it modifies. The tricky part here is the "agreement." The Predicate Adjective, like any adjective, must, I repeat, *MUST* agree with the noun or pronoun it modifies.

ADVERB

An Adverb modifies a Verb, an Adjective, or another Adverb.

Verb -- She sings *beautifully*. In this case, the adverb answers the question, "How?" How does she sing? She sings *beautifully*. Notice how the Adjective "beautiful" becomes an Adverb by adding the suffix "-ly." How are Adverbs formed from Adjectives in the language you are studying?

Adjective -- The book is *very* good, and *well* written. The Adverbs *very* and *well* modify the Adjectives "good," and "written." This is very easy to understand, if you can pick out the Adjectives.

Adverb -- He completed the assignment *very* quickly. "Quickly" is an Adverb; *very* is an Adverb modifying "quickly."

Be sure you understand the concept of what an Adverb is. As you go through the lessons in your textbook, be aware of all the uses of Adverbs, how they are formed, and how they relate to other parts of the sentence. The following are the main classifications of Adverbs that will help you with the language you are studying.

ADVERB of Cause (See also **Interrogative ADVERB**)
Another way of designating an Interrogative Adverb. *Why*, for what reason(s), etc. Examples: *Why* do you like Latin? For what reasons?

ADVERB Clause (See **CLAUSE**)

Comparison of ADVERBS (See **COMPARISON**)

Interrogative ADVERB
When, where, why, and *how* are the main Interrogative Adverbs. Examples: *When* did he arrive? *Where* are the apples? *Why* is he here? *How* does it work? *How much* do you want? *How many* did they buy?

Memorize the Interrogative Adverbs used in the language you are studying. Practice using them.

ADVERB of Manner
These Adverbs answer the question, How? Examples: How did he walk? He walked *slowly*. How are they doing? They are doing *well*.

ADVERB of Place
These Adverbs answer the question, Where? The answer may be *here, there, in, out, up, down, around, somewhere, anywhere, nowhere, everywhere*.

ADVERB (Continued)

Pronominal ADVERB

In French, when the adverb "there" is a combination of a preposition and a pronoun substituted for a place, it can then be expressed by a single term known as a Pronominal Adverb. For example, the sentence, "He goes to the library," can be changed to "He goes to it," and "to it" becomes "there." "He goes there." In French, " Il va a la bibliotheque," becomes "Il *y* va." "y" is the Pronominal Adverb which is a combination of the preposition "to" plus "it" meaning the place (the library), and the position of "y" in the sentence is in accord with the position of pronoun objects. The Pronominal Adverb is treated like a Pronoun Object.

ADVERB of Time

The adverb of time answers the question, "When?" The answer is usually *now, then, later, immediately, soon,* and *how often*? It indicates *date, duration, how long, how frequently,* or *at what intervals*?

AGENT

The importance of the "agent" is usually associated with passive constructions. The "agent" is the "doer" of the action. In the passive construction the agent is expressed as the object of the preposition "by." For example, "The ball was thrown <u>by</u> the boy." If we make the sentence active it would be written, "The boy threw the ball." Note that the "agent" in the passive construction performs the act, but is not the subject of the verb. In the active construction, the agent becomes the subject of the verb. "The boy (agent) threw (verb) the ball."

AGREEMENT

Most language teachers will give gold stars to students who truly understand the concept of "agreement." The simplest type of "agreement" is between Subject and Verb in a Clause or sentence. If the Subject is singular, the Verb must be singular. For example, "The girl sings well." You also have to know the "Person," and "Number" of the Subject. "The girl" is Third Person. You can arrive at the "Person" of the Subject by substituting a Personal Pronoun. In this case, "she" could be substituted for "the girl." "She" is Third Person--by definition. The Verb then must agree with the Subject (she). The Third Person singular of the Verb "to sing" is "sings."

In the language you are studying, there can be other forms of Agreement that do not have counterparts in English. For example, all Adjectives *agree* in Gender and Number with the

AGREEMENT (Continued)

Nouns or Pronouns they modify. In English, it is easy to recognize the difference between Feminine and Masculine Nouns, because we have a Neuter Gender for all Nouns and Pronouns that are neither Masculine nor Feminine. This can be confusing to you when you study a language that has no Neuter Gender. You have to *memorize* the Gender of every Noun so that you can have the proper Agreement with modifiers (Adjectives). For example, the word "table" is Feminine. In French you memorize the word as "la (Feminine Article) table;" in Spanish, "la mesa." In the dictionary or glossary the word will always be given with the Gender. For example, "table - mesa f." You must memorize the word *and* the Gender. Recite the Noun with the Article so you will automatically remember the Gender. There are many clues that will be helpful, for example, Nouns ending in the letter "a" are usually Feminine (la mes_a_). You will find other clues in your text, and your teacher will also give you clues.

REMEMBER: If you know the *Gender* of all Nouns, you will not have difficulty with Agreement. The singular or plural forms are self evident.

ANTECEDENT

This means "to go before." The "antecedent" is a Noun or Pronoun referred to by another Noun or Pronoun that follows. For example, "The *book* that is on the table is mine." This is the type of sentence that illustrates the most important (and often confusing) aspect of the significance of an "antecedent." The word "book" is the antecedent of the (Relative) Pronoun "that." Why is the "antecedent" so important? The reason is because you get the *Gender*, *Number* and *Person* of the Relative Pronoun ("that") from the antecedent ("book").

In French and Spanish "book" is *Masculine*, it is also *singular*, and *Third Person* (it). Why is it so important to know the Gender, Number, and Person of the antecedent? Because it is the only way to know the Gender, Number and Person of the Relative Pronoun (that). This will be treated at greater length in the section on **RELATIVE PRONOUNS**.

Another example of the use of an "antecedent" is in a sentence such as, "Sally drove her car to New York." "Sally" is the antecedent of the Pronoun "her." If the sentence were, "Sally drove *his* car to New York," we would have to look elsewhere to know the antecedent of "his."

REMINDER: The antededent is a source of information for the proper form of the Pronoun which follows.

ANTERIOR (See **TENSE**)

APPOSITIVE

An expression with the same meaning and syntax as a preceding expression. For example, "The boy next door, Al Smith, is on vacation." "Al Smith" is the appositive. "The boy" and "Al Smith" are the same person. The important thing to remember about an appositive is the grammatical similarity with the Noun (or Pronoun) to which it refers.

ARTICLE

The Definite (the, singular and plural) and the Indefinite Article ("a," "an"-singular; "some," "any"-plural) are Adjectives. They must therefore agree in Gender and Number with the Noun or Pronoun they modify. Memorize the Definite Article when you learn any new Noun. If the Noun begins with a vowel, memorize the Indefinite Article because of the elision, or omission of the vowel of the Definite Article. "L'ame" (the soul-French) is feminine. "La ame" is phonetically improper. Memorize the word as "une ame," and you will eliminate the difficulty.

You *must*, I repeat *MUST* know the Gender of *every* Noun. Never, I repeat *NEVER* put off learning the Gender. See the section above on **AGREEMENT**. Remember, masculine and feminine Nouns in English are easy to remember because of our neuter forms. The language you are studying, with or without a neuter form, will have many Nouns whose Gender will appear to be illogical and must consequently be memorized with the proper Gender.

AUXILIARY VERB

Auxiliary Verbs are "helping" Verbs. The important ones for you are the forms of "to be," and "to have." The *help* they provide is in the formation of the "compound" tenses (see also **TENSE**), and also with a principal Verb to specify a certain time or manner of action. In English there are many more uses of auxiliary Verb forms that you are likely to encounter in the language you are studying. This creates difficulty. For example, the "will," or "shall" auxiliaries that we use to form a future tense are not part of the form in the future of most of the Verbs in the foreign language you are studying. The future is contained in the ending of the Verb, but translated with an auxiliary in English. For example, "I will take" is simply "Yo tomar*e*." Remember, auxiliaries like will, shall, may, might, would, should, or could cannot usually be translated into the language you are studying word for word. This will be discussed in greater detail in the section on **TENSE**.

The forms of the auxiliary verbs "to be" and "to have" are used to form all of the compound tenses. If you know all of

AUXILIARY VERB (Continued)

the forms of these two auxiliaries, you can form all of the compound tenses by combining the form of the auxiliary with a participle. For example,

I eat. (Simple Tense)

I *have* (auxiliary) eaten (past participle). (Compound Tense)

I *had* eaten.

I *will have* eaten.

I *would have* eaten.

See the sections on **VERB** and **TENSE** for a fuller discussion.

C

CARDINAL (See **ADJECTIVE**)

CASE (Latin and German)
In Latin and German, nouns, pronouns, and adjectives have characteristic endings (inflections) that indicate subject/object, possession and relationships to other words and parts of the sentence. In English, French, and Spanish, the order of the words in the sentence gives us the main aspects of the meaning of the sentence. In Latin and German, the endings or inflections are the critical determiners of the meaning of the sentence. This can be confusing because we are so accustomed to looking for meaning in what we feel is a logical process. With practice and lots of application, you will become very much at ease with this somewhat different type of linguistic logic.

Ablative CASE (Latin)
This Case was used by the Romans when they wanted to limit or modify the meaning of a Verb, either with or without the use of a Preposition. The meaning usually implies (by what) *means*, (by whom) *agent*, (with whom) *accompaniment*, (how) in what *manner*, (from what place) *where*, (when) *time*. The English Prepositions usually used with the Ablative Case are "by," "with," "from," "in," "on," or "at."

Accusative CASE (Latin and German)
This case is used to express a direct object. For example, I threw the ball. "the ball" would be in the Accusative Case. It is the Direct Object of the verb "threw." (See **OBJECT**)

CASE (Continued)

The Accusative can also be used with certain prepositions, usually denoting motion or movement.

Dative CASE (Latin and German)

This case is used to express an Indirect Object. The prepositions "to," or "for" are usually used or implied in the association. For example, "I threw the ball to Jim." "Jim" is the Indirect Object. I threw the ball, not Jim. The Preposition "to" could have been implied in the following English sentence. "I threw Jim the ball." Be sure you check the sentence carefully to be certain that a Prepostion is implied or understood.

Genitive CASE (Latin and German)

This case is used mostly to express possession. In English we can do this with an 's. "The boy's book." The sentence could also be written as "The book of the boy." The Genitive can usually be distinguished by the use of the Preposition "of" to show possession.

Nominative CASE (Latin and German)

This case is used most often to designate the subject of a finite Verb. "The soldiers (Nominative) left."

Vocative CASE (Latin)

The Romans used the Vocative Case to call or address a person or thing directly. It is usually recognized in English by the use of "O." For example, "O Caesar," or "O Fortune." With one exception, the Vocative Case has the same form as the Nominative.

Locative CASE (Latin)

This case is used to express "place where" reserved mostly for names of cities and towns.

CAUSE (Latin)

The Ablative Case can be used to express a Cause or Reason. For example, "Wolves are feared *because of* their strength."

CAUSATIVE VERB

This is A Verb that causes or *makes* something happen. For example, "The teacher *makes* the students work." The construction is usually used with another Verb.

CEDILLA (See **ACCENT**)

CIRCUMFLEX (See **ACCENT**)

CLAUSE

A Clause is a group of words with a subject and a predicate. As such, it can be considered to be a simple sentence. As a rule, however, it is part of a compound or complex sentence. The different types of clauses you need to be familiar with are listed below.

Adjective CLAUSE

An Adjective Clause is a group of words with a subject and a predicate that modify a Noun or Pronoun. In other words, the Adjective Clause functions just like an Adjective. For example, "The book *which is on the table* is mine." The Clause "which is on the table" modifies the antecedent "book." Note that the Clause "which is on the table," has a subject-*which*, and a predicate-*is on the table*. The clause in this case is a Relative Clause, or one that is introduced by a Relative Pronoun (See **PRONOUN**). If the subject of the clause, "which," is confusing, it should be clarified when you become more familiar with the section on Relative Pronouns.

Adverb CLAUSE

The Adverb Clause is used to express:

Cause: He ate *because* he was hungry.
Comparison: The lesson was clearer *than* he thought it would be.
Concession: *Although* he became ill, he played.
Condition: *If* it rains, take your umbrella.
Manner: He ran the race *as* (in the manner) he was told.
Place: He went *wherever* the books were sold.
Purpose: He worked hard *in order to* succeed.
Time: He was advised to take the test *whenever* he was ready.

Under certain circumstances, the Verb in an Adverb Clause is in the Subjunctive Mood. This will be discussed in the sections on **MOOD** and **VERB**.

Dependent CLAUSE

The Dependent Clause cannot stand alone. It depends on another part of the sentence for its complete meaning. For example, "I believe that the team will win." The Dependent Clause is "that the team will win." The idea *depends* on the main verb, "I believe." If you ask the question, "I believe what?" The answer is the clause itself, "that the team will win." (Dependent Noun Clause)

Another name for Dependent Clause is Subordinate Clause.

CLAUSE (Continued)

Important Note: Many uses of the SUBJUNCTIVE MOOD will be in a Dependent Clause introduced by certain types of verbal expressions. This will be discussed in the section on the **SUBJUNCTIVE**.

Independent CLAUSE

The Independent Clause *can* stand alone. It contains a complete and independent thought or idea. For example, *"The book* that is on the table *is mine."* The Independent Clause, the one that can stand alone is underlined. "The book is mine." It is a complete thought. The relative clause "that is on the table," is the Dependent or Subordinate Clause. It needs the Main or Independent Clause to complete its meaning.

Another name for Independent Clause is Main Clause.

Noun CLAUSE

A Noun Clause is used in the same way that a Noun is used. It can be either Subject or Object. For example, *Subject*: "*That it will rain today* is certain." The Noun Clause is underlined. It serves as Subject of the Verb "is." The Pronoun "It" can take the place of the underlined Clause.

Object: "He believes *that you are right*." The underlined Clause is the Direct Object of the Verb. "He believes what?" The answer (Direct Object of "believes") "that you are right."

More advice about the importance of understanding the concept and use of the CLAUSE. Review this information until it is thoroughly familiar to you. The more you know about the different aspects of CLAUSES, the more successful you will be in the language you are studying.

COGNATE

This is a very important linguistic term that can help you significantly increase your foreign language vocabulary. A foreign language cognate word looks or sounds similar to the same word in English. For example, English "cold" is a cognate of the German "kalt." English words ending in "tion" are mostly cognate in French and Spanish, and often in German. There are many cognate classifications that you can learn and become aware of. It will not only help you increase your vocabulary, but it will also help you make better guesses about the meaning of many words that you come across in your reading selections for the first time.

COMMAND (See IMPERATIVE)

COMPARISON of ADJECTIVES and ADVERBS
There are **three degrees** of Comparison:

> **Positive**
> **Comparative**
> **Superlative**

The **Positive Degree** is simply the existence of the quality itself, with no statement of a relationship to a similar quality in any other person or thing. For example,
> Adjective: "The ball is *round*."
> Adverb: "The dog walks *slowly*."

In both examples, the qualities are expressed without any type of measurement or comparison. "Round" is "round." "Slowly" is just that, "slowly," nothing more.

The **Comparative Degree** shows that a relationship exists to a *greater* or *lesser* extent.
> Adjective: "The ball is *rounder* (more round) than an orange," "The ball is *less round* than a bearing."
> Adverb: "The dog walks *slower* (more slowly) than my cat," or (somewhat awkwardly stated) "The dog walks *less slowly* than my cat."

Both Adjective and Adverb examples of the Comparative Degree are stated in the form of a relationship--"more" or "less" than something or someone else. Remember, Comparative means "more," or "less." You will usually *compare* two items, or two groups. One is either "more," or "less" than the other in regard to some specific quality or qualification.

The **Superlative Degree** expresses either the *greatest* or the *least* of an existing quality. The word "superlative" means the topmost or bottommost level.
> Adjective: "The ball is roundest (most round), or least round of all."
> Adverb: "The dog walks slowest (most slowly), or least slowly of all."

The signs of the Superlative Degree are "most," "least," or the ending "est." In addition to the above regular types of comparison, there are also irregular forms for some Adjectives and Adverbs. Memorize them. Be sure to remember that the Adjectives will have to *agree* with the Noun or Pronoun they modify. Adverbs do not *agree*. The language you are studying has specific requirements for the formation of the Comparative and Superlative Degree forms. Once you understand the principles of **Comparison**, you should be able to use them without any difficulty.

COMPOUND TENSE (See TENSE)

CONDITIONAL SENTENCE

There are two basic clauses in a Conditional Sentence: (1) the Conditional Clause, introduced by "If," and (2) the Result Clause. For example, "If you study, you will succeed." "Studying" is the condition. "Success" is the result. This type of sentence can have a specific sequence of tenses, depending upon the language you are studying. In other words, the condition clause is in the present tense and the result clause is in the future tense. Be sure you follow the proper sequence, as indicated in your textbook. You will also want to be thoroughly familiar with the information in the section on Verb TENSE in this Glossary.

CONDITIONAL TENSES (See TENSE)

CONJUGATE

This means to "Conjugate" a Verb in a specific tense. The forms are as follows: 1st, 2nd, 3rd Person singular; 1st, 2nd, 3rd Person plural. For example, the verb "to go," in the Present Indicative:

	Singular	Plural
1st Person	I go	We go
2nd Person	You go	You go
3rd Person	He, She, or It goes	They go

Note: The instructions to "conjugate" are always twofold: tense and mood. The reason is that some of the tenses are used in both Indicative and Subjunctive Moods. The verbal system is a major part of what you must know in absolute detail. Master it from the very beginning. Look up every term you don't completely understand. Use this Glossary, and any other reference you have, especially your textbook.

CONJUGATION

Verbs can be classified or grouped according to similarities. This helps you remember them along with the sets of endings that pertain to each of the groups. The groups are designated by Roman (Ordinal) Numerals. First, Second, Third, etc. Be sure to keep these classifications in mind when you come across a new Verb and don't forget to place the new Verb in the proper classification or Conjugation.

CONJUNCTION

Conjunction can be a word or words that join words, phrases, or clauses. There are two basic types: coordinating and subordinating.

The commonest coordinating conjunctions are "and," "but," "or," "nor," and "for." These conjunctions join or link

CONJUNCTION (Continued)

two clauses, phrases, or groups of words of equal rank. In other words, the ideas expressed do not *depend* upon each other for specific meaning. For example, "Joan is my sister *and* Sam is my brother." The sentence contains two separate and equal ideas that could be expressed alone, or as equal parts of the same sentence. The only problem you could have with this category of conjunction is how to express those conjunctions that come in pairs. For example, "both...and," "neither...nor," "not only...but," "not...not," and a few others of similar nature. Your text will give you the specific way to translate these expressions. Memorize it and practice it.

Subordinating Conjunctions have additional importance and grammatical significance. They introduce a subordinate clause that can require the verb in the clause to be in the indicative *or* subjunctive mood. The most common of the subordinating conjunctions is *that*. For example, "I think *that* you are intelligent." The main clause is "I think," and the dependent or subordinate clause is "*that* you are intelligent." The subordinate clause is introduced by the conjunction *that*. (Remember, "that" can also be a pronoun. Be sure you know the difference.)

Some other subordinate conjunctions are "however," "until," "as soon as," "before," "while," "as though," "whether," etc. Learn all of these as they come up in your text. As you become more advanced in the language, know when and under what circumstances the subordinate conjunction introduces a clause that requires the subjunctive mood.

CONTRACTION

This means "making smaller." It happens when one or more letters is omitted or replaced by an apostrophe.

COPULATIVE VERB

These are also known as *linking* verbs. They join or link a subject to its complement. The most common copulative or linking verb is "to be." The important thing to remember, especially if you are taking Latin or German, is that what follows is always Predicate Nominative. Other common copulative verbs are "appear," "seem," and "become." The *link* is always such that the subject and what follows are essentially the same. For example, "The man is my father." "Man" and "father" are the same. If you try this with non-copulative verbs, it won't work. The object may be associated with the subject, but they are not the same thing. Substitute any non-copulative verb for "is" in the example above, and you will understand what I mean.

D

DATIVE CASE (See **CASE**)

DECLENSION (Latin and German)
Declension refers to classifications of Nouns, Pronouns and Adjectives according to endings or inflections that are similar. It is the counterpart of CONJUGATION, which is the classification system for Verbs. Declensions are ranked as First, Second, Third, Fourth, and Fifth. It is important to memorize the declension of every Noun, Pronoun and Adjective when you first come across it in your textbook, dictionary, or reading assignment. Memorize the Gender also.

DEFECTIVE VERB
A Defective Verb is one that lacks one or more parts needed to form a complete conjugation.

DEFINITE ARTICLE (See **ARTICLE**, and **DEFINITE ARTICLE** under the heading **ADJECTIVE**)

DEGREE (See **COMPARISON**)

DEMONSTRATIVE ADJECTIVE (See **ADJECTIVE**)

DEMONSTRATIVE PRONOUN (See **PRONOUN**)

DEPENDENT CLAUSE (See **CLAUSE**)

DEPONENT VERB (Latin)
A verb that has *only* passive voice forms, but has active meaning. The principal parts will be passive. Memorize them and be sure to give the proper translation.

DESCRIPTIVE ADJECTIVE (See **ADJECTIVE**)

DIMINUTIVE
A Dimunitive Noun indicates something or someone small, young, or endeared. It can also be someone or something that is disliked or belittled. The Diminutive is usually formed with a suffix or an internal change. For example, "book" becomes "booklet." Learn how to form the Dimunitive in the language you are studying. It is a form that you will use consistently, especially in conversation, and if you plan to travel where the language is spoken.

DIRECT ADDRESS (See **ADDRESS**)

DIRECT OBJECT (See **OBJECT**)

DISJUNCTIVE (See also **PRONOUN**)
A Disjunctive Pronoun is a pronoun object that is *not* joined

DISJUNCTIVE PRONOUN (Continued)

to the verb. The Disjunctive can be the object of a preposition or it can be used alone for emphasis in addition to the regular subject or object of the Verb. For example, "As to *me*, I think he is right." The Pronoun "me" is Disjunctive. It is "not joined" to the Verb.

E

ELISION

Elision is The omission of a vowel, consonant, or syllable to make pronunciation easier. For example, in French "le amour" ("the love," or simply "love") becomes "l'amour." When Elision occurs (in French) you will not have immediate recognition of the gender of Nouns that begin with a vowel or mute "h." *Be sure to memorize the gender.* Use the indefinite article (un or une). Throughout this Glossary, I will continue to stress the importance of knowing the gender of *every* noun! It will save you lots of time and trouble as long as you study the language.

ELLIPSIS (ELLIPTICAL SENTENCE)

The omission of a word or words in a sentence is known as Ellipsis. The meaning is understood. The problem is that an Eliptical Sentence in English may not be Elliptical in the language you are studying. For example, in English, Relative Pronouns and the Conjunction "that" can often be omitted with no effect on the meaning. For example, "The book (which or that) you want is on the table," or "I think (that) he is here." You cannot omit the Pronoun or the Conjunction when you translate the sentence into the language you are studying. *If you suspect that a sentence in English is elliptical, reconstruct it with all of the words that have been omitted.*

EMPHASIS

This relates to subtle changes in the meaning of a word or words by changing the normal order of the word or words in the sentence. The beginning or the end of the sentence are the usual positions for added emphasis. For example, *to learn* is the purpose of going to school." The normal word order would be, "The purpose of going to school is to learn."

ENDING

Verbs, Nouns, Pronouns, and Adjectives change form and meaning by changes in the ending. In Latin and German, these changes are known as "inflections." In French and Spanish, the principal changes are in the verbal forms. These changes must be memorized and "overlearned." Recite the

ENDING (Continued)

forms over and over again until you can do them instinctively. There is more information on this subject in the section of the VERB.

EXPLETIVE

An Expletive is a word that takes the place of another, both in meaning and syntax. The two most common are "it," and "there." For example, "<u>It</u> is my turn." The expletive "It" refers to whatever is meant by "my turn." There are specific rules for the use of these expletives in the language you are studying. Be sure you understand them.

"It," and "there" are also known as "Impersonal," and "Anticipatory."

F

FEMININE (See **GENDER**)

FINITE VERB (See **VERB**)

FIRST PERSON (See **PERSON**)

FUTURE TENSE (See **TENSE**)

FUTURE PERFECT (See **TENSE**)

G

GENDER

Gender refers to Nouns. In Latin and German (and English) there are three Genders: Masculine, Feminine, and Neuter. Although all three of these would seem to be self evident, there are some exceptions. Make sure you memorize them. Don't ever, I repeat *EVER* forget the Gender of a noun.

In Spanish and French there are only two Genders: Masculine and Feminine. This creates a real difficulty because all the Nouns that are neuter in English are either Masculine or Feminine in French and Spanish. This means that you have to memorize the Gender of all those neuter Nouns. There are some helpful hints that you can use, for example nearly all nouns ending in "tion" are Feminine. If you consciously set out to learn and remember the Gender of every Noun, you will avoid serious confusion and frustration later on. I cannot overemphasize how important it is to remember the Gender of *every* Noun you learn.

GENITIVE CASE (See **CASE**)

GERUND
The Gerund is a **verbal noun**. Its importance is mainly for students of Latin. The Gerund may be declined in all cases except the Nominative. In English the Gerund ends in "ing." For example, "he loves **hunting**." "Hunting" is the Direct Object of the Verb "loves." It is derived from the Verb "to hunt," and is used in this example as a Noun. Your textbook will have adequate explanatory information on the use and formation of the Gerund in Latin.

GERUNDIVE
This is a verbal adjective, with importance for students of Latin. I distinguish the Gerund (verbal Noun) from the Gerundive (verbal Adjective) by using the similarity of the "ive" in both "Adject_ive_" and "Gerund_ive_." Both Gerund and Gerundive end in "ing" in English. The following is an example of the Gerundive: "The living sea..." Your textbook will explain the form and the use of the Gerundive.

GRAMMAR
Grammar is the formal structure of a language which includes the rules for proper usage, pronunciation, and word order. See also **SYNTAX**.

GRAVE ACCENT (See **ACCENT**)

H

HISTORICAL PRESENT (See **TENSE**)

HORTATORY SUBJUNCTIVE
The use of the Subjunctive in an **independent clause**. Nearly all uses of the Subjunctive are in dependent or subordinate clauses. The Hortatory is used as a command, and is also known as the "Jussive" Subjunctive in Latin. For example, "Let there be light." (Fiat lux) This is a special use of the Subjunctive. It will be described in your textbook.

I

IDIOM

An expression that cannot be translated literally. An Idiom in one language will not likely be an Idiom in another language. This can be a serious problem, because idioms make up a large part of the spoken language. An expression such as "He kicked the bucket," would be meaningless in a

IDIOM (Continued)

direct translation into another language. Your textbook and foreign language dictionaries will be helpful. The greater your knowledge of idioms, the easier it will be to use the language for practical and personal benefit. Be conscious of idioms, how they are used and what they mean.

IDIOMATIC

This simply refers to the use and translation of Idioms.

IMPERATIVE MOOD (See **MOOD**)

IMPERFECT (See **TENSE**)

IMPERSONAL ADVERB

The use of the Expletive "there." For example, "*There* are three books on the table." See your text for the proper use of this adverb in the language you are studying. It is also known as an "Anticipatory" adverb.

IMPERSONAL PRONOUN (See also **EXPLETIVE**)

The use of the Expletive "it." For example, "It is my turn to play." See your text for the proper use of this pronoun in the language you are studying.

INDEFINITE ADJECTIVE (See **ADJECTIVE**)

INDEPENDENT CLAUSE (See **CLAUSE**)

INDICATIVE MOOD (See **MOOD**)

INDIRECT ADDRESS (See **ADDRESS**)

INDIRECT OBJECT (See **OBJECT**)

INFINITIVE (See **VERB**)

INFINITIVE PHRASE

The Infinitive can be used as a Subject or an Object, by itself, or in a phrase. For example, "*To sing* is her ambition." The Infinitive "to sing" is the Subject of the Verb "is." In the sentence "She likes *to sing*," the Direct Object of the Verb "likes" is "to sing." Remember, the sign of the Infinitive, "to," does not appear in Spanish, French, or Latin. The ending of the Verb will indicate the form of the Infinitive, which will be translated in English as "to -----."

INFLECTION (Latin and German)

A change in the ending or part of the word to indicate a change in the syntactic relationship of the word within the sentence. This relationship in Spanish and French (also

INFLECTION (Continued)

English) is determined by word order. Word order in Inflected languages like Latin and German can be much more varied, since the Inflection determines the essential meaning. As you progress to higher levels in German and Latin, you will discover the subtle differences in meaning that can be expressed with variations in the word order.

INTENSIVE PRONOUN (See **PRONOUN**)

INTERROGATIVE ADJECTIVE (See **ADJECTIVE**)

INTERROGATIVE ADVERB (See **ADVERB**)

INTERROGATIVE PRONOUN (See **PRONOUN**)

INTRANSITIVE VERB (See **VERB**)

IRREGULAR VERB (See **VERB**)

L

LIAISON

This refers to pronunciation. For example, in French a final consonant which by itself would be silent, is pronounced when followed by a word that begins with a vowel or a mute "h." This is called "liaison," or "joining" of the two words so that the sound is more natural, and easier to articulate. "Les" (pronounced by itself as "lay") would be pronounced "laze" (phonetic spelling) when followed by a word beginning with a vowel or mute "h." "Les amis." (Phonetically-"Lazamis").

LINKING VERB (See **VERB**)

M

MANNER (See **ADVERB** and **CLAUSE**)

MASCULINE (See **GENDER**)

MODIFIER

This refers to Adjectives and Adverbs.

MOOD (or **MODE**)

Mood refers to Verbs. It indicates the manner in which the action of the Verb is stated or how the action should be regarded. The two main Moods are the Indicative and the Subjunctive. Some grammarians consider the Imperative to be a Mood. Below are definitions and examples of what you

MOOD (Continued)

should know about this very important part of learning a foreign language.

Imperative MOOD

This is the Command or Request form of the Verb. The word Imperative itself means something that must be done, must not be avoided. Therefore a Command or a strong Request. For example, "Study for the test," "Go home," or "Be on time." Notice that the subject of an Imperative is not expressed. It is *understood*. It is most often "You." Each language has special forms for the Imperative. In English we use "you" for the second Person singular and plural. The language you are studying will have a separate form for both of these second Person forms. Be sure you learn them. Actually, the second Person singular in English is "thou," however, it is so rarely used that many grammarians have all but eliminated it. You should know that it does exist.

Indicative MOOD

The Indicative Mood is the most common. The action stated by the verb is very "matter of fact." If a question is asked, it is usually a real or factual question. For example, "I like candy." "Do you like candy?" "I believe that he is my cousin." These are all examples of Indicative statements. They are very straightforward. There is no doubt, anxiety, fear, or any other subjective type of emotion. The great majority of Verbs are in the Indicative Mood, which is why the greatest part of the Verbal System consists of Indicative forms.

Subjunctive MOOD

The Subjunctive means "joined under." The verbs are most often in Subordinate or dependent clauses, which explains why the word "Subjunctive" is used. Since the Subjunctive is used in the dependent clause, its use will depend upon what is stated in the main clause. When you memorize the forms of the Subjunctive, it would be helpful if you recited them as if they were subordinate. In other words, get in the habit of using the Subjunctive as it is used most often. Your text will identify the principal types of expressions in the main clause that require the use of the Subjunctive in the dependent clause. These include expressions of doubt, possibility, impossibility, wish, desire, fear, negative belief, and other similar feelings. They are much more "subjective" than the indicative statements. Remember, however, that the "subjectivity" is determined by the verb in the main clause, not the verb in the dependent clause.

SUBJUNCTIVE (Continued)

The tenses of the Subjunctive will be discussed in the section on VERBS.

Note: A comparison of the use of the Subjunctive in English will not be much help. Be sure you understand the precise uses in the language you are studying.

MOTION

This relates to the use of verbs. Verbs of "motion", like "to go," "to run," or "to climb," have special characteristics that you need to be aware of. Some may be conjugated (compound tenses) with the auxiliary "to be" instead of "to have." Some may also be Intransitive (see **VERB**). Be very attentive when your teacher discusses this concept, or when you read about it in your textbook.

Note: You may have thought that all verbs represent some type of "motion." This is not true. "Action," or "being" are more applicable and appropriate. "Motion" is a separate and distinct concept.

N

NEGATION

Negation is some form of "denial." We usually think of a sentence with "not" in some part of it. "He does *not* want to go." This is the simplest form of Negation. There are other forms such as "neither," "nor," "never," "none," "nothing." The adverb "only" can also be used negatively.

NEUTER (See **GENDER**)

NOMINATIVE (See **CASE**)

NOUN

A Noun is a part of speech designating a person, place, or thing. One of the main characteristics about Nouns that you must, I repeat MUST, remember is the Gender of the Nouns in the language you are studying (see GENDER). In English, Nouns can be either masculine, feminine, or neuter. It makes life much easier. But when there are only two Genders, Masculine or Feminine, (in both Spanish and French) then all the Neuter Nouns, like "table," "pen," or "stone," have to be either Masculine or Feminine. If you fail to memorize the Gender of these Neuter Nouns, then you will have trouble with the Adjectives that must agree with them. There are certain classes of Nouns that will usually be either Masculine or Feminine. This will help overcome some

NOUN (Continued)

of the difficulty. However, you must understand how very important it is to memorize the Gender of every Noun you encounter either in a Vocabulary in your textbook or in a reading assignment. The best way is to memorize the Noun *and* the Definite Article, (French) "le"-Masculine, and "la"-Feminine at the time you learn the Noun. If the Noun begins with a vowel or "h" mute, memorize the Indefinite Article, "un"-Masculine, "une"-Feminine.

There are two other important uses of the Noun as a concept:

NOUN CLAUSE (See **CLAUSE**)

PREDICATE NOUN

This is important for students of Latin and German. A Noun is in the Nominative Case when it follows the predicate and means the same thing as the subject, and explains or describes the subject. For example, "My mother is a good cook." "good cook" describes "My mother." The Predicate Noun follows a Copulative Verb. (See **COPULATIVE**). The Predicate Noun is also known as "Attribute," "Complement," or "Subjective Complement."

O

OBJECT

The term Object refers to the Object of a Verb, or the Object of a Preposition. The Object can be a Noun, Pronoun, Clause, or Phrase. We will first consider the different aspects of the Object of a Verb.

Direct OBJECT

The Direct object of a Verb receives the action of the Verb *directly*. You can substitute either "What?" or "Whom?" for the Object, and if the answer is the sentence itself, then the Object is Direct. For example, "I threw the ball." Question: "I threw what?" Answer: "I threw the ball." "The ball" is the Direct Object of the Verb "threw." In Latin and German, the Direct Object is in the Accusative Case.

The Direct Object of a Verb can also be a Noun Clause. For example, "I think (that) I will go to the game." Question: "I think what?" Answer: "(that) I will go to the game." "That," in parentheses, can be omitted in English, but *not* in the language you are studying. When the Direct Object is a person or persons, the question "Whom?" can be answered by the sentence. For example, "I saw Jane." Question: "I saw whom?" "I saw "Jane." (**Note:** "whom" is the Object form of "who.")

OBJECT (Continued)

The Direct Object of a Verb can never, I repeat *NEVER* be the Object of a Preposition.

Indirect OBJECT

The Indirect Object of a Verb receives the action indirectly, or as the Object of a Preposition. The Indirect Object can be identified by answering the question "to or for what?" or "to or for whom?" For example, "I threw the ball to Jane." Question: "I threw the ball *to whom*?" Answer: "to Jane." (I did not throw Jane, I threw the ball *to* Jane.) "Jane" is the Indirect Object of "threw."

Note: In English, the sentence could be written, "I threw Jane the ball." (See **ELLIPTICAL SENTENCE**) The Preposition "to" can be omitted, but it is clearly understood. If you have any doubt whether the Object is Direct or Indirect, use the question/answer method. See also the sections **TRANSITIVE** and **INTRANSITIVE** under **VERB**.

In Latin and German, the Indirect Object is usually in the Dative Case. Consult your text for the uses and Prepositions that govern the Case of the Object.

OBJECT of a Preposition

The Object of a Preposition can be a Noun or a Pronoun. It can be alone, with modifiers in a phrase, or as a clause. The Noun or Pronoun will always be in the Object form, and is known as the Objective Case in English. For example, "She gave the books to *me* and (to) *him*." When the object of the preposition is a pronoun used as the Indirect Object of a Verb, you need to be aware of the pronoun form and the position in the sentence in the language you are studying. In English the Pronoun Objects, both Direct and Indirect, always come *after* the verb. This is not the normal position in most cases in the language you are studying. For example, In the sentence above, "She gave the books to me," would appear in French and in Spanish in the following word order: "She to me gave the books." Latin and German will also have rules for the placement of Pronoun Objects. Practice the forms to understand and appreciate the *logic* of their use.

When a Pronoun is the Object of a Preposition and is separated from the verbal part of the sentence, the pronoun is called Disjunctive (Disjoined). Your text will give you the proper forms. (See the section, **DISJUNCTIVE**)

ORDINAL ADJECTIVE (See **ADJECTIVE**)

P

PARADIGM

A Paradigm is a list or table of inflections for Nouns, Pronouns, and Adjectives, called DECLENSION; for Verbs the forms are called CONJUGATION. The term is used mostly in the inflected languages, Latin and German. It is equally appropriate, however, in any language.

PARSING

This means describing a word or words grammatically, telling the part of speech, all the inflected forms, and syntactic relationships. Your textbook and your teacher will give you the specific details of what you are expected to do. It is used most often in Latin and German.

PARTICIPLE (See also **ADJECTIVE** and **VERB**)

The Participle "participates" in being at the same time both a Verb and an Adjective. In English the Participle does not show person or number. In the language you are studying, it will follow the rules for agreement of Adjectives when modifying a Noun or Pronoun. As verbs, Participles have tense and voice; they may take a Direct or Indirect Object or other construction used with a particular Verb. They may also be modified by an adverb or an adverbial phrase. There are four tenses of the Participle with which you need to be familiar. They are listed below alphabetically:

Future Active PARTICIPLE

You will study this form in Latin. It is translated as being "about to do something."

Future Passive PARTICIPLE

Used mainly in Latin. It is translated as an action "about to be done."

Past PARTICIPLE

This is the regular "ed" in English. It can be used as an adjective, for example, "the *baked* bread," or strictly as a verb in the compound tenses, for example, "They *have baked* the bread." It is usually the Fourth Principal Part of the Verb in Latin. (See **PRINCIPAL PARTS**)

When the Past Participle is used as an adjective, as in the example, "the *baked* bread," the Participle will follow all the rules for the Agreement of Adjectives.

In Latin the Adjective form of the Past Participle is also known as the Perfect Passsive Participle. The "baked bread," for example could be translated as the "bread, *having been baked*."

PARTICIPLE (Continued)

Present PARTICIPLE

The Present Participle is the "ing" form in English. In the verbal form it can take a Direct Object or other construction. For example, "He fell while *riding* his bike." There is a comparable form in the language you are studying.

As an Adjective, the Present Participle will follow all the rules for the agreement of Adjectives in the language you are studying.

It is also used in the Progressive forms in English. This can be quite confusing because the Progressive forms may not be directly translated in the language you are studying. For example, "I give," in English is very similar to the Progressive form "I am giving." You cannot translate "I am giving" literally in the language you are studying. It is simply the First Person Singular of the Present Tense.

Look carefully in your textbook for the ways to translate the tenses as you study them. Remember, the Present and Past Progressive forms in English cannot ordinarily be translated literally in the language you are studying.

PARTITIVE

This means "part," or it indicates a form of possession. For example, "John's book," is really "The book of John."

Another important aspect of the Partitive construction is the meaning of "some," or "any," which indicates a "part" of the whole. It may be formed by a combination of the Preposition "of" and singular or plural of the Definite Article.

PARTS OF SPEECH

There are eight Parts of Speech. Except for Interjection, all others are listed separately in this Glossary. Some grammarians do not consider the Interjection to be a true Part of Speech. The following is a very brief description of all the Parts of Speech (including Interjection).

NOUN: A person, place, or thing.

PRONOUN: Takes the place of a noun or another pronoun.

ADJECTIVE: Modifies a noun or pronoun.

VERB: Denotes action or a state of being.

PARTS OF SPEECH (Continued)

ADVERB: Modifies an adjective, verb, or another adverb.

PREPOSITION: A word or term that shows relationship between a word that follows it known as the object, and a word before it to which it is related.

CONJUNCTION: Joins or connects words, phrases, clauses, or sentences without establishing a relationship between or among the elements.

INTERJECTION: Denotes strong or sudden feeling and is an independent word, with no relationship to other parts of the sentence. It is not, as such, a true Part of Speech. It is usually punctuated with an Exclamation Point.

PASSIVE VOICE (See VOICE)

PASSIVE PERIPHRASTIC (Latin)
In spite of the horrendous name, the Passive Periphrastic conjugation is a combination of the Gerundive (Adjective) plus a form of "to be."

PAST (See TENSE)

PERFECT (See TENSE)

PERSON
There are three Persons, with both Subject and Object Forms:

	SINGULAR	
	Subject	**Object**
1st Person	I	Me
2nd Person	You (Thou)	You
3rd Person	He, She, It	Him, Her, It
	PLURAL	
1st Person	We	Us
2nd Person	You	You
3rd Person	They	Them

There are also Personal Possessive Adjectives and Pronouns. Memorize the forms and get in the habit of using them correctly. Whenever you hear the terms First, Second, or Third, think automatically of Personal Pronouns. Remember

PERSON (Continued)

also that the Second Person Singular in English is really "thou" and its corresponding forms. These forms are so rarely used that they are often not even listed in most grammars. The Second Plural form is used for both Singular and Plural. However, the Second Singular still remains in the language you are studying. The forms have specific uses under specific circumstances. Be sure to learn all of these uses.

PLUPERFECT (See TENSE)

PLURAL

An aspect of Number. Plural means two or more. The significance is in the formation of plurals. Be sure you are aware of the different ways, and also the rules for agreement of adjectives.

POSSESSIVE (See ADJECTIVE and PRONOUN)

PREDICATE

The Predicate is the part of a sentence that follows the Subject. In other words, the (finite) Verb and everything that follows. The importance of the Predicate has a lot to do with the type of Verb that is used: action or state of being. In Latin and German, the Case of Predicate Nouns, Pronouns and Adjectives will be determined by the type of Verb. (See COPULATIVE) In Spanish and French, you will have to be aware of the rules for agreement of Adjectives that modify the subject of the sentence.

PRESENT (See TENSE)

PREPOSITION

A Preposition is a word that joins or connects a noun or pronoun with a verb, adjective, or another noun or pronoun. The Preposition not only joins the elements, but also indicates a relationship between them. For example, "He spoke to the girl." The Preposition "to" connects the Verb "spoke" with the object of the Preposition, "girl."

In Latin and German, Prepositions determine the Case of the Nouns, Pronouns, and Adjectives that form the Prepositional Phrase. This is all explained in your textbook.

In English, the Preposition is sometimes understood and may be omitted. For example, in the sentence, "He threw John the ball," "John" is really "to John," which means that "John" is an Indirect Object. Be sure you know when the Preposition is understood in English, and how it affects the form of the Object. If you have any doubts, reconstruct the sentence and include any Prepositions you think may be omitted but understood in the English sentence.

PRETERITE (See **TENSE**)

PRINCIPAL PARTS OF THE VERB

In Latin, there are four Principal Parts of the Verb. You memorize all of them with each Verb. The Principal Parts provide you with the stem for all of the tenses in the verbal system. The process is very structured in Latin. Your teacher can give you a similar stem-system for the formation of the tenses in the language you are studying. If you try to memorize tenses without using a system, you will be doing too much work, and it will often be very frustrating. Learn and use the stem whenever possible. The endings are not difficult to master.

PROGRESSIVE (See **TENSE**)

PRONOUN

The definition of a Pronoun is deceptively simple: a Pronoun takes the place of a Noun, or another Pronoun. A thorough knowledge and understanding of all the different types of Pronouns and their uses is *absolutely indispensable*.

I will describe and explain alphabetically the different types of Pronouns and give you examples of their usage which will help you understand more clearly the logical and grammatical ways that these Pronouns fit into the structure of the language you are studying.

Conjunctive PRONOUN

The Conjunctive Pronoun is joined or connected to the Verb. (The Disjunctive Pronouns are not joined or connected to the Verb) For example, "I gave *it* to *him*." "It," and "him" are Conjunctive Pronouns; they are both Objects of the Verb "gave."

Demonstrative PRONOUN

This is similar to the Demonstrative Adjective. The forms in English are "this," "that," "these," "those," "the former," and "the latter." They are called Demonstrative because they point out, show, or demonstrate. You can distinguish the Demonstrative Pronoun from the Demonstrative Adjective by the fact that the Adjective will *always* be followed by a noun. For example, "This book," "these people." The Pronoun takes the place of the Noun and is simply "this," (implying "this book") and "these" (implying "these people"). Your textbook has the forms of the Demonstrative Pronouns in the language you are studying.

Disjunctive PRONOUN

A Disjunctive Pronoun is a Pronoun Object that is *not* joined or connected to the Verb. The Disjunctive Pronoun can be the object of a Preposition, or it can

PRONOUN (Continued)

be used alone for emphasis along with the regular Subject or Object of the Verb. For example, "I, I will not go under any circumstances." The first "I" is used for emphasis. It is Disjunctive. "This present is for *them*." "Them" is also Disjunctive. It is the Object of the Preposition "for."

Some of the Disjunctive Pronouns in English will be in the Subjective Case, for example, "*I*, I will not go..." "I" is in the Subjective Case (Objective Case would be "me"). It may be different in the language you are studying. Be sure you know the rules.

Indefinite PRONOUN

The Indefinite Pronoun conveys a general or indefinite idea or impression. It is used specifically to avoid the use of a Noun. The most common Indefinite Pronouns in English are "somebody," "anybody," "everybody," "nobody," "something, "anything," "nothing," "anyone," "someone," "no one," "none," "several," and "some." These Pronouns have a variety of different forms in the language you are studying, particularly the negative forms, "nobody," and "nothing." Review them very carefully and be sure you understand how the negatives are used. In English, a double negative makes the expression positive, as in "Nobody never goes there," actually means "Somebody goes there." In the language you are studying you may find that the negative form of the Indefinite Pronoun can be used with another negative component, which gives the appearance of a double negative. It is not the same in English.

Intensive PRONOUN

By now you should have the idea that the names of these Pronouns are exactly what they imply. An Intensive Pronoun "intensifies" or strongly "emphasizes" another Pronoun or Noun. For example, "I, myself, saw the accident." The subject "I" is intensified or emphasized by the addition of the "myself." The Intensive Pronouns are:

	Singular	Plural
1st Person	Myself	Ourselves
2nd Person	Thyself, Yourself	Yourselves
3rd Person	Himself, Herself, Itself	Themselves

PRONOUN (Continued)

Remember, they "intensify," and "emphasize." Another example, "He did it himself," or "He, himself, did it."

There is a tendency to confuse the Intensive Pronoun with the Reflexive Pronoun. They look alike, but the Reflexive Pronoun is the Direct or Indirect Object of a Verb. More on this below in the section on Reflexive Pronouns.

Interrogative PRONOUN

The Interrogative Pronoun asks for an explanation of a situation that tends to be somewhat indefinite, but nevertheless expects an answer. The Interrogative Pronoun can refer to both persons and things. It can be the Subject of the sentence, the Direct or Indirect Object of a Verb. The Table below describes the Interrogative Pronoun in all of its possible forms in English. It should give you the information you need in order to use the correct form of the Interrogative Pronoun in the language you are studying. Use the Table as a guide to determine which Interrogative Pronoun you should use.

	Subject	Direct Object	Indirect Object
Person	Who	Whom	Whom
	Which	Which	Whose
			Which (One, Ones)
Thing	What	What	What
	Which	Which	Which (One, Ones)

There is no difference between the Singular and the Plural forms of the Interrogative Pronouns above. The form "Which (One)" or"Which (Ones)," in which the word "One," or "Ones" is usually implied, is the same in English for both persons and things.

One glance at the Table and you can see the difficulty. Except for "who" and "whom," there are no differences among the forms. (Even "who" and "whom" have lost much of their grammatical difference.) However, this is not at all the case in the language you are studying. The forms are different and you have to know why they are different, and what the correct forms are. This requires some memorization, plus the ability to know immediately the difference between a Subject, Direct and Indirect Object. For example, in the sentence, "*What* do you want?" "*What*" is the Direct Object of the

PRONOUN (Continued)

Verb "want."

And let's not forget "*Whose*?" Think of it as a combination of "to" or "of whom." For example, "Whose son are you?" can be reworded as, "Of whom are you the son?" Awkward? Yes, but it will help you understand how to translate the Interrogative "Whose" in the language you are studying. "*Whose*" is always indirect. *It denotes possession.* If you remember that much, and always reword "whose" using the proper Preposition, you will arrive at the proper translation.

Reconstruct the Table with the proper forms of the Interrogative Pronouns in the language you are studying Add the Plural forms. Use examples. Remember, the difference between a Direct or Indirect Object.

This represents a brief overview of the Interrogative Pronoun. It contains a great deal of grammatical content with which you must be familiar. Use the Table and lots of examples. Reword English sentences so you can understand the concepts more clearly. Once you break down the English form into its grammatical parts, you will understand the intricacies of this subject.

Personal and **Possessive PRONOUNS**

The Personal Pronouns refer to persons, with the exception of "it," which can refer to things or ideas. The Personal Pronouns can be Subject, Object, or Possessive. See the Table below:

Singular	Subject	Object	Possessive
1st Person	I	Me	Mine
2nd Person	You (Thou)	You (Thee)	Yours
3rd Person	He, She, It	Him, Her, It	His, Hers, Its
Plural			
1st Person	We	Us	Ours
2nd Person	You	You	Yours
3rd Person	They	Them	Theirs

The only real problem you might have with the Personal Pronouns could be with the Object forms. In English we use the Subject at times when you might be required to use an Object form in the language you are studying. For example, "It is *he*," is correct in English, but might require the Object form in the language you are studying.

PRONOUN (Continued)

Use the Table above as a model. Construct the proper forms in the language you are studying. In Latin and German, you will have to know the different Case forms for all of the Personal and Possessive Pronouns.

Reflexive PRONOUN

The Reflexive Pronoun looks like the Intensive Pronoun. See the Table below:

	Singular	Plural
1st Person	Myself	Ourselves
2nd Person	Yourself (Thyself)	Yourselves
3rd Person	Himself, Herself, Itself	Themselves

Reflexive Pronouns differ from Intensive Pronouns in one important aspect: the *Reflexive pronoun is either the Direct or Indirect Object of the Verb* while the Intensive Pronoun "intensifies" or "emphasizes" the Noun or Pronoun, which may be either Subject or Object of a Verb, or in a Prepositional phrase. "Reflexive" means "reflect." The action of the Verb is "reflected" back to the Subject of that Verb. For example, "He likes himself." Question: "He likes whom?" Answer: "He likes himself." "He" and "himself" are the same. "Himself" is the Direct Object of the Verb "likes." The Reflexive Pronoun is either a Direct or Indirect Object. This can be an important distinction to make if (as in French) there is a question of Agreement of the Past Participle with a preceding Direct Object.

When a Verb is used with a Reflexive Pronoun, the Verb is called Reflexive. This is not as important in English as in Spanish, French, and Latin, and to a lesser extent in German. The use of a Reflexive Pronoun can change the meaning of a Verb. Be aware of this when you come across the Verb in a Vocabulary Section or a reading assignment. When the meaning changes by the use of a Reflexive Pronoun, *be sure to memorize the verb and the Reflexive Pronoun* together with the meaning. The fact that we don't use the Reflexive Pronoun as extensively in English can be somewhat confusing. There is logic, however, in the presence of the Reflexive Pronoun. If it gives you a problem, get in the habit of reconstructing (rewording) the English to include the Reflexive Pronoun. For

PRONOUN (Continued)

example, in English the verb "to wonder" in French becomes "to ask oneself." It is Reflexive. When "I wonder about something," I really "ask myself about something." If you become accustomed to rewording, you will appreciate the logic of the Reflexive forms.

Relative PRONOUN

The Relative Pronoun *relates* which is another way to say "is *associated with.*" It is *associated with* an *antecedent,* which is the word or words that precede the Relative Pronoun. The Relative Pronoun introduces a Relative Clause.

Note: The Relative Clause is *always an adjective clause.* It modifies the *Antecedent.*

The Relative Clause is *always* Dependent (Subordinate).

The following is an example of a sentence with a Relative Pronoun and, of course, a Relative Clause. "The girl *who lives next door* is my friend." I have underlined the Relative Clause. The Relative Pronoun is "who." The *Antecedent* is "girl." The clause "who lives next door," is a Relative (Adjective) Clause, and it modifies the Antecedent, "girl." The Main Clause, the one that can stand alone (Independent) is "The girl is my friend."

Another important aspect of the Relative Pronoun in the sentence above is that "who" is the *Subject* of the Verb in the Relative Clause. You should also recognize that the antecedent "girl" is Feminine Singular. The form of the Relative Pronoun often depends on the syntax of the Antecedent, and also whether the Relative Pronoun is the Subject, Direct or Indirect Object of the Verb in the Relative Clause.

Stated as a Rule: The Relative Pronoun gets its Person (1st, 2nd, or 3rd), Gender (Masculine, Feminine or Neuter) and Number (Singular or Plural) from the Antecedent; the Case (Subject, Direct or Indirect Object in Spanish and French; Nominative, Genitive, Dative, Accusative or Ablative in Latin and German) is determined by the use of the Relative Pronoun in the Relative Clause. If you remember this rule, you will understand the absolute essence of how to use a Relative Pronoun.

To state the rule more succinctly: *THE RELATIVE PRONOUN gets PERSON, GENDER, and NUMBER from the ANTECEDENT. CASE is determined by its USE IN THE RELATIVE CLAUSE.*

PRONOUN (Continued)

Let's illustrate by going back to the example on the preceding page: "The girl <u>who</u> lives next door is my friend." The problem with the English sentence is that you get no clues from the Pronoun itself ("who") as to its Person, Gender, or Number; we do know, however, that the form "who" has to be the Subject (Nominative in Latin and German). The Antecedent is "girl," and therefore the Relative Pronoun has to be 3rd Person, Feminine, Singular. Since we know that the Relative Pronoun is 3rd Person Singular, and also the Subject of the Verb in the Relative Clause, then the Verb in the Relative Clause has to be 3rd Person Singular in order to agree with the Subject which is, of course, the Relative Pronoun "who." In other words, the Verb "lives" is 3rd Person Singular because "who" is 3rd Person Singular. If "who" were 3rd Person Plural (the sentence would be "The *girls* who *live* next door are my friends.") notice that the Verb in the Relative Clause becomes "live," which is 3rd Person Plural.

If the Antecedent is 1st Person Singular, and the Relative Pronoun remains Subject, for example, "It is *I who* am here today." The Verb "am" agrees with the Relative Pronoun "who," which is the First Person Singular Subject of "am" the Verb in the Relative Clause.

If this seems complicated, it will become much easier with practice. Always identify the Antecedent and get the information you need. Separate the Relative Clause from the rest of the sentence and you will quickly learn the Case. Now you have *all* the *information* you need. The next step is to select the precise form of the Relative Pronoun for the language you are studying. The following Table should be helpful. Change all the English forms to those used in the language you are studying. In Latin and German, look up the Declensions in your text.

Note how few clues you get from the forms in English.

Antecedent	Subject	Direct Object	Indirect Object
Person(s)	who, that	whom, that	whom, whose, that
Thing(s)	which, that	which, that	which, whose, that

PRONOUN (Continued)

"Whose" denotes possession, and can refer to both persons and things. For example, "The book whose cover is brown is mine," or "I saw the boy whose sister won the contest."

Remember, the Indirect Object forms are always the Object of a Preposition. For example, "The man *to whom* you spoke is my brother."

Another small problem you might encounter in the use of Relative Pronouns is that the Relative Pronoun can often be omitted in English. For example, "The book you want is on the table." The Relative Pronoun, "that," or "which" is omitted, but clearly understood. "The book (that or which) you want is on the table." *You cannot omit the Relative Pronoun in the language you are studying.* How do you know when it has been omitted? Whenever you have a Dependent Clause in a sentence in English with no Pronoun, Adverb, or Conjunction preceding it (introducing it) then the Pronoun, Adverb, or Conjunction has been omitted. You have to reconstruct the sentence including the Pronoun, Adverb, or Conjunction. In a short time you will know immediately every time the omission occurs.

Note: The word *"what"* can be used as a Compound form of a Relative Pronoun. When it is used as such, it can be reworded in English to "that which," for example, "I like *what* (that which) you are doing." The Relative Pronoun is "which," and the Antecedent is "that." Consult your textbook for the proper use of this construction in the language you are studying.

Reciprocal PRONOUN

"Reciprocal" means "mutual." What happens to one happens to the other. The Reciprocal Pronouns are "each other," and "one another." They are often used without any differentiation, however, "each other" may often refer to two, while "one another" refers to more than two. Each language has its own convention for the use of Reciprocal Pronouns. Look up the exact usage for the language you are studying.

R

REFLEXIVE PRONOUN (See **PRONOUN**)

REGULAR VERB (See **VERB**)

RELATIVE PRONOUN (See **PRONOUN**)

RESULT CLAUSE (See **CLAUSE**)

S

SENTENCE: Simple, Compound, Complex

Simple SENTENCE

The Simple Sentence expresses a *single idea*. The minimum requirement for a Simple Sentence is a Subject and a Predicate. For example, "Jane runs." In the case of an Imperative (command) the Subject is understood. For example, "Run." The Subject that is understood is "You."

Compound SENTENCE

The Compound Sentence contains two or more separate ideas joined by a Coordinating Conjunction (the most typical are "and," "but," "both," "or"). For example, "John bought a book, *and* I bought a magazine." These are two separate ideas each with a separate Subject and a separate Predicate *joined* by the Coordinating Conjunction "and."

Complex SENTENCE

A Complex Sentence contains a Main (Independent) Clause, and one or more Subordinate (Dependent) Clauses. The Dependent Clause may be introduced by a Pronoun, Adverb, or Subordinating Conjunction. These are the types of sentences that you need to understand in detail, mainly because the Pronoun, or Subordinating Conjunction may be omitted (but clearly understood) in the English Sentence. For example, the Complex Sentence, "I think that John will win the match," could also be written, "I think John will win the match." In the second version, the Subordinate Conjunction "that" has been omitted, which can be confusing since the Subordinate Conjunction *cannot* be omitted in the language you are studying.

Relative Pronouns can also be omitted in English but not in the language you are studying. In fact, I omitted the Relative Pronoun in the expression I just used, "the language (which or that) you are studying.

Determine whether a Relative Pronoun or a Subordinate Conjunction has been omitted in English. If so, reword the Sentence by inserting the omitted Pronoun or Conjunction. Become accustomed to doing this and many of the problems associated with Complex Sentences will no longer exist.

SEQUENCE OF TENSES

This relates to Complex Sentences. There are specific rules for various constructions which you will be required to learn in the language you are studying. The sequence represents a logical relationship of time as expressed by the Verb Tenses. The possible difficulty you may have is that the same Sequence or logic may not be what you find in the English sentence. Be aware of what the Sequence is in the language you are studying, and also the logic for the Sequence. For example, in the sentence, "I hope (that) my father comes home this evening," in French would require the use of a future tense in the Dependent Clause. "I hope my father *will come* home this evening." The logic is that "my father" has not yet come home, therefore the thought should be expressed in the future. In English, either the present or the future would be acceptable.

You will find that there is more leeway in the use of Tense Sequence in English than in the Language you are studying.

SIGN

This is the Preposition "to," used in connection with an Infinitive in English. The Infinitive is always given with the Sign, "*to* run," "*to* dance," "*to* love," etc. The Sign does what signs do, they *tell* us something. In this case, the Sign tells us that the Verb is an Infinitive (See VERB for the difference between the Infinitive and the Finite form of Verbs). Can we have an Infinitive without a Sign in English? Yes. For example, "His mother made him *eat* his vegetables." "*Eat*" is a complementary Infinitive, without the use of the Sign. I mention it because, with the exception of German, the other languages (French, Spanish, and Latin) do not use a Sign or Preposition with the Infinitive. Therefore, you have to be able to recognize the Infinitive in some other way. The *Ending* will tell you whether the Verb form is an Infinitive. In each language, the *Ending* of the Infinitive will also tell you which Classification or more appropriately, which Conjugation the Verb belongs to.

Remember, the *Ending*, not the Sign, will tell whether the Verb is an Infinitive.

SIMPLE SENTENCE (See SENTENCE)

SIMPLE TENSE (See TENSE)

SINGULAR

This is used to designate NUMBER. Singular is obviously One. But you have to be consciously aware of what the Singular forms are for Nouns, Pronouns, and Adjectives, and the Singular Verb forms for the proper agreement of Subject and Verb. Remind yourself consistently that some part of the sentence is either Singular or Plural.

STEM

The Stem is the base-part of the word to which an ending is added. The Stem plus the Ending (or Inflection) form the whole word. We don't think of Stems in English as much as you have to in the language you are studying. In Spanish and French, the Stem is mainly used with the Verb System. In Latin and German, the Stem is important for Verbs, Nouns, Pronouns, and Adjectives. The Stems follow definite patterns and give you clues to various regularities and irregularities in Conjugations and Declensions.

STRONG VERB (See VERB)

SUBJECT

The Subject of a Sentence, Clause, or Infinitive is a word or words that require a Verb to express a thought, action, or state of being. In other words, the "Subject" is always "the Subject of something," and the "something" is some form of a Finite Verb or an Infinitive. In Latin and German the Subject of a Finite Verb is always in the Nominative Case, while the Subject of an Infinitive in Latin, German, and English is in the Accusative (or Objective) Case.

The Subject of a Finite Verb in French or Spanish is in practically all respects similar to English. You should have no difficulty with the translation. The Subject of an Infinitive is a different matter. When the Subject of the Main Clause and the Subject of the Infinitive are the same, it is often permissable to use the Infinitive in your translation. For example, "I want to swim." If I change the Infinitive to a Dependent Clause, it would read, "I want that I swim." I realize how awkward it is, however, it does illustrate the same Subject in both the Main Clause and the Dependent Clause: "I." If I change the Subject in the Dependent Clause, for example, "I want him to swim," we have a different situation. You cannot use the Objective (or Accusative) form "him" as the Subject of an Infinitive in French or Spanish. You must use a Dependent Clause. It would be, "I want that he swim." It sounds awkward in English, but it makes no difference.

Remember, when the Subject of an Infinitive in French and Spanish is different from the Subject in the Main Clause, convert the Infinitive to a Finite Verb in a Dependent Clause; The Subject of the Infinitive becomes the Subject of the Dependent Clause. Avoid the tendency to try for a literal translation, which in this case will not work.

SUBJUNCTIVE (See MOOD, VERB)

SUBORDINATE CLAUSE (See CLAUSE)

SUBORDINATE CONJUNCTION (See CONJUNCTION)

SUBSTANTIVE

Another expression for Nouns and other words or word groups used as Nouns.

SUPERLATIVE DEGREE (See **COMPARISON**)

SUPINE (Latin)

The Supine is a Noun form derived from a Verb and used only in the Accusative, Dative, or Ablative Case.

SYNOPSIS OF A VERB (Pertains mainly to Latin)

This is the arrangement or Conjugation of a Verb in one Person and Number only in all or specifically designated tenses. For example, a Synopsis of the Verb "to see" in the Present and Future Indicative, Third Person Singular would be, "he sees," and "he will see." A complete Synopsis would include all Verb Tenses. The purpose is to test your knowledge of the Verbal System.

SYNTAX

Syntax is often used synonomously and incorrectly with Grammar. Syntax essentially means explaining the word relationships in a Sentence, Clause, or Phrase, according to the Rules of Grammar. Grammar is the more inclusive term. Your teacher might ask you to explain the Syntax of a particular word or construction. The explanation would be based on the Rules of Grammar.

T

TENSE

Tense means "Time." It is deceptively simple. The problem is that the Tenses in English are not identical to the system of Tenses used in the language you are studying and it makes translating somewhat difficult. In many respects, the English Tenses tend to create most of the problem because you expect to make direct translations of forms and constructions that either may not exist or cannot be translated literally. What I will do in this section is take each Tense or Tense-related concept separately, explain its use, and what the counterpart is in English. The Tenses and related concepts will be discussed alphabetically.

Anterior TENSE

An Anterior Tense is another way of saying Past Tense.

Compound TENSE

A Compound Tense is formed by the use of some form of the Auxiliary plus a Past Participle. For example, "I have eaten." The Auxiliary is "have," and the Past

TENSE (Continued)

Participle is "eaten." Together they form a Compound Tense, which implies more than one component part.

Conditional TENSE

This is the "should" or "would" form of the verb. In English "should" and "would" are Auxiliaries used with what looks like the Infinitive without the "to" sign. For example, "He *would* go to the game, if he had a ticket." In English, this Conditional statement is expressed in a Compound form. In the language you are studying, a Conditional statement is expressed as a Simple Tense, or as a single form. The Conditional Tense is most often used in the Result Clause of a sentence that contains an "if" statement and the Result that would take place. For example, "*If* you had the tickets, I *would* go with you." The Conditional Tense is used in the "I would go with you" Clause, which is the Result or what would happen "if" something else ("you had the tickets") took place.

Note the Sequence of Tenses in the two clauses: Past (Imperfect) in the "if" Clause, and Conditional in the Result Clause. This is an important aspect of the use of the Conditional Tense. It is part of a Sequence that follows a pattern similar to the requirement in French as follows:

TABLE		
	"IF" CLAUSE	"RESULT" CLAUSE
Example:	**Present** If you *have* the tickets,	**Future** I *will go* with you.
Example:	**Past (Imperfect)** If you *had* the tickets,	**Conditional** I *would go* with you.
Example:	**Pluperfect** If you *had had* the tickets,	**Conditional Perfect** I *would have gone* with you.

Be sure you know what the requirments are in the language you are studying. In Latin the Mood changes to Subjunctive in the Conditional Sentence (includes both the "if" and the Result Clause). In German, the Subjunctive is also used in some Conditional Clauses when there is an element of doubt or improbability, while in English the Subjunctive Mood is used in Conditions that are Contrary to Fact.

TENSE (Continued)

Note: Do not confuse the use of the Conditional auxiliary "should" with the use of "should" meaning "obligation." For example, "I *should* leave early," implies obligation and can be reworded as "ought to." "I *ought to* leave early." See your textbook for the correct use of this type of statement.

Conditional Perfect TENSE

This is also known as the Past Conditional, which means that the Condition "would have existed" under a set of possible circumstances. Look at the second example in the Table above and notice the Sequence of Tenses. The Conditional Perfect Tense is a Compound Tense, which means that the Verbal expression will have an Auxiliary plus a Participle.

The Syntax of Conditional and Conditional Perfect Sentences will vary depending upon the language you are studying. See your textbook for the rules.

Future TENSE

The Future Tense is used to describe an action or a state of being that *will* occur at some point in time beyond the immediate Present. The Future is expressed in English by the Auxiliary "shall" or "will." German also uses an Auxiliary to form the Future Tense. Spanish, French, and Latin *do not*.

There are times when the Future Tense *must* be used in the language you are studying, but in English either a Present or Future Tense may be used. For example, in French, the Future Tense is used after the Adverb "when." In English we say, "When he arrives (Present) we will leave." In French, the wording is "When he *will arrive*, we will leave." The logic for the use of the Future in the French is based on the fact that the action (arriving) has not yet taken place, and should therefore be considered as a Future action. In English the Present *can* express an action or state of being that may have a Future aspect or connotation. Unfortunately, tenses in English cannot always be literally translated into the language you are studying.

Future Perfect TENSE

The term Perfect always means "Past." Future Perfect means Future in the Past. If that sounds like a contradiction in terms, it is really perfectly logical. To illustrate, consider the three divisions of time: Past, Present, and Future. Let's take the Past as a separate time span or entity. Every action or state of being that falls into the Past is over, done, complete.

TENSE (Continued)

That is a given definition, and we accept it. The next step is to look more closely at the actions or states of being that are expressed in the Past. Some may be *more* Past than others and we call them Pluperfect. "Plu" means "more." "Pluperfect" means "more than Perfect," or in strict grammatical language, "more than Past." An example is "When I came home, my brother *had eaten*." Both tenses are Past. But something happened even before "I came home." Something is even "more" Past than the statement "I came home." In other words, the "more than" Past action was over, and then "I came home." (See the section on **Pluperfect**)

If an action or state of being can be "more" than Past in the Past, why not have an action or state of being that *will* be over, done, complete, *after* something else has happened in the Past? In other words, a Future in the Past, in grammatical terms, a Future Perfect. For example, "When I come home, my brother *will have eaten*." In other words, *after* I come home, something else, some other action which has not yet taken place (Future), will be over (Past). Otherwise known as the Future Perfect--Future in the Past.

In using the Future Perfect, check the rules for the Sequence of Tenses that you should follow. The Future Perfect is always used in relation to another Tense.

Historical Present TENSE

At times, a writer or author will use the Present Tense to describe a Past action in order to make it seem more immediate and vivid.

Imperfect Indicative TENSE

This Past Tense does not have an exact counterpart in English. "Imperfect" means "not Perfect," in the sense that the actual beginning or completion of the action or state of being *cannot* be precisely pinpointed as to when it took place in the Past. For example, the sentence, "I fell," or "I have fallen," leaves no doubt whatsoever about the fact that at a specfic point in the Past, "I fell." That's it. It's over, and done.

But if I said, "When I *was* young, I *used to fall*," or "I often *fell*," I would be describing, I repeat DESCRIBING something that does not have a neat, precise beginning and endpoint in the Past in the same way that a statement such as "Yesterday, I fell and bruised my arm" is Past. "I used to fall," or I often fell" have no specific beginning or ending. All we know is that the action is over, done, and in the Past. In a sense,

TENSE (Continued)

"I used to fall," or "I often fell" are DESCRIPTIVE statements. They DESCRIBE a characteristic of me over a non-specific period of time in the Past.

The Imperfect Tense is also called the Past Descriptive Tense. When a writer chooses to use it he wants to be more descriptive. In English the Imperfect is implied when "was," "were," or "used to" are used.

In the first part of the example above, "When I *was* young," "*was*" describes a state of being in the Past. There is no definite point in time when I started being "young," or when I stopped being "young." All we know is that I am no longer "young." Being "young" for me is over. It is Past. But not in the same sense that a statement such as "Yesterday I fell and bruised my arm," is Past.

Remember, we do not have an exact counterpart of the Imperfect Tense in English. You have to recognize it in the ways I noted above. Be aware of it when you come across it in your reading assignments. With practice, you should become quite accustomed to using it properly and appreciating its descriptive quality.

Imperfect Subjunctive TENSE (See also **MOOD, SUBJUNCTIVE**)
This Tense is usually used in specific Sequences that are related to the rules for the use of the Subjunctive in the language you are studying.

Past Definite TENSE
This is the designation of a simple (meaning a single form) Past Tense, which in French is used primarily in literary works. In other words, it is practically never used in the spoken language. You have to learn it (the stem plus endings) because it will appear in much of what you read.

Past Indefinite TENSE
This is a Compound Tense, similar to the Present Perfect in English. It is formed by the Present Tense of the Auxiliary Verb plus the Past Participle. For example, "I have eaten." The Auxiliary in the Present Tense is "have"; the past participle is "eaten." In French, the Past Definite is also used to translate the Simple Past. "I ate," in English would become "I have eaten" in French.

Past Perfect TENSE (See **PLUPERFECT**)
The Past Perfect is formed by the Past tense of the Auxiliary plus the Past Participle. For example,

"They *had eaten*, when I came home." It is really a Past in the Past, or "more than Past." See the section on PLUPERFECT for a more detailed description.

Past Subjunctive TENSE

See your textbook for the proper use of the Past Subjunctive. See also the section on the Subjunctive in this Glossary.

Perfect TENSE

Perfect means Past. In English, the Perfect is used in combination with Past (Perfect), Present (Perfect), and Future (Perfect). Each is a Compound Tense. The Past, Present, and Future are the Tenses of the Auxiliary Verb. For example, the Verb "to eat"

Past Perfect	I *had* eaten.
Present Perfect	I *have* eaten
Future Perfect	I *shall have* eaten

The Past Perfect is also known as the Pluperfect, more than Past. (See **Pluperfect TENSE**)

The Present Perfect is not the usual term for this Compound Tense in the language you are studying. Consult your textbook for the correct designation.

Remember: *Perfect* means *Past.*

Pluperfect Indicative TENSE

This is the same as the Past Perfect in English. It is a Compound Tense, with the Auxiliary in the Past Tense. For example, "I *had* eaten."

Pluperfect means "more Past." It means that an action or state of being existed *before* another action or state of being took place. For example, "When my brother *came* home (Past action), I *had* already *eaten*." The action "*had eaten*" took place *before* "my brother came home." Both actions are Past; one action is "more Past" than the other. "Had eaten" is more Past, and is therefore called Pluperfect, which means "more Past." Consult your textbook for the proper form of the Pluperfect in the language you are studying.

Pluperfect Subjunctive TENSE (See also **MOOD, SUBJUNCTIVE**)

Consult your textbook for the appropriate Tense Sequence and other conditions under which the Pluperfect Subjunctive should be used.

TENSE (Continued)

Present Indicative TENSE

The Present Indicative Tense describes an action or state of being that exists now, or in certain constructions as a near Future. As simple as it may seem, the Present Tense can be confusing due to the several ways it can be expressed in English that cannot be literally translated in the language you are studying. For example, the Present Tense of "to give" in English can be: "I give," "I do give," and "I am giving." Each is the Present Tense and would usually be translated as a single, simple tense in the language you are studying. The problem is that in English the Present Tense can be expressed as a Simple Tense ("I give"), or as a Compound Tense ("I do give," or "I am giving."). The form "I am giving," is Progressive (see **PROGRESSIVE**). Consult your textbook for the correct translation of this form of the Present Tense.

The Present Tense in English can also be used at times when the Future could be required in the language you are studying. For example, "When *I see* you, I will give you the book." The Verb *"see"* in the first part of the sentence is in the Present Tense, but clearly has Future meaning.

Present Subjunctive TENSE (See also **MOOD, SUBJUNCTIVE**)

Consult your textbook for the proper use of the Present Subjunctive.

Present Perfect TENSE

The Present Perfect is a Compound Tense formed by the Present Tense of the Auxiliary and the Past Participle. Consult your textbook for the proper use of this tense in the language you are studying.

Preterite Indicative TENSE

This is the Simple (meaning no use of an Auxiliary) Past Tense. For example, "I gave." The Preterit is usually used to translate a Simple Past action; it can also be used to translate the Present Perfect in English, " I have given," and also "I did give."

PROGRESSIVE CONJUGATION

The Progressive construction is formed with an Auxiliary and the "ing" form of the Verb. For example, "I am giving," "I have been giving," "I was giving," "I will be giving," etc. These are troublesome forms because there are few exact counterparts in the language you are studying. "I am giving" is usually considered as a Simple Present Indicative Tense, and would be translated as if it were, "I give," or "I do

TENSE (Continued)

give." There are ways to translate the Progressive idea in the language you are studying, but the translation will not likely be a direct counterpart of the Progressive form in English.

Consult your textbook for the best ways to translate the Progressive forms. For example, "I was giving," would likely be translated by the Imperfect Tense.

SEQUENCE (See SEQUENCE OF TENSES)

SIMPLE TENSES

The Simple Tenses require a single Verb form to express an action or state of being. For example, "I give" is a Simple Tense. Compound Tenses require some form of an Auxiliary Verb plus a Participle to express an action or state of being. For example, "I have given," or "I have been giving." A Verb Tense can be either Simple or Compound.

The problem you may encounter is the use of a Simple or Compound Tense in English, and the opposite in the language you are studying. For example, "I have given" (Compound) may be translated by a Simple Past Tense in the language you are studying. As you become more familiar with the Verb System in both languages, the difficulties will diminish.

THIRD PERSON (See PERSON)

V

VERB

A Verb is used to express an action or a state of being. It is the one indispensable Part of Speech. There can be no sentence without a Verb. Even if the Verb is missing, it is still there. It is *understood*. You can't get rid of it.

AGREEMENT

There are two main Agreement functions associated with Verbs. The first is the Agreement between Subject and Verb. For example, "He gives," has a Subject that is Third Person Singular ("He"), and a Verb that is also Third Person Singular ("gives"). Although this may seem quite simple to understand, you need to be able to *identify the subject of every verb*. For example, what are the Subjects of the Verbs in the following sentence: "The book that *has fallen* from the shelf *is* now on the floor." The Subject of the first Verb, "has fallen" is

B 50

VERB (Continued)

the Relative Pronoun, "that." The Person and Number of the Subject "that" are Third Person, Singular. The Verb "has fallen" must agree with the Subject; "has fallen" is therefore Third Person, Singular.

If you were confused by the Relative Pronoun, refer to the section on **Relative PRONOUN** under **PRONOUN**.

The Subject of the other Verb is "book," which is Third Person, Singular; the verb "is," therefore *agrees* with its Subject.

Be certain that you locate the subject of every Verb in the sentence. Be certain to check the Agreement of every Verb-Subject combination in the sentence.

Agreement can also involve the Past Participle. Consult your textbook for the appropriate rules, and look up any terms you do not understand in this Glossary.

Auxiliary VERB

An Auxiliary Verb is used with any Compound Verb form. In English the Auxiliary can be any form of "to be" or "to have," plus all the forms of "can," "do," "may," "must," "shall," and "will." You should not have any problems with the forms of "to be," and "to have." For the most part, these Auxiliaries can be translated, however, "can," "do," "may," and "must" will have separate rules for their use in a sentence; "shall," and "will" are used with Future constructions.

In other words, be sure you know what the English Auxiliary couterparts are in the language you are studying. There are times when a form of "to have" will be translated with a form of "to be." For example, the intransitive expression "I have gone," requires the use of the Auxiliary "to be" in the French translation. The Auxiliaries are extremely important, and will be troublesome if you do not know precisely when and where to use them, which ones to use, and what forms they should take.

Causative VERB

This means "causing" something to happen. The Causative idea is mainly expressed by placing the Auxiliary "make," "have," or "get" before the Infinitive of the Verb in question. For example, "He makes (causes) me laugh," or "He got (caused) me to laugh," or "He had (caused) me put the books on the shelf." Consult your textbook for the correct use of this construction in the language you are studying.

VERB (Continued)

Copulative VERB (COPULA)

The Copula joins the Predicate to the Subject by means of the Verb "to be." For example, "My father *is* a carpenter," "He is good," or "They are tall." The Copula announces the Predicate. It is not itself a "predicate," it merely *links* the Predicate to the Subject. In addition to the forms of "to be" there are a number of other Linking Verbs that are "Copulative," such as "seem," "look," "get," etc. Consult your text-book for the proper use of each of these Copulative Verbs in the language you are studying.

Defective VERB

A Defective Verb lacks one or more parts needed to form a complete Conjugation. All of the Auxiliaries except "to do," and "to have" are defective. Defective Verbs in English may not necessarily be defective in the language you are studying, and vice versa.

Finite VERB

A Finite Verb is limited or restricted by Person and Number and can therefore be the Predicate of a sentence. For example, "They give." The Verb "give" is Finite. It is Third Person, Plural. It is also the Predicate of the sentence. The word "finite" literally means something that can be measured. In the grammatical sense the measurements are Person and Number.

Infinitives and Participles are not Finite which means they are not limited or bounded by Person or Number, and as such cannot function as the Predicate of a sentence.

INFINITIVE

The Infinitive is literally and gramatically "infinite" in the sense that it is not limited, restricted, or bounded by Person or Number. (See **Finite VERB** above). In English, the Infinitive is usually identified by the sign "to." For example, "I like *to swim*." You will identify the Infinitive in the language you are study-ing by the ending of the Verb, rather than by the use of a Preposition.

The following are several important aspects of the Infinitive that you need to understand:

• *The Subject of a Dependent Infinitive.* For example, "I want *him* to play." In English, Latin, and German, the Subject of the Infinitive can be expressed in the Accusative or Objective Case as in the example above. In Spanish and French, when the Subject of an

VERB (Continued)

Infinitive is different from the Subject of the Verb in the Main Clause, the Subject of the Infinitive becomes the Subject of a Dependent Clause, and the Infinitive becomes Finite. To illustrate, the sentence "I want him to play," must be translated as "I want *that he play*," as awkward as it may seem.

● *Tenses of the Infinitive.* There are three Tenses of the Infinitive that may be used regardless of the Tense of the Main Verb. They are:

Present Infinitive: indicates **the same time** as that of the Main Verb. For example, "I like (Present) *to swim*," or "I liked (Past) *to swim*." In both examples, the Present Infinitive is used to indicate either the Present or the Past time of the Main Verb, "I like," or "I liked."

Perfect Infinitive: indicates *time before* that of the Main Verb. For example, "He is sorry *to have lost* the match." He lost the match *before* he became sorry.

Furure Infinitive: indicates time *after* that of the Main Verb. This is used mainly in Latin. For example, "I think he is *about to throw* a forward pass." He has not yet thrown the pass. Consult your textbook for the correct way to express this type of action.

The Passive forms of the Infinitive can also be formed in the Present, Perfect, and Future. (See **VOICE**)

The uses of the Infinitive in English can be misleading if you attempt a direct translation. Try to think of the uses in relation to the syntax requirements in the language you are studying.

Intransitive VERB

An Intransitive Verb does not require a Direct Object to complete its meaning. For example, "The airplane has landed." The idea is complete. We are not left dangling with a question such as "What?" or "Whom?" (See **Transitive VERB** below) All Copulative (linking) Verbs are Intransitive. Many Verbs can be both Intransitive and Transitive.

Be aware of the fact that a Verb can be used either Transitively or Intransitively in English but in the opposite way in the language you are studying.

VERB (Continued)

Irregular VERB

An Irregular Verb does not have the same forms either in the stem or the endings that are found in regular Verbs in the same Conjugation. For example, in English, the Verb "to think" is Irregular in the Past Tense. "I thought," etc. The regular Past would be, "I thinked."

Irregularities are always identified in the Tense(s) where they occur.

You will also find that Irregularities tend to follow patterns. When you learn the patterns, the Irregularities are easier to remember.

Note: Mastery of Irregular Verb forms requires prior mastery of all the Regular Verb forms.

Regular VERB

Regular Verbs use the stem and endings associated with the regular forms of the Verbs in a given Conjugation.

Transitive VERB

A Transitive Verb requires a Direct or Indirect Object to complete its meaning. For example, if you say, "He likes," the thought is left dangling. The question immediately arises: "What" or "Whom" does he like? The answer has to be that "He likes something or someone."

A Transitive Verb can also be used Intransitively. For example, in the sentence, "He slams the door," the Verb "slams" is Transitive. He "slams" what? He "slams" the door. However, in the sentence, "The door slams," the Verb "slams" is Intransitive, which means that no Object is required to complete the meaning. "The door slams" is a complete thought. No question arises.

Be sure you understand what is also contained in the sections on **Direct OBJECT**, **Indirect OBJECT**, and **Intransitive VERB**.

VOCATIVE CASE (See CASE)

VOICE

There are two Voices in English and also in the language you are studying: Active and Passive.

VOICE (Continued)
  Active VOICE

      A Verb in the Active Voice means that the Subject of the Verb performs the action or state of being. For example, in the sentence "The sun shines," the Subject "sun" does the "shining."

      Active refers to the relationship between the Subject and the Verb. The Subject *does* the "acting."

  Passive VOICE

      The Subject of a Verb in the Passive Voice *does not*, I repeat, *DOES NOT* perform the action. The action is performed by someone or something else. The Subject of a Verb in the Passive Voice is *acted upon* by someone or something. For example, "The boy was struck on the arm by a branch." "The boy" is the Subject of the Verb "was struck," but the boy did not perform the act. The act was performed *by* a branch.

      Note that the Passive Voice consists of a form of the Auxiliary "to be" plus the Past Participle.

      The tense of a Passive Verb is determined by the Tense of the Auxiliary Verb. For example, "The ball *is* thrown." "*Is thrown*" is Present Passive. "The ball *will be thrown.*" is in the Future Passive.

      Consult your textbook for specific and required uses of the Passive Voice in the language you are studying.

END OF GLOSSARY TERMS

Index of Grammatical Terms

TOPIC AND PAGE NUMBERS

A

C

H

Historical Present, 46
Hortatory Subjunctive, 21

I

Idiom, 21-22
Idiomatic, 22
Imperative, 22,24
Impersonal Adverb, 22
Impersonal Pronoun, 22
Indefinite Adjective, 5, 10
Independent Clause, 14
Indicative Mood, 24
Indirect Address, 4
Infinitive, 52-53
Infinitive Phrase, 22
Inflection, 22-23
Intensive Pronoun, 33-34
Interrogative Adjective, 5
Interrogative Adverb, 7
Interrogative Pronoun, 34-35
Intransitive Verb, 53
Irregular Verb, 54

L

Language Learning Skills, 1-2
Liaison, 23
Linking Verb, 17
Listening Skills, 2

M

Manner, 7, 13
Masculine, 20
Modifier, 4-7;
Mood, definition, 22-23; imperative, 24; indicative, 24;
    subjunctive, 24-25
Motion, 25

N

Negation, 25
Neuter, 20
Nominative Case, 12
Noun, definition, 25-26; noun clause, 14; predicate noun, 26
Number, singular, 41; plural, 31

O

P

R

S

Second Person, 30
Sentence, simple, 40; compound sentence, 40; complex sentence, 40
Sequence of Tenses, 41
Sign of the Infinitive, definition, 41
Simple Sentence, 40
Simple Tense, 50
Singular, 41
Speaking Skill, 1
Stem, 42
Subject, 42
Subjunctive, 24-25
Subordinate Clause, 13
Substantive, 43
Superlative, 15
Supine, 43
Synopsis of a Verb, 43
Syntax, 43

T

Tense, definition, 43; anterior, 43; compound tense, 43-44;
    conditional, 44; conditional perfect, 44-45; future, 45;
    future perfect, 45-46; historical present, 46; imperfect
    indicative, 46-47; imperfect subjunctive, 47, past definite, 47;
    past indefinite, 47; past perfect, 47-48; past subjunctive, 48;
    perfect tense, 48; pluperfect indicative, 48; pluperfect
    subjunctive, 48-49; present indicative, 49; present subjunc-
    tive, 49; present perfect, 49; preterite indicative, 49;
    progressive conjugation, 49-50; simple tenses, 50
Third Person, 30-31

U

Understanding Skill, 2

V

Verb, definition, 50; agreement, 50-51; auxiliary, 51; causative
    verb, 51; copula, 52; defective verb, 52; finite verb, 52;
    infinitive, 52-53; intransitive verb, 53; irregular verb, 54;
    regular verb, 54; transitive verb, 54
Vocative Case, 12
Voice, active, 55; passive voice, 55

W

Writing Skills, 2

A Final Word To You, The Student

You now have enough information, examples, explanations, and instructions to develop the best possible learning and thinking capabilities. You may never have realized how much there was to learn about "learning," or "thinking." There is, however, one very strong impression that I would like to leave you with: Knowing what the skills are, and how to use them, is not enough. You must practice them over and over again until you know what to do *instinctively*. I repeat:

KNOWING WHAT THE LEARNING SKILLS ARE AND HOW TO USE THEM IS NOT ENOUGH. YOU MUST PRACTICE THEM OVER AND OVER AGAIN UNTIL YOU KNOW WHAT TO DO INSTINCTIVELY.

GOOD LEARNING and GOOD LUCK!

Herman Ohme

Los Altos, California
October, 1986